UNIX™ SYSTEM V
PRIMER

Mitchell Waite is president and founder of the Waite Group, a San Rafael, California based producer of high-quality books on personal computing. Mr. Waite has coauthored 15 computer titles, with over 750,000 copies now in print. He is an experienced programmer fluent in ten computer languages, who has also studied nuclear engineering, built bio-feedback machines and robots, and written poetry. A pioneer in the personal computer book field, Mr. Waite has been involved in computers since 1976 when he bought his first Apple I from Steven Jobs. When he has free time he swims, plays racquetball, and races motorcycles.

Stephen Prata is a professor of physics and astronomy at the College of Marin in Kentfield, CA. He received his B.S. from the California Institute of Technology and his Ph.D. from the University of California, Berkeley. His association with computers began with the computer modeling of star clusters. He currenty is involved with teaching UNIX® and the C language at the College of Marin. Dr. Prata is coauthor of the Sams/Waite *UNIX® Primer Plus*. Dr. Prata and his wife, Kathleen, live in San Rafael, CA. Their interests include travel, table tennis, and photography.

Donald Martin is chairman of the Physics, Astronomy, and Energy Science Department at the College of Marin in Kentfield, CA. He received his A.B. from the University of California, Berkeley, and his M.A. from San Jose State University. He has long been interested in the problems that students have in developing their reasoning and critical thinking skills. Recently, this interest has led him to the Logo computer language, a course he now teaches on a UNIX-based system at the college. Mr. Martin is coauthor of the Sams/Waite *UNIX® Primer Plus* and *Apple LOGO Programming Primer*. His hobbies include reading, running, and traveling with his wife Kay, and his family.

UNIX™ SYSTEM V PRIMER

by
Mitchell Waite, Donald Martin,
and Stephen Prata

Howard W. Sams & Co., Inc.
A Subsidiary of Macmillan, Inc.
4300 West 62nd Street, Indianapolis, Indiana 46268 U.S.A.

International Standard Book Number: 0-672-22404-6
Library of Congress Catalog Card Number: 84-51098

Edited by: *Welborn Associates*
Illustrated by: *T. R. Emrick*

Printed in the United States of America.

PREFACE

UNIX* SYSTEM V is a new, powerful and comprehensive computer operating system developed at AT&T Bell Laboratories. An operating system is the software that breaths life into a computer. It gives the computer a "personality;" it manages the resources of the system; it runs programs; and it handles interactions between you and the computer. Compared to other operating systems, UNIX offers much greater freedom of action and many more comprehensive aids to the user. With these features, the UNIX operating system is growing in popularity, especially in education, where it has been continually improved and expanded. Today, over 80% of American universities use UNIX.

In the past, AT&T has elected to treat UNIX as an "exclusive" operating system, available only on large and expensive mainframe and minicomputers. But recently, with the advent of powerful 16/32-bit microprocessors, AT&T has entered the computer marketplace to establish UNIX as an industrial standard. Today, UNIX is becoming available at a reasonable price on small but powerful microcomputers. Market researchers expect that over 300,000 UNIX-based computer systems will be sold in 1985, many of them priced under $10,000.

Understandably, AT&T settled on a modified version of its own in-house UNIX, added some improvements, and labeled it "standard" UNIX SYS-TEM V. As UNIX SYSTEM V comes to market, there is a need to explain its operation to new users: whether they are secretaries, businesspersons, students, scientists, homeowners, or hobbyists. That is the purpose of this book. **UNIX SYSTEM V Primer** is the first book to teach you how to completely master the UNIX SYSTEM V operating system. The book presents the powerful and fascinating features of UNIX SYSTEM V in a clear, easy-to-follow manner.

The book differs from most UNIX books in several significant ways. First, the entire powerful family of **ex** editors is included, of which the familiar **vi** is a subset. Second, the amazing subject of shell scripts and shell

---

* UNIX is a trademark of AT&T Bell Laboratories.

programming is covered in detail. Programming the shell produces highly portable UNIX applications. Third, there is abundant material on the **sed** stream editor. The **sed** performs excellent pattern matching and substitutions on text files. There is also material on UNIX filters, text **cut** and **paste**, and the text formatting utilities **nroff** and **troff.** These utilities allow you to do powerful text formatting, such as controlling type styles and sizes, line widths and lengths, etc. We cover complex forms of **find** and **awk,** and include a new helpful **UNIX Startup Card**. Finally we have improved our delivery and added additional information to make learning UNIX easier and faster.

The authors of this book have not only used UNIX for many years, but have extensive experience teaching it as well. These experiences have helped them identifiy the problems of the new user so they can steer you around the pitfalls that await the unwary beginner. The authors hope this book helps you fully appreciate and enjoy the powers of the UNIX SYSTEM V operating system.

MITCHELL WAITE
DONALD MARTIN
STEPHEN PRATA

This book is dedicated

To our families and friends for your love and understanding

ACKNOWLEDGMENTS

Any book attempting to teach the use of a computer operating system to beginners would surely be useless without copious amounts of human feedback and testing of the manuscript. This is especially true for the UNIX system because of its large number of built-in facilities and commands. Further, since UNIX is becoming so popular (even as a 16/32-bit operating system for micros), it is critical that the teaching of its operation be carefully explained and completely tested. We have been fortunate to have several people contribute to the testing and critiquing of our original manuscript and we would like to pay tribute to them here.

First, we would like to thank Jon Foreman, Dan Putterman, and Michael Lindbeck at the College of Marin for the many technical discussions we held regarding UNIX. We are particularly indebted to Brian Harvey, who made numerous technical contributions to our first book, *UNIX Primer Plus*.

The good people at Howard W. Sams gave us the strong support necessary to make this book a real visual treasure, and we would like to give them our sincere regards.

We also wish to thank our colleagues at the College of Marin for their help and support: Bob Petersen, Dick Rodgers, Bernd Enders, Fred Schmitt, and Nancy Zimfirescu. And, of course, our sincere appreciation to the numerous students who struggled through our earliest efforts at creating a user-friendly introduction to UNIX. A special thanks to Wayne Kristoff and Phebe Packer of Motorola Inc. for their technical advice and help.

Finally, thanks to Bob Johnson for his fantastic cartoons and help in illustrations.

Even with this wonderful support, we may have allowed an error or two to creep into this book. For them, we are responsible.

CONTENTS

CHAPTER 1

CHAPTER 2

CHAPTER 3

CHAPTER 4

CHAPTER 5

CHAPTER 6

CHAPTER 7

CHAPTER 8

CHAPTER 9

CHAPTER 10

CHAPTER 11

CHAPTER 12

APPENDIX A

APPENDIX B

APPENDIX C

APPENDIX D

APPENDIX E

APPENDIX F

APPENDIX G

APPENDIX H

How To Use This Book

Whether you are new to computers or an experienced programmer, this book will give you a good introduction to the UNIX operating system and to many of its important application programs. Here are a few suggestions on how you might use this book.

The best way to learn UNIX is to use it. When you start reading the book in earnest, sit down at a terminal and duplicate our examples. Improvise your own examples. You may be surprised occasionally, but you won't hurt the system.

Glance through the first seven chapters. These chapters contain the *basic* ideas and commands that you will need. We furnish analogies, pictures, and stories to provide mental hooks on which you can hang these concepts. If you are a casual UNIX user, you may not need to read beyond these chapters.

Read the beginning of Chapter 5. It discusses the two editors we cover, and you can decide which one better suits your needs. To a large degree, the presentation of the editors is independent from the rest of the book, so you can switch back and forth between studying an editor and reading the other chapters.

Try the Questions and the Exercises at the end of each chapter. They should give you more confidence in your new skills and they may clarify a point or two for you.

The later chapters explore a variety of the more interesting and powerful UNIX commands and features. You may wish to just browse through them, picking up on those commands and uses that most interest you.

Use this book as a reference book. Our summaries document a large number of UNIX commands. You also can use this book as a lead-in to the official UNIX manual. The manual is rather terse and it is written for knowledgeable users; the summaries and examples that we provide can help you to understand the manual.

Leave the book lying in a prominent place. Your friends and other visitors will be very impressed.

Have fun!

1

Introduction to UNIX

In this chapter, you will find:

- Introduction
- An Overview of UNIX
- What Is an Operating System?
- The History of UNIX
- The UNIX Philosophy
- What Can UNIX Do for You?
- The Electronic Office
  - Word Processing
  - Electronic Filing
  - Electronic Mail and Networking
  - Electronic Data Bases
- Programmer's Support Tools
- Who Should Read This Book?

1   INTRODUCTION TO UNIX

Introduction

Did you know that there are more than 15,000 UNIX installations around the country that are supporting over 400,000 users? Furthermore, the recent introduction of dozens of relatively inexpensive ($5,000–$25,000) computer systems capable of running UNIX means that in the next few years many more of us will become members of the New Information Age.

This book will help you take that step. It is designed to introduce newcomers to the powerful magic of one of the world's most successful operating systems.

An Overview of UNIX

A computer needs special programming called "software" to make it work. UNIX systems have two kinds of software: (1) the operating system software, and (2) the "application" or "utility" software. The operating system software is what breathes "life" into the computer. It behaves somewhat like our subconscious, taking care of a myriad of everyday "housekeeping" details. If the operating system is doing its job, you can do your tasks without ever needing to worry about the computer's inner workings.

The other kind of software, the utilities or application software, does *our* work. This software might include an "editor" (a program that lets you write, change, and store text and data), electronic mail programs, business applications, languages for programming (such as Pascal), and so forth.

UNIX consists of both kinds of software. The term UNIX, then, refers to both the operating system and to a host of useful application programs. In this book, we will just briefly describe the operating system part of UNIX and will spend the majority of our time on how to use the powerful UNIX utilities.

What Is an Operating System?

Those who have suddenly found themselves caught up in computers, and in computing, will find terms, such as "operating system," "utilities," "multiuser," and the like, to be confusing when they are first encountered. We will make a small digression at this point to explain exactly what an operating system is, why it is necessary, and what it does. Those of you who are already familiar with operating systems may want to skip ahead to the next section.

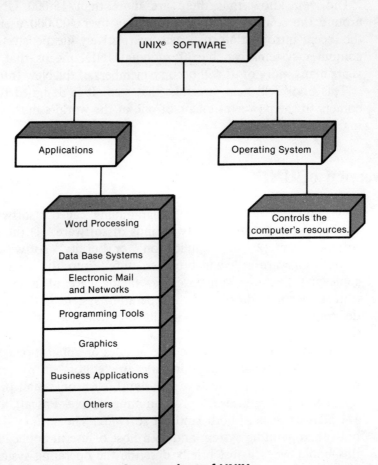

An overview of UNIX.

In a very rough way, an operating system is like a teacher in a classroom. The teacher gives out assignments, schedules use of equipment, and, in general, coordinates student activities.

In a much more restrictive way, the operating system coordinates the inner workings of the computer. The operating system relies on an internal clock within the computer to help make simple scheduling decisions, such as when to send information to the printer or when to load and execute user programs. Operating systems, themselves, are just programs created to reduce the amount of programming required of you and me, especially the programming that is required to take care of routine and repeated tasks.

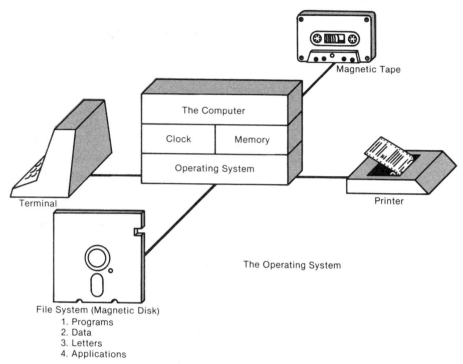

The operating system.

An operating system can also be defined as the *link* between the computer and the computer user. Its purpose is to provide the user with a flexible and manageable means of control over the resources of the computer. The three primary functions fulfilled by all operating systems are:

1. *Set up a file system.* A "file" is a block of information stored in the computer. Files can hold letters, programs, budgets, schedules, and anything else that you can type on a typewriter. In UNIX, we can write new files, add to old files, copy files, rename them, or move them elsewhere, all by giving rather simple commands. The UNIX file management system keeps all unnecessary details "hidden" from the computer operator, making it very easy to use, unlike some other systems.

19

2. *Provide for the loading and execution of user programs.* "Loading" a program consists of placing the program instructions into the proper locations; "executing" a program means to run the program. In providing this service, the operating system lets you run programs that might be written in a high-level language, such as Pascal or BASIC, as well as run programs already written and stored in the file system. Again, the purpose of the operating system is to make this task as simple as possible.

3. *Provide a communication link between the computer and its accessories.* These accessories, sometimes called "peripheral" devices, or "input-output" devices, include terminals, printers, and information storage devices, such as magnetic tapes and magnetic disks.

In addition to these three basic functions, a variety of more elaborate features are found on the newer or larger operating systems such as UNIX. Some additional features in UNIX include:

1. *Provide multiuser time sharing.* This means that several people at different terminals can use the computer at the same time. This process resembles the workings of a kitchen in a restaurant. The staff in the kitchen divides its time preparing and serving several customers simultaneously, sending out the soups, salads, main courses, and so on. An efficient staff will give each patron the feeling of being waited on as if he or she were the only customer. An efficient time-sharing computer will give you the same sensation.

2. *Provide multitasking.* This feature allows one user to run several computing jobs simultaneously, allowing the user to set different priorities for each job as appropriate.

Along with these basic housekeeping operations, UNIX has a library of application and utility software that has grown over the years to provide an essential service to thousands of users. We will take a brief look at how UNIX has evolved into what it is today.

The History of UNIX

During the early 1960s, computers were expensive and had small memories. For example, one middle-priced work horse of that day, the IBM-1620, had only 24K of memory, and was capable of storing about 40,000 numbers. The primary design criteria for all software—languages, programs, and operating systems—was to use memory efficiently and to make programs simple for the computer. This was usually at the cost of being unwieldy for the programmer and other users.

UNIX grew out of the frustrations that programmers faced when working with this early time-consuming software. UNIX was born in 1969 at Bell Laboratories, the prestigious research arm of the American Telephone and Telegraph Company. Surprisingly, it began when one man, Ken Thompson, decided to try to create a less expensive and more hospitable programming environment.

Ken Thompson was working on a program called *Space Travel* that simulated the motion of the planets in the solar system. The program was being run on a large computer made by General Electric, the GE645, which was using an operating system called Multics. Multics was developed at MIT and was one of the first operating systems designed to handle several users simultaneously. However, its use on the GE computer was expensive and awkward. Each run of the *Space Travel* program costs over $70.00. Thompson found a little-used smaller computer made by Digital Equipment Corporation called the PDP-7. He began the burden of transferring his *Space Travel* program to run on the smaller computer. In order to use the PDP-7 conveniently, Thompson created a new operating system that he christened UNIX, as an offshoot of Multics, since it incorporated the multiple-user feature of that system. Thompson was successful enough in this effort to attract the attention of Dennis Ritchie and others at Bell Labs, where they continued the process of creating a useful environment.

The combined work of Dennis Ritchie and the others quickly progressed to the point where UNIX became operational in the Bell Labs system in 1971. Like most software (and hardware, too), UNIX evolved from the best ideas of its predecessors. During the early 1970s, UNIX ran primarily on computers that were manufactured by Digital Equipment; first on the PDP-7 and, then, on the PDP-11/40, /45, and, finally, blossoming on the PDP-11/70 where it achieved widespread acceptance throughout Bell Labs. During the same time, universities and colleges, many of which were using the PDP-11/70 computers, were given license to run UNIX at minimal cost. This shrewd move by AT&T eventually led to UNIX being run at over 80% of all university computer science departments in the United States. Each year, thousands of computer science students graduate with some experience in running and in modifying UNIX.

UNIX, like most operating systems, was originally written in what is called "assembly language." This is a primitive set of instructions that controls the computer's internal actions. Since each computer model has its own particular set of internal instructions, moving UNIX to another computer would involve a significant programming effort. The solution to this problem, and perhaps the key to UNIX's popularity today, was Ken Thompson's decision to rewrite the operating system in a higher level language—one less primitive than assembly language.

The language was called B. Soon it was modified extensively by Dennis Ritchie and rechristened C (in 1973). As a general-purpose language featuring modern commands, C is much easier to understand and use than assembly language. Although not as efficient as assembly language in terms of the speed with which the computer carries out its manipulations, C is much more convenient. This convenience has encouraged users to modify and improve UNIX, thus creating a tremendous amount of additional UNIX software, especially in the areas of word processing and programming support.

The use of C makes UNIX easily portable to other computer systems. Only a very small fraction of UNIX is still written in assembly language. Today, UNIX can be run on a host of other computers besides the PDP-11 series, including the large IBM, Honeywell, and Amdahl computers.

Probably more important (for us potential computer users) is the fact that C compilers (a compiler translates C into the host computer's internal language) are now available for every major 16-bit "microprocessor" on the market.

Microprocessors form the "brains" of microcomputers. One significant fact about microprocessors is that their sophisticated, complex, electronic circuits are all contained in a single small package called a "chip." The first microprocessor was a 4-bit chip made by Intel in 1970. It was followed by the 8-bit chip which launched the microcomputer revolution of the late 1970s. Today, we have 16-bit and 32-bit microprocessors that promise even greater computing power at lower cost.

The net result of these advances in hardware is that UNIX can now run on newer, relatively inexpensive, microprocessor-based computer systems. For example, in the late 1970s, a PDP-11/70 time-sharing system with 15 terminals might cost $150,000. In the 1980s, a microprocessor-based system with 15 terminals can be installed for about $35,000. Single-user UNIX systems can cost as little as $5,000.

Today, there are several dozen companies manufacturing microprocessor-based computer systems that will run UNIX. UNIX has already established itself as one of the major operating systems for these new breeds of computers. In addition to UNIX itself, there are several UNIX "look-alikes,'' or enhanced UNIX systems.

There are two major reasons why UNIX has achieved such widespread acceptance. First, and probably the most important, is the fact that UNIX is adaptable. Since UNIX is written in the language C, it is fairly easy to modify and can continue to evolve, incorporating the best ideas that are currently available. This adaptability not only applies to adding new software created by experts, but it also allows casual users, even beginners, the power to modify UNIX commands, using the "shell script" feature described in Chapter 9.

UNIX SYSTEM V

In January of 1983, AT&T announced that for the first time it was licensing a new "standard" version of UNIX for the commercial OEM (Original Equipment Manufacturer) marketplace. This version was called UNIX SYSTEM V, and was based on the UNIX that AT&T was using internally. It contained many of the best features of the UNIX that was in use at most universities at that tine (Berkeley UNIX, also called 4.1 bsd). AT&T also announced that it was becoming a software supplier and would offer full support for developers of UNIX. In addition, the licensing fee for UNIX SYSTEM V became much more reasonable than previous versions.

At the same time that AT&T announced UNIX SYSTEM V, it also announced that it was licensing the top three semiconductor manufacturers of 16/32-bit microprocessor chips to develop rigorous "standard" versions, or "ports," of UNIX for these chips. Each "port" would consist of a 16/32-bit microprocessor, a ROM, and a set of disks containing the entire UNIX SYSTEM V operating system. Motorola completed the first port of SYSTEM V to receive port acceptance by AT&T Bell Labs.

The SYSTEM V port was not a trivial undertaking: AT&T required manufacturers to reproduce 98% of all the known bugs in UNIX SYSTEM V. The insistence by AT&T for a rigorous UNIX standard port means that, except for speed, UNIX SYSTEM V software will run the same, regardless of the computer it is running on. The net result of this standardization is that software developers are assured that their programs will work on the largest number of machines. To computer hardware manufacturers and designers, it means that they can focus energy on squeezing more speed and performance out of the computer, without having to worry about software compatability. Of course, the overall performance of a UNIX SYSTEM V 16/32-bit microprocessor based computer will still depend on the talents of the engineers that design the complete system. But regardless of performance, to the end user, a UNIX operation in one system will work exactly the same in any system.

The UNIX Philosophy

The major design factors behind UNIX were to create an operating system and supporting software that were simple, elegant, and easy to use. Elegant, in this context, generally means using a good programming style and thrifty memory management.

These design characteristics led to the following maxims among UNIX builders.

1. Make each program do one thing well. These simple programs often are called "tools."
2. Expect the output of every program to become the input to another, yet unknown, program. This means simple tools can be connected to do complex jobs.
3. Don't hesitate to build new programs to do a job. The library of tools keeps increasing.

The net result of these maxims is that UNIX systems are sometimes said to embody Schumacher's dictum that "small is beautiful." Each UNIX program is a compact, easily used tool that does its job well.

The verdict on UNIX software is already in. Thousands of students, teachers, programmers, secretaries, managers, and office workers have found that UNIX's friendly environment and quality software have become time-saving tools that improve their productivity and employ their creativity.

The picture on page 25 was created to give you a peek into the UNIX toolroom and to sum up some of the ideas presented here.

What Can UNIX Do for You?

As we mentioned earlier, in addition to the UNIX operating system, which manages the internal workings of the computer system, UNIX provides a host of built-in software. An easy way to get a quick overview of these UNIX features is to divide this software into two major categories. These software categories could be called the Electronic Office and the Pro-

gramming Support areas. Since this book is for beginners, most of the UNIX software we will discuss deals with the services that we describe under the term, ''The Electronic Office.''

The Electronic Office

The concept of an electronic office is still young and changing. Most discussions of what it involves center around four interrelated functions. These are:

1. Word Processing.
2. Electronic filing.
3. Electronic mail and networking.
4. Electronic data bases.

Word Processing

UNIX has dozens of tools to help you do word processing. These tools go by such names as editors, text formatters, spellers, and even syntax checkers to test your sentence structure. With these tools, here's what you can do.

You can throw away the liquid correction fluid, correction tape, scissors, erasers, paper clips, scotch tape, and all the old tools you used for dealing with printed words on paper. You now deal with words inside an electronic memory. They can be moved and changed easily, quickly, and efficiently, allowing you to type in your words without thinking about the appearance of your finished product.

A text "formatting" program permits you to turn a ragged right margin into a beautiful, professional looking, typeset format just by using a few keystrokes. Or, suppose you want to add a new sentence in the middle of your many paged document? No problem. Simply enter the editor "insert" mode and start typing away. Because the editor has an electronic brain, it can instantly shift all the text in its memory forward to make room for new words and do it without losing its paragraph structure. Or, suppose you spelled the same word incorrectly in 157 places? Quick work for your editor . . . ; merely enter the "search and replace" command and the computer will automatically change all occurrences of the misspelled word as you sit back comfortably and sip on your cafe mocha. Other things you can do with simple key operations include the moving of paragraphs and blocks of text, doing boldface, underlining, superscripts, and subscripts.

These UNIX tools allow you to do things that would require days of work using a standard typewriter, such as converting a long double-spaced document to a narrow column width, single-spacing a document that is suitable for publication, printing individually addressed copies of the same letter, sorting and merging mailing labels, proofreading and correcting large documents for spelling and syntax errors, and generating an index.

This kind of power will change your writing experience drastically. The ability to change words quickly and easily gives them a new malleability. Words become like wet clay. You rework the same sentence over and over, deleting old words with hardly a care until the words say exactly what you mean. Because of the fluid nature of the work, you become braver. Your creativity tends to flow more freely because you're not concerned with how the typing looks. Neither are you hampered by the fear of putting an idea in the wrong place, for you can easily move the words around later. You create and let the machine manage the words.

Electronic Filing

Supporting the word processing function and providing even more services is the electronic file system. To visualize the file system, imagine that all

of the written information you now store in a file cabinet or on shelves were placed in an electronic file cabinet.

A file can contain anywhere from one to several thousand words or numbers. Anything you can type on a typewriter can be placed in a file. Each

Once you have a file system set up and your information stored there, here's what you can do. Using just simple commands, you can get a listing of the titles of every document or file, or you can read any one file in its entirety, or you can scan (search) the first 10 lines (or the last 10 lines) of a number of files looking for specific information. Better still, suppose you want to find a certain letter that was sent to you about a specific product. No problem. You can let "UNIX do the walking." A simple command will scan one or more files searching for the product name. Phone listings, product listings, bills, and bookkeeping can all be kept on file and scanned in the UNIX file system. And the best part about the UNIX file system is that the files can be organized in exactly the same way you might arrange them in a cabinet.

You can build categories of files. For example, you might group together all of your travel files in one drawer (called a directory in UNIX), insurance records in another drawer, clients' accounts in a third drawer, and so on. Files can be easily moved from one drawer to another, copies can be placed in several drawers, or files can be cross-referenced. Files can be added together, cut in two, or merged alphabetically. In fact, all of the word processing functions described earlier can be applied to any of your files, even though you may not have originated them.

Electronic Mail and Networking

Another related, necessary, and very useful function of the electronic office is electronic mail and networking. As you might have noticed by our comments at the beginning of this chapter, electronic communication is the glue that holds together the Electronic Office. With electronic mail, you can emerge from the doldrums of paperwork shuffling into the more creative and rewarding task of information processing. For example, in writing letters, you have all the advantages of word processing that were described earlier. And, you can send copies instantly to anyone on the UNIX system.

One extremely valuable use of electronic mail occurs when two or more people collaborate on a letter, book, report, plan, or any typewritten document while using the word processor/mail system. Each person can write his or her portion of the plan, mail it to someone else for changes or additions, and then receive a new copy back again. No paper or postage is involved. These plans, as well as any UNIX file containing any kind of written information, can be mailed (transmitted) easily and simply with just a few keystrokes.

Another useful and related feature of UNIX mail is the "reminder" service. If you keep a diary of your important dates in a file called "calendar," the UNIX operating system will send you mail each day reminding you of your day's schedule.

In addition to sending "local mail" to people connected up to your computer, another feature of the UNIX mail system is its ability to send mail to other UNIX computer systems anywhere in the country. This is done by one UNIX computer automatically telephoning other UNIX computers using a device called a "modem" and, then, sending "mail" over the phone lines. There are several such telephone "networks" that offer this service; some, such as USENET, are devoted exclusively to UNIX computer systems.

Sending electronic signals over telephone wires can be relatively slow (about one page of text per minute). Other types of networks, such as Ethernet, allow several UNIX computers to be connected together, sharing resources at very high speeds. Ethernet is a local network for use in one or more adjacent buildings.

Meanwhile, over the horizon, there are various satellite networking systems.

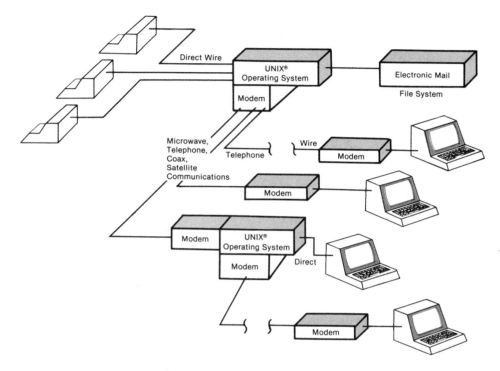

Electronic mail and networking.

However, no matter which network or what kind of computer you have, if it's running the UNIX operating system, you can communicate with other UNIX systems using all the resources of the word processing and electronic filing system plus the electronic mail features we have described in this book.

Electronic Data Bases

The electronic data base is essentially an extension of the filing system. In fact, the UNIX file system already has the features of a very simple data base. For example, if you placed all the phone numbers you use (or even a whole telephone book full of numbers) into one or more UNIX files, you can search those files for a particular name and number with just a single command. Or you could pull out all the names beginning with "John" and place them in a new file.

A simple data base is just a collection of information that you can add to or delete from, or can sort in various ways. It can be searched using key

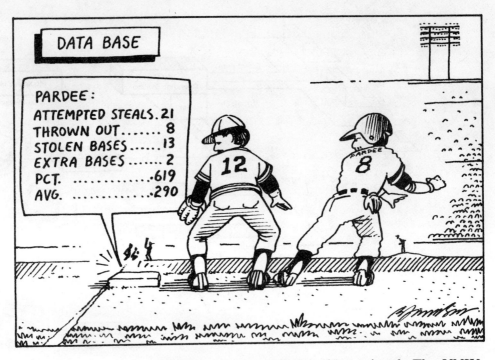

words and specific information can be copied and/or printed. The UNIX file system can do all of this easily as we will show you in later chapters.

There are more powerful data base systems, such as ''INGRES,'' available for running under UNIX. These systems have more sophisticated searching and storing techniques. To give you a simple example (using the telephone book again), you might want to find all the phone numbers listed under ''John,'' living on ''Beachside Avenue,'' but *not* all those starting with the numbers 454-. The beauty of a data base system like INGRES is that you can pull out specific information and can create a new data base from it extremely fast and easily.

Although UNIX can easily set up both small data bases (using ordinary file commands) and sophisticated data bases (using a specialized program), UNIX is not designed to handle large volumes of high-speed transactions such as a bank or airline might use.

The future of electronic data bases looks especially promising for business firms. Payroll, sales, and employee records, inventories, clients' records, and economic data can all be placed right at your fingertips for easy access.

However, to make the maximum use of data bases, they must be tied into the electronic office. The features of word processing, electronic filing, and electronic mail give the data base user additional powers. For example, you could extract specific information about an inventory, add a few remarks, and mail the result to several other people.

UNIX has all four of these features ready to go.

It should be emphasized again that these four features of the electronic office add together synergistically so that the total is much greater than just the sum of its parts. You can purchase computer systems and software that would do two or three of these functions or provide these services to just a few people. However, when all these services are provided to the majority of the office workers in a company, it can radically change the nature of their work. It has already been demonstrated that these features improve productivity and communications, save money, and improve the general attitude people have towards work. That's why organizations large and small, local and national, such as the National Research Council of England, have adopted UNIX as their software standard.

Another key element in the use of these electronic tools is "user-friendliness." How easy is it to use them? How much time do they save? Is it worth spending the time to learn how to use them? In the case of UNIX and the Electronic Office, we believe the answer is an overwhelming "YES." The thousands of employees at Bell Labs, AT&T, at colleges and universities, and in other businesses and industries have already discovered this fact.

Besides the electronic office features described above, another major service of UNIX is to help programmers solve programming problems, as we will briefly discuss in the next section.

Programmer's Support Tools

UNIX was originally developed to make life easier for the programmer. However, it turned out that programmers wanted the electronic office programs just as much as everyone else. Thus, both types of UNIX software have evolved side by side and are widely used. The programmer's support tools can be classified into four major areas. These are:

1. *Programming Languages and Compilers.* All of the major languages (FORTRAN, BASIC, Pascal, COBOL, etc.) can be run under UNIX. This means that if UNIX has a standardized form of a language (for example, Standard FORTRAN 77), then any FORTRAN 77 programs written anywhere in the country (and there are thousands of

these) can be run on your system and vice versa. In addition to the most popular languages, dozens of other languages, such as SPITBOL, APL, LOGO, RPG, RP-1, and so forth, have been placed on specific UNIX systems.

Of course, since UNIX is written in C, that language is available and widely used to write programs. A "compiler" translates programs written in the high-level languages into the primitive instructions that the machine can understand.

In Chapter 8, we show you how to write and run programs that are written in different languages.

2. *Command Line Interpreter* (called the *shell*). The "shell" is the link between most users and the computer. It is a program that accepts commands that you type into the computer and, then, executes them. The shell contains over 100 built-in commands just ready for your use. Actually, there is more than one version of the shell. The shell provided with the standard Bell Labs version of UNIX is called the *Bourne shell* after its developer. The other widely used current shell is called the *C shell* and was developed at the University of California, Berkeley. Most of the features we discuss in this book are common to both shell versions, but some are exclusive to the C/Bourne shell. In this book, we will explain over 60 commands and what they will do for you.

The shell can be used as a programming language having many of the features of C. The programmability of the shell, which few other systems offer, plus the large number of built-in commands that the shell already knows, gives programmers exceptional flexibility and power. This power is enhanced by the "pipe," a UNIX concept that has since been widely copied. Pipes, as we will discuss later on, allow programs or commands to be coupled together. The output of one program becomes the input to another, etc.

3. *Programmer debugging tools.* The first time a program is written, it rarely runs correctly. Usually, the program has errors or "bugs" that need fixing. UNIX, like most systems, has built-in programs that help locate these errors. However, we will not be discussing these programming aids in this book. If you're interested in reading further, you might look at the articles suggested in Appendix B.

4. *The Programmer's Workbench.* This package of UNIX tools is especially valuable for team-oriented programming projects. These software tools maintain a complete record of all changes made to a pro-

gram as it is written. They also allow programs to be tested in part as they are developed. The package also simplifies the task of transferring programs to other computer systems. The Programmer's Workbench is available from Bell Labs. We will not discuss it in this book.

All of these support services for programmers, together with the adaptability of the UNIX software in general (written in C), are the main reason that UNIX is gaining such wide popularity.

Who Should Read This Book?

As we mentioned in the preface, the goal of this book is to introduce UNIX's marvelous tools to both the beginning and the experienced computer user. The tools that we have chosen to present are those most needed for work in an electronic office and those needed to write and run simple programs in various computer languages, such as Pascal, FORTRAN, or C. So if you are a secretary or manager in an office, or a student in a computer science class or a computer hobbyist, who is interested in UNIX, this book is for you. We hope you will enjoy learning UNIX as much as we have enjoyed writing this book.

2

Getting Started: *login, passwd, and who*

In this chapter, you will find:

2   GETTING STARTED: *login, passwd,* and *who*

Frederick Porteous Ramshead III answered the door. Outside stood a small, white-haired woman with rosy-red cheeks, a merry grin, and an avaricious glint in her eyes,

"Freddie Pet, let me in!"

Frederick made way, noting the small suitcase in her hand.

"Grandma! You haven't left Grandpa again! And my name is Frederick, not Freddie Pet."

"Of course I haven't, and of course it is, deary. Now offer your dear Granny a seat and a pitcher of lemonade."

"Yes, yes, please make yourself comfortable. But why . . . , I mean, to what do I owe the honor of this visit?"

"Freddie, I am here to make you a wonderful offer, one that will change your life for the better—and you certainly can use that!"

"That's wonderful, Grandma," beamed Frederick, while inwardly groaning. He recalled the 20 newspaper subscriptions she sold him last year so she could win that trip to Disneyland.

"You have a computer terminal, right?"

"Right, Grandma." She had sold him one last Christmas.

"Well, I'm going to give you access to a UNIX system."

"A UNIX system?"

"You're sure quick on the uptake, Pet. Yes, a UNIX system." Grandmpa spilled open the suitcase, liberating a mass of documents, brochures, and contracts. She fixed Frederick with a steely gaze. "Now pay attention to what I am going to tell you."

An hour later, a triumphant Grandma left with a nice new check, and a dazed Frederick Porteous Ramshead III sat down at his terminal, wondering what he had gotten into this time. He attached the modem and dialled the number Grandma had given him. Soon the following display appeared on his screen:

```
Grandma's Old-Fashioned UNIX
Login:
```

He typed in the login name Grandma had given him: freddie (someone already had taken frederick). The terminal responded with

```
password:
```

He typed in the password Grandma had given him: pet. The system responded with

```
WELCOME TO GRANDMA'S OLD-FASHIONED UNIX, WHERE
VALUE AND QUALITY ARE NEVER COMPROMISED.
$
```

What did that "$" mean? Did it indicate that Grandma was getting a percentage of his computer payment? Oh, now I remember; that was the signal that UNIX was ready for his next command. Grandma called it the UNIX "prompt." The first thing he wanted to do was change the "password" Grandma had given him. He typed in the **passwd** command and changed his password to "hotshot." Ah, that was better.

What next? He tried **date** and the system displayed today's date and time. Frederick set his calendar watch by it. Next, he typed in **cal 11 1912** to find out on what day of the week Grandma was born. The UNIX system showed the month of November, 1912. Then he typed **who** to find out who else was logged in. Hmmm, was "pierre" his brother? Had Grandma hit him up, too? Well, he'd better learn some more about the system. He picked up the nice looking book Grandma had left him and opened it up.

An hour later, much more knowledgeable about the UNIX file system, he sat back, typed in <control-d> and gave a sigh of relief. *This* time, Grandma really had done him a favor. UNIX *was* going to improve the quality of his life.

Getting Started

How do you get involved with UNIX (aside from the obvious method of being hustled into it by your grandmother)? For many, it is a matter of circumstances. UNIX is by far the leading computer operating system used on our college and university campuses; large numbers of students learned their first computing knowledge on UNIX systems. Now, college graduates, in increasing numbers, are entering business and industry and are demanding access to UNIX and UNIX-like systems. Computer manufacturers are responding to this demand by offering a wide range of microcomputer and minicomputer systems.

Another possibility is that you might buy time on a UNIX system. Some universities and private companies are now offering this service at very reasonable rates. And recently, we have started to see the introduction of UNIX operating systems on some of the more expensive home personal computers. This last possibility is perhaps the most attractive. With your own computer, you don't have to wait for open terminals or open phone lines, and you don't have to see your work slowed down by heavy demands on a time-sharing system. Yet, if you want, you still can tie into other UNIX systems with your modem and you can share information and programs with other UNIX users.

We'll suppose that by choice or fate, you now are involved with UNIX. So let's begin our study of the nitty-gritty of UNIX. We'll begin by showing you how to get started on a UNIX system. The first sections of this chapter describe the major characteristics of a typical terminal that you might use to communicate with UNIX. Then, we'll discuss the "login" and "password" process in detail. Finally, we'll look at the first of many simple, yet powerful, commands in the UNIX shell.

Establishing Contact With the Shell

Lured on by the wonders of UNIX, you want to unleash its powers. But how do you get in touch with the system? The precise details will vary from system to system, but the following general features will hold:

1. You need a means to communicate with the system; normally the means will be a keyboard and a screen display. That is what we will assume you have.
2. You will have to tell the system who you are by "logging in." (Computers that handle multiple users are usually selective about whom they deal with.)
3. You may have to give the system a password. (Computers are not too good at recognizing faces, so they may need a password to reassure them that you are who you say you are.)
4. When you are done, you need to "logout" to tell the UNIX system you are done. Otherwise the system will just sit there, waiting for your next instructions.

Now we will go over how these features are implemented.

The Keyboard

If you have seen a typewriter, you should find the typical computer terminal keyboard at least vaguely familiar. It will have keys bearing symbols such as D and U; you may recognize them as the English alphabet. The top row of letters on the standard keyboard start with the letters QWERTY. There also are keys bearing the likenesses of the digits—5, 3, and so forth. Then there is an assortment of other symbols—#, *, ~, @, etc. Some of these symbols (or characters, as they are called) are not usually found on a typewriter. Then there are keys bearing words or abbreviations of words—keys such as RETURN (C/R on some keyboards), CTRL (for control), break or BREAK, SHIFT, and ESC (for escape). Many of these keys have been added to the standard keyboard just to make life easier for us computer users. The convention we will use to indicate which keys to push as part of a UNIX command will be to place the key name inside < > symbols. Thus we might say, push the <return> key or the <esc> key. In addition, we will always use lowercase letters to indicate keys even though some keyboards list their letters in uppercase. When we want you to type out the letters in a command, we will place the letters in boldface, as in "type the **who** command."

Other special keys and their meaning to UNIX will be discussed later in this chapter. In the following figure, we present a typical keyboard.

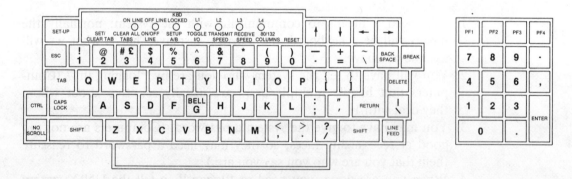

Standard keys.

It would be nice if there were a standard keyboard layout, but not all keyboards are identical. Fortunately, there is a standard "character set" that most keyboards carry. It's called the ASCII (pronounced askee and standing for American Standard Code for Information Interchange) character set. You can find a copy of this set of characters in Appendix C. It includes the uppercase and lowercase alphabets, the ten digits (0–9), punctuation marks, and an assortment of symbols including " ", the blank or space that we find between words. Unfortunately, although different terminal manufacturers agree on where to place the alphabet and the numbers, they mostly go their separate ways when it comes to deciding where to physically place the other characters of the ASCII set. So if you learn on one terminal, be alert when you use a different kind of terminal that some keys will be in a different location. Also, be aware that many terminals have special keys not found in the ASCII character set, for example, keys with special editing or graphics uses.

Using the keyboard is a straightforward procedure; you depress a key to send the symbol on it to the computer. To send a 6, depress the <6> key. There are a few additional facts you should know.

1. Some keys bear two symbols. Ordinarily, the lower of the two characters is sent when the key is depressed. To send the upper character, depress one of the <shift> keys at the same time you depress the character key. For example, on the keyboard shown earlier, you must depress a <shift> key, hold it down, and then press the <6> key to send the & character.

2. Standard terminals (there are exceptions) transmit lowercase alphabetic characters unless the <cap lock> key is on or if a <shift> key is used at the same time. Thus, depressing the <a> key transmits an a (lowercase), but depressing the <a> key while pressing the <shift> key transmits an A (uppercase). This combination often is represented by <shift-a>. The <cap lock> key acts like you are permanently holding a <shift> key down, except that it only affects the letters. Thus, if the <cap lock> key is engaged, hitting the <b> key produces a B, but hitting the 6 key produces a 6, not an &. To get an & with the <cap lock> on, you must use the <shift> key as before. *Note:* Often the actual keys on the terminal are labeled with uppercase letters, but since they nonetheless normally transmit lowercase letters, we will use labels like <a> rather than <A> to stand for the key.

3. Additional characters are produced by depressing a regular key and pressing the <control> key or <ctrl> key. For example, pressing the <control> key while hitting the <d> key smartly produces a character called <control-d>. We will use the notation <control-d> to indicate when this character is to be typed. It sometimes is displayed on the screen as ∧d and sometimes it is not displayed at all. It is truly

one character although it takes two symbols to represent it on the screen. Such "control-characters" are often used for special purposes in computer systems.

4. On many typewriters, the lowercase letter "l" and the numeral "1" are interchangeable. This is not so for a computer keyboard. If, in your typing, you have used the letter "l" for the number "1," you must break the habit. The same situation holds true for the uppercase letter "O" and the digit "Ø" (zero). They are *not* interchangeable.

5. Develop a good touch. Many keyboards will repeat a letter if you hold a key down too long. You may find yourself typing lines like "Myy ssincereest apoloogiees.." if your terminal is sensitive and your fingers are not.

There is one key we wish to spotlight now; this is the <return> or <c/r> (for carriage return) key. On an electric typewriter, depressing this key advances the paper a line and returns the typewriter to the left-hand margin of the page. It performs a similar function on a computer terminal. More importantly, depressing the <return> key tells the system that you have finished that line. For example, we soon will discuss the UNIX command **who.** If you are on the system and type the letters w-h-o and nothing else, nothing will happen. A useless command? No, the problem is that UNIX doesn't know you are finished. You could be a slow typist working on **whoami** or **whoa there, black thunder, i think i see trouble ahead.** What you need to do is press the <return> key! Depressing the <return> key tells the system, "Okay, I'm done; take it from here." Thus, the correct way to use the **who** command is to type

who <————————————————————————————— <return>

where <return> stands for the return key, not for typing the word "return." At first, we will remind you a few times to hit the return key after each new line command, but later we won't bother—we have confidence that you will soon be hitting <return> automatically. (A lot of times people bang the <return> key when the system seems to be "stuck." This usually is harmless and occasionally even helps.)

Logging In

The first step in using a UNIX system is to login. The word "login" comes from the old shipping era when you would fill out the daily "log" with a record of activities. In our context, we are signing into the "log" of the UNIX system. We will assume that you are at a computer that uses a screen display that is turned on and you are rarin' to go. The first key you should push is the <return> key. UNIX should respond with something like

```
Welcome to UNIX VERSION 7.3. Enjoy Your Computing
Login: □  <─────────────────────────────────── (cursor)
```

Immediately after the colon in "login:", there should appear a rectangle of light, or else an underscore mark (blinking on some terminals), called the "cursor." The cursor is nothing less than your guiding light; it shows you where your next letter will be placed on the screen. Now you type in your login name. (What's your login name? It is a name by which you are known to the UNIX system and it usually is assigned to you by the folks running the system. Let's assume your login name is "sneezy.") Each time you type a letter, it appears on the screen and the cursor moves over a space. *Don't* put in a space before or after your name; the space is just another character, so adding a space would make the name different. Login names normally are in lowercase letters only, so type "sneezy," not "Sneezy" or "SNEEZY." Finish up with a <return>. This, then, is the line:

```
Login: sneezy  <────────────────────────── <return>
```

The Prompt Character

If your account has been set up without a password, and if the system recognizes "sneezy" as a valued client, there will be a pause while the system sets up things for you. It may give you some messages, and then it will display a "prompt," which is a special symbol at the left of the screen that tells you UNIX is in operation and waiting for your next command. Each time you give UNIX an instruction, it will give you a new prompt symbol when it has finished and is ready for the next instruction. The standard prompt usually is a "%" or a "$". We will assume the prompt is a $. The <return> and the $ serve the same purpose as "over" in CB talk; <return> tells UNIX that you are done and it is its turn, and $ tells you that UNIX is done and it is your turn.

The Password

What if you do have a password or what if the system does not recognize "sneezy" as a login name? In either case, the system responds to the previous line with

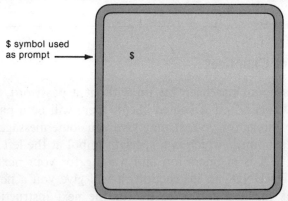

$ symbol used
as prompt →

The UNIX prompt.

password:

You then type in your password. The letters you type *will not* appear on the screen as you type them. (After all, what good is a password if someone can look over your shoulder and read it off the screen!) Again, follow with <return>. (It may happen that your account will be set up so that you neither have nor need a password to use the system.) If you have no password and still get this message asking for one, then you've blown it. The system doesn't recognize you, but being a bit cagey, it asks you for a password anyway. The login procedure won't continue unless you give some password (anything) at this point, so fake one. This won't get you on the system, but it will cause the system to revert to asking for your login name again. At this point, you may notice that you mistyped your login name. For example, suppose in answer to "password," you (sneezy) type

```
snowwhite
```

for your password. UNIX then compares the password you typed with its record of sneezy's password. If the two agree, you are welcomed to the system and presented with the system prompt. If you typed either your login name or password incorrectly, the system responds with

```
Login incorrect
Login:
```

and you get to try again. You can repeat this as many times as necessary unless the powers-that-be are worried about CPU thieves and have installed a trap to catch repeated attempts to login.

Setting Up and Changing Passwords

It is a simple matter to give yourself a password if you lack one. Once you are logged in and have the UNIX prompt, you type in the command

```
passwd <————————————————————————————— <return>
```

Notice that the command **passwd** is in lowercase letters. Also note that the command is **passwd** and not **password**. This saves you time in typing a command you may use once a season, if that often. (For some people, these UNIX abbreviations are a minor system foible, since the abbreviations are harder to remember than the full word.) After you type in this line, UNIX will respond with

```
changing password for sneezy
New password:
```

You then type in your choice of password. It will not appear on the screen. Then, hit < return >. UNIX will respond with

Retype new password:

This is to check to see that both you and UNIX have the same word in mind. Since you don't see what you type, this check is valuable. If the two words you typed in disagree, UNIX responds with

```
Mismatch-password unchanged
$
```

The return of the $ prompt means UNIX is finished with the **passwd** command. If you want to continue, you have to start over again by typing **passwd** and < return >. You should get used to the fact that when UNIX does something successfully, it *doesn't* say "good" or "correct." Instead, it just gives the old prompt.

If the words you typed did agree, UNIX will accept the new password and you will have to use it the next time you log in. It is a good practice to write down your password and keep it somewhere handy.

To change your password, you go through the same procedure, except there is one extra step. After you type **passwd** and < return >, UNIX will ask

```
old password:
```

You type it in, follow it with < return >, and the procedure continues as described above. This step is a precaution to keep your friends from jokingly changing your password when you get called away from the terminal for a moment.

What sort of passwords can you use? Generally, a password should contain at least one nonnumeric character and should be at least 6 characters long if you use only uppercase or only lowercase characters. (You can get away with 4 characters if you use a wide variety of character types.) Thus, some unacceptable passwords are 007007, pip, and doog. Some acceptable examples are cowboy, hog666, TOADLIFE, 747F22, and rPg@2. Oh yes, make sure you remember your password. If you forget it, you will have to deal with whoever administers the system.

Logging Out

The process of signing off when you are done is called "logging out." To log out, you need the UNIX prompt showing. Thus, you can't log out in the middle of the **passwd** process. If the prompt is showing, just type

```
<control-d>  <——————————————————————————— <return>
```

(This means hold down the <control> key while hitting the <d> key once.)

This should log you out, and the screen should now show your system's standard welcome message:

```
Welcome to UNIX VERSION 7.3 Enjoy Your Computing
Login:
```

You can now walk away feeling that you have said goodbye properly to UNIX and that the terminal is ready for the next user.

There are things you can do that will cause the system to not log you out right away after you give the <control-d> command. We assume you don't know how to do these things yet. Later, we will give some examples (such as background jobs running) and tell you what to do.

Correcting Typing Errors

Even the most talented fingers sometimes stumble as they sweep across the keyboard, and even the most talented minds sometimes have second thoughts about commands they have typed. One of the major advantages of an interactive system such as UNIX is that it gives you the opportunity to see and correct errors immediately.

The mechanics of making corrections depends on the terminal you use and on how your particular system has been set up, so what we will describe here are just possible examples. You'll have to check out what works on your system.

Erasing Characters

The key most commonly used to "erase" a character (usually moving the cursor back one space and removing the offending character) is the <backspace> key. For example, if you type

```
passqr
```

and, then, press the <backspace> key twice, the cursor will back up (move left) over the last two letters, erasing them at the same time, and leaving the word

```
pass
```

The user then can correctly complete the command by typing a ''w'' and a ''d'' to produce

```
passwd
```

Another common choice for erasing characters is <control-h>; this means depressing the ''control'' key and hitting ''h'' key once. Yet another choice that is widely used on ''hard-copy'' terminals is the ''pound'' or ''number sign'' (#) key. This choice works somewhat differently since a hard-copy terminal cannot erase parts of text on a screen. In this case, using the ''#'' key erases the character from the computer's memory but not from the screen. Thus, the correction for the last example would appear this way on the screen:

```
passqr # # wd
```

The first # cancels the ''r'' and the second # cancels the ''q.'' When you hit <return>, **passwd** is transmitted to the computer.

For all these examples, you can't erase a letter in the middle of a word without also erasing all the letters after the erroneous one. For example, to correct

```
pusswd
```

you would type, using the #-example,

```
pusswd # # # # # asswd
```

Here you had to erase (from right to left) the d, w, s, and s to reach the u. We then had to retype the letters s, s, w, d after replacing the u with an a. Other less common keys used to erase characters are the <delete> key or the <rub> key. (These last two keys are sometimes used to ''interrupt'' a process. See the next section.)

Canceling Lines and Interrupting a Command

A character that cancels a whole line instead of just one letter is called a "kill" character. For example, on our system, the kill character is <control-x>. (Note that <control-x> is considered a single character even though it involves two keys—<control> and <x>—depressed simultaneously.) Thus, the sequence

passwd <————————————————————— <control-x>

produces a blank line; **passwd** is deleted.

Some systems use "@" as kill character. Usually, in this case, the line is not erased from the screen, just from what is transmitted. For example, the following sequence will transmit **passwd:**

osddef@passwd <————————————————————— <return>

Another special character is the "interrupt" character, which usually is generated by a <control-c> or a <del> (delete) key. This causes the system to "interrupt" what it is doing. It will not only erase lines but will halt many procedures after they have started running. This is the common way to stop the computer from doing something and returning to the shell ($).

The <break> key sometimes will do the same thing: "interrupt" a process. However, on some systems, <break> will lock up a terminal, not only interrupting UNIX but, also, the user. We suggest that you *do not* use <break>.

Some Simple Shell Commands

Suppose you have logged on successfully by answering the login: and password: questions properly. The UNIX prompt appears on the screen, telling you that UNIX is ready to obey your every command. After your first flush of joy and power, you may wonder "What do I tell it to do?" There are literally thousands of legitimate possible answers to that question and, in this section, we will look at three of the simplest: the commands **date, cal,** and **who.** These are examples of "shell commands," which are standard commands recognized by the shell program. We choose these three commands because they are easy to understand and useful.

The Bourne Shell and the C Shell

The shell is that part of the UNIX operating system that acts as an intermediary between you and the computer. It relays your commands to the computer and returns its responses to you. As we write this book, there are two main varieties of shells in widespread use. The first is the Bourne Shell, named after the man who developed it. It is the shell that comes with the standard Bell Labs release. (It may vary slightly from older to newer releases.) The second is the C Shell, developed at the University of California at Berkeley, and included as part of Berkeley Software Distribution (BSD) packages. Most of what we say in this book applies equally well to both shells, but there are differences. This book is written for the Bourne shell. See the book *UNIX Primer Plus* for a C-shell version.

How can you tell which shell you have? You can ask. You can try using a C-Shell-only feature and see if it works. Usually you can tell by the prompt. The Bourne Shell normally uses a $ as the main prompt, and the C Shell normally uses the % as the main prompt.

We've talked about the shell as being the liaison between you and the computer. Let's see how that works in the context of shell commands. First, after you log in, the shell provides you with a prompt (a $, we're assuming). It's now ready for your move. You then give it a command, such as **date**, and hit <return>. The shell then identifies this command as something it knows and causes the command to be executed, usually giving you an output on the screen. Whether it gives you an output or not, you will know when it is finished since the shell sends another prompt to the screen to let you know it is your turn again. If you type in a command it doesn't recognize—**getlost,** for example—the shell lets you know with a response like

```
getlost: not found
```

Now, let's try out one of the commands that does work; the **date** command.

The *date* Command

The **date** command displays the current date and the time on the screen. To use it, type **date** after the prompt. (Recall that commands to be typed literally will be given in boldface.) Thus the line will appear as follows:

```
$ date
```

UNIX provides the $, you provide the word **date.** (Don't forget that you have to hit the <return> key. In a way, the <return> key is *your* prompt to UNIX while $ is its prompt to you.) This line of instruction is known technically as the "command line." The result of giving this command is that UNIX prints out the date. It would look something like this:

```
Tue Jun 1 14:49:19 PST 1985
```

Note that UNIX uses a 24-hour clock and gives the time to the second. The full sequence of command and response would look like this:

```
$ date
Tue Jun 1 14:49:10 PST 1985
$
```

You can now give another command after the last prompt.

As we introduce each new command, we generously will supply you with a summary of the command. Here is the summary for **date.**

Summary: date—gives date and time		
name	**options**	**argument**
date	none	none
Description:	When you type **date**, UNIX returns the date and time of day to you.	

Although **date** has no options or arguments, we will give a brief explanation of what those terms mean now. Some commands perform "operations" such as printing or listing information. These types of commands often need something to operate on. The name of the thing operated on is called the argument. Many commands are not complete without an argument and some commands can have more than one argument. For example, to print two files one after the other, you would use a print command and the names of the two files. These two file names would be two arguments.

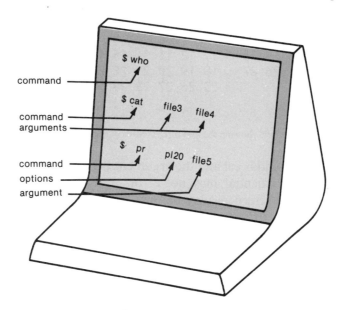

Commands, options, and arguments.

Options generally are variations on the command. For example, a printing command may have an option to double-space the output.

Our next command gives an example of arguments.

The *cal* Command

You might want to use the **cal** command next; this does not give information about California, but rather it prints out a calendar. This command takes you up a level in sophistication for it requires an argument. This argument does not mean to give UNIX any backtalk it means, as we mentioned above, to provide additional information. In this particular case, we have to supply the command with the year for which we want the calendar. Thus, the command line to produce a calendar for the year 1776 would look like this:

```
$ cal 1776
```

When we push <return>, the display shows:

```
                          1776
        Jan                   Feb                   Mar
 S  M Tu  W Th  F  S    S  M Tu  W Th  F  S    S  M Tu  W Th  F  S
    1  2  3  4  5  6             1  2  3                      1  2
 7  8  9 1Ø 11 12 13    4  5  6  7  8  9 1Ø    3  4  5  6  7  8  9
14 15 16 17 18 19 2Ø   11 12 13 14 15 16 17   1Ø 11 12 13 14 15 16
21 22 23 24 25 26 27   18 19 2Ø 21 22 23 24   17 18 19 2Ø 21 22 23
28 29 3Ø 31            25 26 27 28 29         24 25 26 27 28 29 3Ø
                                              31
```

(We are only showing the first three months of the twelve-month display here to save space.)

The command is **cal** and the argument is **1776.**

The full calendar may not fit on your screen. You can hit <control-s> to stop the screen display before January rolls up off the screen and, then, hit any key to start it up again. (Some systems may use different keys for this.)

You also can get just the calendar for one month by typing the number of the month before the year. You can use either a one-digit or a two-digit number for the month; thus May is 05, or 5. Here is the command line to get the calendar for July 1872:

```
cal 7 1872
```

Summary: cal—provides a calendar		
name	**options**	**arguments**
cal	none	[month] year

Description: This command provides a calendar for the year typed in after the command; there must be at least one space between the command and the year. The year should be in the range of 0-9999 AD. You can get the calendar for just one month by preceding the year with the number of the month, numbered from 01 to 12.

Example: To see the calendar for May 1942, type **cal 05 1942**

The month is an "optional argument," meaning it can be omitted. The year is not optional, however, you must give it. We can represent the form of this command by

```
cal [month] year
```

The brackets around "month" tell us "month" is an optional argument. You don't actually type in the brackets when you use the command. In this book, the fact that neither [month] nor year is in boldface tells us that we don't type those words literally but, instead, type in a value for them.

You can use **cal** for future calendars (up to the year 9999) as well as for the present and the past.

The *who* Command

UNIX is a time-sharing system, which means several people can use the system at the same time. In recognition of the inquisitive human nature, UNIX has a **who** command. When you give this command, UNIX responds with the list of people logged into the system at that moment. The command and its result might look something like this:

```
$ who
bob             tty04        Aug 23          8:27
nerkie          tty07        Aug 23          8:16
catfish         tty11        Aug 23          8:38
sneezy          tty15        Aug 23          8:52
granny          tty21        Aug 22         23:13
boss1776        tty24        Aug 23          9:01
$
```

The first column gives the login name of the user. The second column identifies the terminal being used. The label "tty" is a throwback to the days when most terminals were Teletype® machines that printed out on paper rather than on a screen. The number of the tty can provide a clue as to where the person is logged in from if you know what room specific terminals are placed in. The remaining columns give the date and the time each user logged in using the 24 hour clock. It looks like granny has been on the system all night, or maybe she forgot to logout again.

Teletype is a registered trademark of the Teletype Corporation.

The **who** command does contain several options, but they are not significant for us at this time.

Summary: who—who's on the system		
name	**options**	**arguments**
who	several	[am I]

Description: This command, when typed without an argument, tells you who is currently on the system. It gives you the user's login name, the terminal name, and when he logged on. If you ask **who am I,** it gives you this information just about yourself and it may also tell you which UNIX system you are on.

Example: To find who's on the system, just type **who.**

In the next chapter, we shall see how to communicate with our fellow computer people using electronic mail.

Review Questions

To help you fix in your mind the material from this chapter, we are providing you with some questions to test your knowledge. We also will provide the answers in order to keep you reassured.

A. Matching Commands

Match the command in the left column to the corresponding description in the right column.

1. who
2. passwd
3. date
4. cal

a. Gives the date and time.
b. Tells who's logged in.
c. Produces a calendar.
d. Lets you choose a password.

B. Questions

1. Identify the arguments, if any, that appear in the following commands:

    a. cal 1984
    b. cal 09 2025
    c. who

2. What's the difference (besides "or") between **passwd** and "password:"?

3. Which of the following is a basic purpose of the UNIX prompt, i.e., the "%" or "$"?

    a. To demonstrate UNIX's ability to produce unusual symbols.
    b. To tell you UNIX is ready to accept a command.
    c. To tell UNIX that you are finished.

4. What happens when you fail to hit < return >?

5. What does the phrase "hit < control-s >" mean?

6. How do you correct a typing error on the same line as the cursor?

Answers

A. 1—b, 2—d, 3—a, 4—c

B. **1.** a. **1984** b. **09** and **2025** c. no argument. **2.** "password:" is a prompt from UNIX asking you to type in your password; **passwd** is a UNIX command that initiates the process of changing your password. **3.** b, of course. **4.** Nothing happens; UNIX just sits patiently, waiting to be told that you are done and that it is its turn to do something. **5.** It means you are to depress the <s> key and the <control> key simultaneously. **6.** It depends on the terminal you use. Generally, terminals use the <backspace> key, or the <rub> key, or <control-h>, or the <#> key.

Exercises at the Terminal

The best way to learn UNIX is to use it. We hope you have been trying out the commands as you read about them. Here are some tasks you can try doing using the material in this chapter.

1. Login to your UNIX system.

2. Type **whp** and correct it to **who.**

3. If you don't have a password, give yourself one now. If you do have one, change it to a new one.

4. Find out how many people are logged in and who has been logged in the longest.

5. Find the time of day.

6. Find out on what day of the week you were born.

7. Find out on what day of the week is January 1, 1991.

3

Electronic Mail and On-Line Help: *mail, write,* and *man*

In this chapter, you will find:

- Electronic Mail
  - The UNIX Mail System
  - Sending Mail to Yourself
  - Reading Your Mail
  - Local Network Mail
  - World-Wide Network Mail
- Electronic Chit-Chat: *write*
- For Advanced Users
- The On-Line Manual
- Review Questions
- Exercises at the Terminal

3   ELECTRONIC MAIL AND ON-LINE HELP: *mail, write,* and *man*

Electronic Mail

Electronic mail is a fairly recent term for a mail delivery system that replaces conventional mail delivery with an electronic computer-based service. Electronic mail can also replace some types of telephone calls and inter-office memos. The form of electronic mail used with UNIX is sometimes called a "mailbox" system. Each user with a log-in account has a "mailbox" file that other users can send mail to.

An electronic mail system has several major benefits:

* You can create the correspondence on your keyboard or terminal and you have word processing capabilities that make entry and corrections easy.
* You can mail identical copies to several users simultaneously.
* You can print paper copies and even have them typeset.
* The mailing process is much faster than postal letters—a message reaches its destination almost instantaneously.
* Electronic mail doesn't interrupt the recipient the way a phone call does; you can read your messages at your leisure.
* The letter can be electronically filed with all the inherent advantages of that process.
* The letters may be mailed locally, such as in a local UNIX time-share system, or letters may be routed through one of several world-wide distributing networks, such as USENET.
* No stamps, envelopes, or paper are required and no trips to the post office are needed.

The major disadvantage of this type of electronic mail is that the recipient must log into his or her account to notice whether mail has been sent or not. Other forms of electronic mail can overcome this disadvantage. For example, mail can be printed on paper at the receiving end and, then, be hand-delivered like an office memo or telegram.

The UNIX Mail System

The UNIX mail system uses the command word **mail** (**Mail,** on some systems) to initiate both the sending and the receiving of mail. The mail system

actually contains several dozen options for preparing, delivering, reading, and disposing of mail. These options are briefly described in the on-line manual (under **mail**). However, most new users can get along very nicely with the simple command sequence we will describe next.

Sending Mail to Yourself

If you want to remind yourself to do something the next time you log onto the UNIX system, the mail system provides an easy service. If your login name is beth, and if you have the shell prompt appearing on the screen, you just type **mail beth** and push <return>. You can now begin drafting your letter. The UNIX mail system does not use a prompt here. Just keep typing, using <return> as you would a carriage return on a typewriter. When you complete the letter, type a lone period at the beginning of a new line. The sequence would look like this:

```
$ mail beth
Take the dog to the vet.
Sign up for the exercise class at school.
Give a big party for Bob.
```

```
.  <————————————————————————————————— (a lone period)
$
```

The next time you log in, or a few minutes later if you stay logged in, the greeting would include the happy announcement "you have mail."

Reading Your Mail

To read your mail is simplicity itself. First, you type **mail.** The system responds by displaying the last letter sent to you and then displaying a prompt sign, the question mark (?). If you want to read other letters in your mail file (mail box), just push <return>. Each letter in your mail file is read from the most recent letter to the first one sent.

Here is a sample mail treat. We'll assume that your login name is **beth** and that while you were away, two people sent mail to you.

```
$ you have mail <————————————————————————— UNIX displays
$ mail <————————————————————————————— you type

>From dick Sat May 15 15:03 1984
Hi Beth,
Are you ready for the big beach party Saturday night?
I'll pick you up at 8:00 pm sharp!
Love,
Dick


?<return> <—————————————————————————— you push

>From bob Sat May 15 15:01 1984
Hello beautiful blue eyes,
don't forget our big date
to go dancing tonight.
See you at 7:30.
Bobbybaby


?<return> <—————————————————————————— you push

end-of-file <——————————————————— UNIX says no more letters

?<return> <—————————————————————————— you push

$ <————————————————————————————————— UNIX displays
```

What happens to the letters after you read them? Nothing. They remain in your mail file until you decide what to do with them. The major choices you have are

1. Delete the letter from your mail file (**d**).
2. Save the letter to any new or old file (**s**).
3. Mail the letter to someone else (**m**).
4. Leave the letter in the mail file ( ).

To select a choice, give the appropriate command (**d, s, m**) right after reading the letter. For example, after reading the first letter, you can type

? d

to delete the letter. If you want to save the letter in a file call **bobstuff,** just give the command

? s bobstuff

If you want to just dump the letter into a large basket to hold for a while, you can use the **s** command without a file name. UNIX puts it into a file called **mbox.** This is called a "default" file for the **s** command.

The "receiving of mail" command has one other major option worth mentioning. Since the disposition of each letter takes place immediately after reading the letter, there needs to be some way to go back to look at (and dispose of) previously read mail. There is. You can use the − command (a minus sign) to display the previous letter. It would be given like this.

? − <─────────────────────────────────── display previous letter

The minus sign command can be repeated to continue back through other letters.

There are a few more "options" to the **mail** command that we have not discussed. We have left them our for simplicity and brevity. If you want to know what your options are when reading mail, type a ? followed by a <return>. If you're eager to try out everything UNIX has to offer, you need to become familiar with the UNIX manual (as well as have a lot of time). The manual will be introduced later in the chapter. Also, there might be some minor changes in how these commands work on your system. The

mail commands seem to be ones that programmers like to fool around with to improve (for example, sending copies to others or to provide an "editor" capability).

Here is the summary for the sending and receiving of mail.

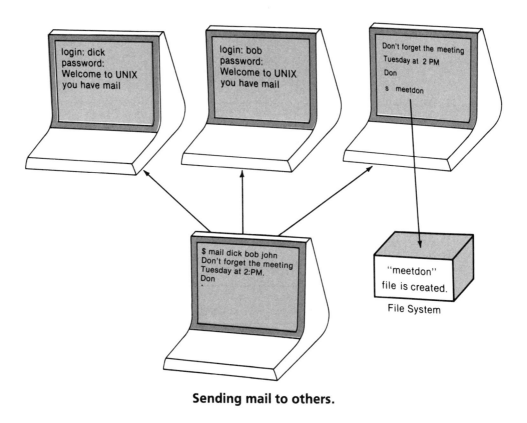

Sending mail to others.

Summary: mail—sending mail		
name	**option**	**argument**
mail	none	[people . . .]

Description: Mail can be sent to one or more people, using login names for the addresses. After you invoke the mail command and push

<return>, there is no prompt or response from the system. You should begin the typing out of your letter and when done, place a period on a separate line.

Options: None

Example: **$ mail dick bob**
             Hi Dick and Bob,
             This is my first letter using the UNIX mail system.
             Will you send me mail?
             Thanks,
             Don
             .

             $

Comments: Remember, when you finish writing the letter, you must type a period (.). A file can be sent over mail by using the redirect commands as follows:

             $ mail dick bob < filename

             This redirect command is discussed fully in Chapter 4.

Summary: `mail`—receiving mail

name	options	argument
`mail`	d, m [person . . .] F ,s [filename]	

Description: The command word **mail** with no arguments is used to check mail out of the post office for reading. The options shown below can then be used to read and dispose of your mail.

Commands: <return> Displays next message. Leaves mail.
             d   Deletes message.
             s [file] Appends message to contents of file or creates new file if none exists.

```
          q          Quits mail.
          m [person] Mails message to person.
Example:  $ mail

          > From bernd Fri Aug 27 15:51:19 1984
          To: beth

          Hello Beth! Don't forget the champagne and marshmallows!
          Burningly, Bernd

          ?q
          $
```

Local Network Mail

Network mail lets you send mail to fellow UNIX users who have login accounts on other UNIX computers. Just as the **mail** command lets you send mail to people on your own UNIX computer, network **mail** lets you send mail to people on other UNIX computers. For example, you might be working for a large company or university with several UNIX computers tied together electronically. Network mail lets you be the "postperson." You can route mail directly to its destination. Network mail is routed by giving the name of the computer (Each computer would be given a name like **daisy, lilac,** or **petunia,** etc.) and the login name of the person receiving the mail. An exclamation point (!) is used to separate all names. Here are two typical addresses

```
$ mail daisy!beth
$ mail lilac!dick
```

The **mail** command sends your mail from your UNIX computer to the computer named **daisy** or **lilac** for delivery to beth and dick.

If for some reason, your UNIX computer is not communicating directly with **lilac,** but you know that **daisy** is talking to **lilac,** then it is possible to route the mail through **daisy** with the following command:

```
$ mail daisy!lilac!dick
```

In this case, the mail goes to the **daisy** computer, which sends it on to the **lilac** computer for delivery to someone with the login name dick. Of course, this type of network mail only works if the computers are electronically connected by wire or phone lines or satellite or by some other means.

World-Wide Network Mail

Suppose that you have a friend using UNIX halfway across the country. Is it possible to send electronic mail to them? Yes indeed. That is, yes, you can send mail anywhere in the country if your UNIX computer belongs to a large network like USENET. With USENET, you can route electronic mail to any other UNIX user in the network. Right now, there are over 900 UNIX computers on the USENET system serving thousands of users. However, in order to route mail through a large network like this, you need a network map.

In a simplified view of a large network, one UNIX computer might communicate with other UNIX computers once every hour or once every six hours by telephone or by other means. Not every computer in the network calls every other computer. In order to limit phone calls and distribute costs, a network map is created with some UNIX computers serving as "nodes" or relay stations and other UNIX computers being at the end of the line. Part of a typical map is shown in the figure below.

Looking at the figure, if **you** wanted to send mail to **beth,** then the mail could be routed by either command (other routes are also possible)

```
$ mail A!E!G!F!beth
$ mail A!C!B!F!beth
```

where the names of the computers are A,B,C,D,E, and F for simplicity.

If network node E was not working due to a severe winter storm or similar calamity, then the mail would not get through. If E was down for some time, it is possible that A would give up trying to contact E and remove the letter from its files and you might never be told that the mail didn't get through. For that reason, it is always helpful to acknowledge mail received, both with network mail and regular mail.

Network mail is part of a larger communications system called **uucp,** Unix to Unix Communications Package. **uucp** has commands that allow file transfer between remote UNIX computers as well as the remote execution of commands. That is, you can send a package of commands from one UNIX computer to be run on another UNIX computer. Another **uucp** command lets you use your computer's modem to dial up or call another UNIX

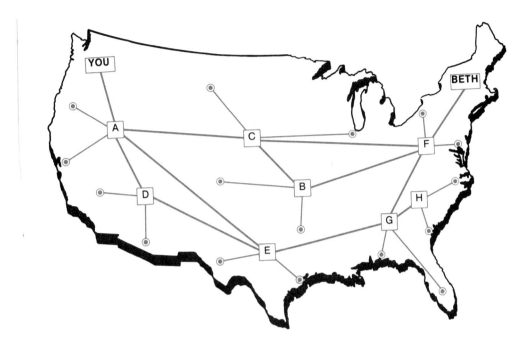

A hypothetical UNIX network.

computer in order to transfer files or run commands. If you're interested in these services, check the manual or a local guru for more details.

Electronic Chit-Chat: *write*

UNIX systems have a second form of electronic communication, one that lets you hold a conversation with another user. This method can work only if the person you want to talk to is logged in and wants to talk back. The first step is to see who is on the system; the **who** command will tell you this. Suppose you spot your old friend Hortense Grigelsby and that her login name is hortense. Then you would give the command

```
write hortense
```

She would then get this message on her screen:

```
Message from abner on tty 14 at 09:56 . . .
```

(We are assuming that your login name is abner.)

Meanwhile, on your screen, the cursor will advance to a line with no prompt. Now each line you type on your terminal will be transmitted to Hortense's terminal when you hit the <return> key. (The line also shows on your screen as you type it.) When you have finished your say, hit <control-d>. This will restore your regular prompt to you and will send the message "EOT" (for "end of transmission") to Hortense's terminal, so that she will know you are done.

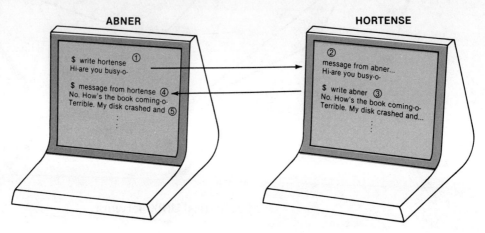

Abner writing Hortense and vice versa.

To get a two-way exchange, once she learns that you are writing her, she can enter

```
write abner
```

Then she can send you messages while you send her messages. On most systems, what she types can appear in the middle of your typing and vice versa. It is best to adopt a sensible code of behavior. A simple one to use, that is similar to CB radio, is to type

```
-o-
```

for "over" when you have completed a thought, and to type

```
-oo-
```

for "over-and-out" when you intend to quit. These are not commands, they are just ways to help you coordinate communication with your partner.

In Chapter 10, we will show you how to block **write** messages using the **msgs** command if you wish to work undisturbed.

Summary: `write`—write to another user

name	options	arguments
write		user login name

Description: **write** transmits lines from your terminal to the other user's terminal. Transmission occurs when you hit the <return> key. Transmission is terminated by hitting <control-d>; this sends EOT to the other user.

Note: To block incoming messages from interrupting your work, use the **mesg** command described in Chapter 10.

For Advanced Users

Who is an advanced user? It might be someone with considerable experience with computers. It might be someone of unusual brilliance. Or, it might be someone with a lot of time on her hands. It might be you. If so, we offer you some additional material to help take you beyond what this book offers. We can do this because the UNIX system itself contains information about UNIX. There is an extensive manual stored in the system memory.

The On-Line Manual

There is a very large document called the UNIX System V User's Manual. It is available in bound printed form; Volume 1 is also stored in a file on disk memory. This second version is called the "on-line" manual. All the UNIX commands and utilities are documented in this manual and you can easily summon this information to your terminal screen. Sound great? It is, except for one point. The manual is written for experienced UNIX programmers, not for beginners. (That's one reason we wrote this book!) This may not be a problem if the command you wish to study is a simple one like **date.** But, for other cases, you may have to put in a goodly amount of trial-and-error work to see how to apply the information to your needs. But, then, that's a great way to learn!

How do you tap into this fount of knowledge? By typing **man** followed by the name of the command you wish to study. For example, to learn all there is to know about **date,** type

```
man date
```

(Don't forget the space between **man** and **date.**)

To learn more about the **man** command itself, type

```
man man
```

(Don't forget the <return> key.) Be prepared to wait a bit; it sometimes takes the system quite a while to find the desired entry. (Oddly enough, the entries are scattered throughout the system.) Here is an excerpt from the UNIX on-line manual as it might appear if we typed **man who.**

```
WHO(1)                    UNIX User's Manual                    WHO(1)

NAME
 who — who is on the system
SYNOPSIS
 who [ — uTlpdbrtas] [ file ]
 who am i
DESCRIPTION
 Who lists the user's name, terminal line, login time,
 elapsed time since activity occurred on the line, and the
 process-ID of the command interpreter (shell) for each
 current system user. It examines the /etc/utmp file to
 obtain its information. If file is given, that file is
 examined. Usually, file is /etc/wtmp, which contains a
 history of all the logins since the file was last created.

 Who with the am i option identifies the invoking user.

 Except for the default —s option, the general format for
 output entries is:
```

```
     name [ state ] line time activity pid [ comment ]
     [ exit ]
```

With options, *who* lists logins, logoffs, reboots, and changes to the system clock, as well as other processes spawned by the init process. These options are:

 −u List information about those users who are currently logged in. The *name* is the user's login name. The *line* is the name of the line as found in the directory /dev. The *time* is the time that the user logged in. The *activity* is the number of hours and minutes since

. . . . . more information follows, but is not shown here . . .

```
FILES
     /etc/utmp
     /etc/wtmp
     /etc/inittab
SEE ALSO
     init(1M) in the SYSTEM V/68 Administrator's Manual.
     date(1), login(1), mesg(1), su(1), wait(2), inittab(4),
     utmp(4).
```

This example follows the typical format of the UNIX Manual entries.

First, under the heading of "NAME," there is the name and a brief description of the command. Next, there is a SYNOPSIS which shows how the command is used.

who [− **uTlpdbrtas**] [file]

This form indicates that the **who** command has several optional arguments, indicated by the presence of brackets.

Then comes a description. As you can see, the description presupposes knowledge about the system (such as what /etc/wtmp is), but you can just filter out the parts that don't yet concern you.

Next comes a section called "FILES." It contains a list of files used by UNIX to run this particular command.

The "SEE ALSO" section lists some related commands and utilities. The numbers in parentheses tell which section of the manual contains the description. Thus, **who(1)** is in the first section and **utmp(4)** is in the fourth section.

The UNIX manual, Volume One, has 6 sections.

1. Commands
2. System Calls
3. Subroutines
4. File Formats
5. Miscellaneous
6. Games

Unless you are quite advanced, you probably will be most interested in Section 1 and, perhaps, Section 6.

Summary: man—find manual information by keywords

name	options	arguments
man	several	section

Description: When used with no argument, this command searches the entire on-line manual for the section containing the keyword. It then prints a description of the command similar to the printed version of the manual.

Example: **man cat**
This command will display on the screen the on-line manual explanation of the command **cat**.
Note: **man** is usually quite slow in carrying out its service, have patience.
Note: To keep the screen from scrolling too much information, try using < control-s >.

Review Questions

Questions

Here are some review questions and their answers to remind you of some of the more important points in this chapter.

1. After giving the **mail** command to send mail, do you get a prompt?

2. How do you finish a letter in order to send it?

3. If you have five letters in your mail file (sent to you), which one gets read first? What command do you give to read the next letter?

4. Give the command to save the last letter read in your **mail** file.

5. How do you get out of the **mail** (receive) mode?

Answers to Questions

1. No. 2. Begin a new line with a period. 3. The most recent one. Use the <return> key. 4. Use the save command **s**. 5. Either use **q** or step through your letters with the <return> key.

Exercises at the Terminal

1. Read your **mail** file (if you have one) to see if it contains any old letters.

2. Send yourself mail, perhaps some reminders of things to do today. When the message arrives at your terminal that you have mail, read it, and save it in a file called **today.**

3. Try the command **who** to see if anyone you know is using a terminal right now. If so, use the **write** command to ask him or her if you can practice sending some mail.

4. Send mail to someone you know (or would perhaps like to know).

5. If you read the section concerning the "on-line" manual, try using the manual on a command you already know about. Then, experiment with it. You can't hurt it.

4

Files and Directories: *ls, cat, and pr*

In this chapter, you will find:

4 FILES AND DIRECTORIES: *ls, cat,* and *pr*

Introduction

The UNIX file and directory system is wonderfully simple yet versatile. The best way to learn its features is to use them, so we strongly urge you to experiment with the commands we will present, even if you don't really need to use them yet.

You need to know three things to use the file and directory system with ease and understanding. First, you need to know the structure of the system. That will be the first topic of the chapter.

Secondly, you need a way of finding out what files you have; the **ls** command will help you there. Thirdly, the **cat** and **pr** commands will handle the next necessity, that of seeing what is in the files. These three commands form the core of our relationship with our files.

Of course, it would be nice to have a way to create files, and that will be the subject of Chapters 5 and 6. However, we will give you a head start in this chapter by showing you a quick and easy way to produce files. (Actually, you already have learned one way—sending mail to yourself!)

That's whats coming up, so let's begin by seeing how UNIX organizes files.

Files and the UNIX Directory System

Files are the heart of the UNIX system. The programs you create, the text you write and edit, the data you acquire, and all the UNIX programs are stored in files. Anything you want the computer to remember for you, you must save in a file. One very important skill to acquire, then, is the ability to create files; we will start you off on that in this chapter. But unless you can keep track of your files, it doesn't do much good to create them. The UNIX directory system is designed to help you with the extremely important task of keeping track of your files.

Just as a telephone directory contains a list of subscribers, a UNIX directory contains a list of files and subdirectories, each of which can contain lists of more files and subdirectories. Let's look at the most basic example of a directory—the "home directory."

When you are given an account on the system, you are assigned a "home directory." When you log in, you can think of yourself as being "in" your home directory. (Later you will learn to change directories but, for now, let's keep you confined to your home directory.) Now, suppose you create a file. You will have to give it a name. (See the box on file names.) Suppose you call it **ogre.** This name will then be added to the list of files in your home directory and, in future instructions, you can refer to the file as **ogre.** After you have created a few files, you can visualize your home directory as looking like the following sketch. (We'll explain the "branches and leaves" stuff in a minute.) Also, you can think of your directory as being your personal filing cabinet and of the files as being labeled file folders.

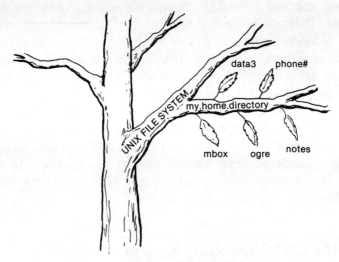

A home directory.

Of course, every other user has his home directory, too, so UNIX needs a way to tell home directories apart. UNIX accomplishes this by giving your home directory a name, usually your login name. Next, UNIX needs a way of keeping track of all these home directories. It does this with a new directory—a directory of directories. Typically, this directory would be called **usr,** and the home directories are termed "subdirectories" of **usr.** The following diagram will help you visualize this.

Notice that the **usr** directory in this example contains some files (leaves) as well as directories (branches). In general, any directory can contain both files and subdirectories.

Is **usr** the ultimate directory? No, that distinction goes to a directory called / and known informally as **root.** (Computers are usually not that informal; they insist on /. However, **root** is easier to say, so we'll use that

The *usr* directory.

name.) All other directories stem directly or indirectly from **root** which, of course, is why it is called **root.** The following sketch (The directory system) represents a complete directory system.

The drawing looks a lot like a tree; the directories are the trunk and the branches, and the files are the leaves. For this reason, the UNIX directory system is often described as having a tree structure. (Here the metaphors get a big confusing, for the **root** directory is the trunk of the tree.)

A different analogy portrays the system as a hierarchy like, say, the organization of an army. At the top is the **root** directory. Serving under **root** is the next rank of directories; **usr, bin,** and the like. Each of these, in turn, commands a group of lower-ranking directories, and so on. The next figure represents the hierarchal view.

The directory system, then, provides structure for the organization of files. It also provides a clear way of specifying the location of a file, and we will explore that in Chapter 7.

What can you do in the UNIX directory system? You can expand it by adding subdirectories (branches) to your home directory, and subdirectories to those subdirectories. You can change directories (move to another limb), moving your field of action to, say, one of your subdirectories. And, you can place files (leaves) in any directory or subdirectory that you control.

The words file and directory are sometimes used with two different

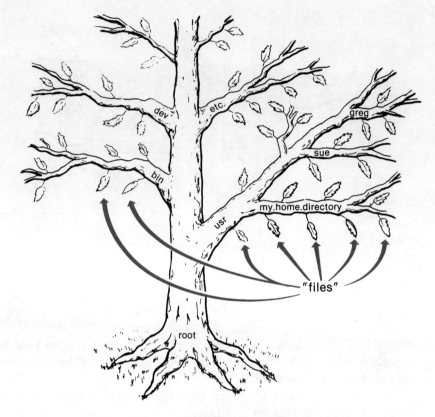

The directory system.

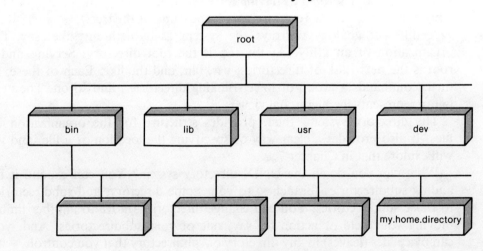

The UNIX hierarchy.

meanings and can create confusion at first. We often talk about the "file system" or the "directory system," where both terms refer to the entire system of files and directories. On the other hand, we say that a file can only contain information; it cannot have directories coming from it. The analogy of the files being like leaves and the directories being like branches of a tree keeps the proper relationship.

File And Directory Names

UNIX gives you much freedom in naming your files and directories. The name can be from one to fourteen characters long, and you can use about any character you want. However, you will be better off if you avoid using characters that have a special meaning to UNIX. In particular, avoid using the following characters: / \ \ " ' * ; - ? [ ] ( ) ~ ! $ { } < >. (It is not, necessarily, impossible to use these characters, just inconvenient.) You can use digits as part of a filename with no difficulty; in fact, you can give names like **22** if you like. However, it does make sense to make the names as descriptive as possible.

UNIX uses spaces to tell where one command or filename ends and another begins, so you should avoid spaces in names. The usual convention is to use a period or underline mark where you normally would use a space. For example, if you wanted to give the name **read me** to a file, you could call it **read.me** or **read__me** instead.

Uppercase letters are distinguished from lowercase letters, so **fort, Fort, forT,** and **FORT** would be considered four distinct names.

UNIX make no distinction between names that can be assigned to files and those that can be assigned to directories. Thus, it is possible to have a file and a directory with the same name; the **snort** directory could have a file in it called **snort.** This doesn't confuse UNIX, but it might confuse you. Some users adopt the convention of beginning directory names with a capital letter and beginning filenames with a small letter.

Listing Directories: *ls*

The **ls** command is used to list the contents of a directory. Let's take a hypothetical example and see how this command is used. Samuel Spade is a new student enrolled in a burgeoning computer science course (called cs1) at a very large university. His UNIX login name is sammy and his instructor has identified his account in the UNIX hierarchy as shown in the following diagram. (In this case, a directory other than/**usr** is being used to house the student accounts.) We'll use black lines to identify directories and blue lines for files.

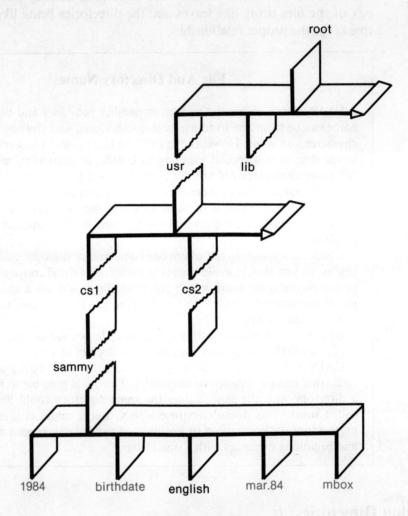

Sammy's directory.

We assume that Sammy is properly logged in and has established contact with the shell as indicated by the $ prompt. At this point, the shell is ready to execute his every whim (command). In our hypothetical situation, if Sammy types

```
ls
```

the system would respond with

```
1984  birthdate  english  mar.84  mbox
```

We'll list the file and directory names horizontally. Your system might list them vertically.

These are the names of the four files and one subdirectory in Sammy's account. The directory is **english,** and it is listed along with the files. How can we tell it is a directory? We can't tell just by looking at this list. Either we have to remember that it is a subdirectory, or else we can use the −**P** options described later.

Well, that is pretty simple, and you probably won't need to know more than this at first. But there is more to **ls** than what we just have seen. For one thing, you can list the contents of just about any directory, not just your own. Secondly, in the words of one version of the on-line manual, "There are an unbelievable number of options."

We will look into some of these options now. If you want to skip ahead, that's okay, but remember to come back to these pages when you need them.

Choosing Directories

If you just type **ls**, you get a listing of your "current working directory." Right now, that would be your login directory but, later, when you learn how to change directories, it will be whatever directory you are currently working in (just like the name says!). To get a listing of files and directories in some other directory, you just follow **ls** with the name of the directory you want to see. For instance, the command

```
ls english
```

would show what is in the directory **english.** Note that there has to be a space between **ls** and the directory name. The directory names may be a little more involved than this example; you will learn all about that when you get to the section on "pathnames" in Chapter 7.

Some *ls* Options

You tell UNIX which options you want by using option flags, just as we described for **who** in Chapter 2. The flag should be separated by spaces from the command name and from any following arguments. Suppose, for example, that Sammy types

```
ls −s
```

The −s option is a "size" option; it gives the size of the file in blocks. (Files are built from blocks having a size of 1024 bytes, in our example.) The UNIX response would look like this:

```
total 17        13 birthdate   1 mar.84
  1 1984         1 english      1 mbox
```

Thus, the file **birthdate** contains 13 blocks or 26 x 1024 = 26,624 bytes.

This might give you a small surprise; try

```
ls −a
```

If Sammy does this, he will find some strange entries!

```
.         .profile  1984       english   mbox
..        .login    birthdate  mar.84
```

The −a option stands for "all," and it lists some things normally invisible to the reader. As we will discuss later, the single period is short for the directory itself, while the double period is short for the parent directory. These entries are part of the scheme that binds directories together, and they need not concern us here. The other new entry is a special file used by UNIX to set up operating conditions in Sammy's directory. We will discuss them in Chapter 10.

The bulkiest and most informative option is the −l, or long, option. For Sammy, this option would produce the following listing:

```
total 17
−rw−r−−r−− 1 sammy     231 Aug 18 12:34 1984
−rw−r−−r−− 1 sammy   13312 Jul 22 16:05 birthdate
drwxr−xr−x 2 sammy     112 Aug 29 10:15 english
−rw−r−−r−− 1 sammy      52 Aug 01 17:45 mar.84
−rw−r−−r−− 1 sammy     315 Aug 28 09:24 mbox
```

The "total" entry shows the number of blocks used. After that comes one line for each file or directory. The first character in each line tells if the entry is a file (shown by a ''−'') or a directory (shown by a ''d''). Next come several letters and hyphens. These describe ''permissions'' to read and use files; we'll take that matter up when we discuss **chmod** in Chapter 10. Then comes a numeral that gives the number of ''links.'' (See the **ln** command in Chapter 7.) Next comes Sammy's login name; this column tells who ''owns'' the file. Next comes the actual length of the file in bytes. Then comes the date and time the file was last changed. Finally, there is the filename.

You can use more than one option by stringing together the option letters. For example, the command

```
ls −la
```

would produce a long listing for all the files revealed by the −**a** option.

The following summary will give a few more options for your pleasure.

Summary: ls—list contents of directory

name	option	argument
ls	[−a,c,l,p,r, s, + others]	[directory . . .]

Description: **ls** will list the contents of each directory named in the argument. The output, which can be a list of both files and subdirectories, is given alphabetically. When no argument is given, the current directory is listed.

Options: −**a** lists all entries.
−**c** lists by time of file creation.
−**l** lists in long format, giving links, owner, size in bytes, and time of last file change.
−**p** marks directories with a /.
−**r** reverses the order of the listing.
−**s** gives the size in blocks of 1024 (may vary) bytes.

Example: **ls −c**
This command will list the contents of the current directory in the order that they were created.

> Comments: Remember that directories contain only the "names" of files and subdirectories. To read information contained in a file, use **cat.** As with many UNIX commands, different UNIX systems may use different letters for options.

Reading Files: *cat*

cat is short for the word "concatenate," which means to link together. However, some people prefer to think of it as catalog. It can be used to display the contents of one or more files on the terminal screen. To display one of the files in Sammy's account, e.g., **mar.84,** you would type

```
cat mar.84
```

The system would then print whatever was in the file named **mar.84.** Here we assume it looks like this:

```
      March 1984
   S   M  Tu   W  Th   F   S
                    1   2   3
   4   5   6   7   8   9  10
  11  12  13  14  15  16  17
  18  19  20  21  22  23  24
  25  26  27  28  29  30  31
```

As you can see, this file contains a calendar for the month of March. Apparently, Sammy has mastered the **cal** command (Chapter 2) and has learned how to save the output. (See "redirection" later in this chapter.)

To read another file, for example, the one called **mbox,** you would type

```
cat mbox
```

If you make a mistake and type

```
cat box
```

UNIX will appeal to your sympathies with

```
cat: cannot open box
```

The **cat** command is summarized in the following table.

Summary: cat—concatenate and print

---

name	option	argument
cat		[file . . .]

Description: **cat** reads each file in sequence and writes it on the standard output (terminal).

If no filename is given, or if "−" is given as a filename, **cat** reads the standard input (the keyboard); a <control-d> will terminate keyboard input. (This latter process is described later in this chapter.)

If the file is too large for a single screen, try using

<control-s> to stop the file information appearing on the screen, or use the **pr** command described next.

Options: **none**

Example: **cat file2**
                   This will print **file2.**

Comments: If no input file is given, **cat** takes its input from the terminal keyboard. Later in this chapter, we show that **cat** and redirect together are very useful. Note: The redirection operator uses the symbol >. You can use **cat** > **file5** to create a new file called **file5** and can enter text into that file. You can use **cat file2 file3** > > **file4** to append **file2** and **file3** to the end of **file4.**

Simple Page Formatting: *pr*

The major problem with **cat** is that it won't wait for you. For example, if we assume the file **1984** is a full calendar, then there isn't enough room to fit it on the screen. **cat** doesn't care. **cat** will fill the screen full, and then continue adding more information at the bottom of the screen, scrolling the screen upwards. The first few months go by too fast to read, let alone reminisce.

There are two ways to handle the problem of screen scrolling. If we have too much information for one screen, for example, when using **cat** or **mail,** we can use <control-s> to stop the scrolling and any key to start it back up. The second way to handle large amounts of information is to use the **pr** or print command.

The **pr** command was created primarily to prepare file information for printing with a line printer (see the **lp** command in Chapter 10). However, like many UNIX commands, **pr** has a host of options, three of which are handy for viewing files.

The **pr** command with no options formats text to fit on a page 66 lines long. When you use it, **pr** puts a five-line heading at the top of the page consisting of two blank lines, an identifying line and two more blank lines. At the bottom of the page, it puts five blank lines. For instance, the command

```
pr mbox
```

would produce the following output

```
< ——————————————————————————————————— (two blank lines)
Jul 27 19:34 1985 mbox Page 1
< ——————————————————————————————————— (two blank lines)
Hi Beth,
How about . . .
< ——————————————————————————————————— (56 lines of text)
                                        (then 5 blank lines)
```

Since most crt terminals only hold 24 lines of text, a straight, no-option, **pr** command is most unsatisfactory. The text scrolls by just like the **cat** command, except that the bottom lines are left blank. The trick is to use the **−l** option to limit the page length to about 20 lines and the **−p** option which pauses before printing each page. The pause option requires a <return> keystroke in order to print a page. The modified **pr** command would look like this.

```
pr −pl20 mbox
```

You might think of the "pl" combination standing for "page-length." In this example, we set the page-length to 20 lines. Remember to hit a <return> to display the first page as well as to display each following page.

There are more than a dozen options available with **pr,** five of which are shown in the Summary.

Summary: pr—prints partially formatted file onto standard output

name	options	arguments
pr	[−d,l,p,t,w + others]	[filenames]

Description: **pr** prints the named file onto the standard output. It divides the text into 66-line pages, placing five blank lines at the bottom of the page and a five-line heading at the top. The heading consists of two blank lines, a line bearing the date, filename, and page number, and two more blank lines.

Options:	−d	doublespace lines
	−l k	set page length to k lines
	−p	pause until a <return> before displaying page
	−t	suppress the five-line head and tail
	−w	set line width to k positions

Examples: **pr myths**

This command prints out the file **myths** as just described; the heading would include a line like:

```
May 1 12:29 1983 myths Page 1
```

pr −pl20 myths

Printing pauses until you hit <return>, then prints 20 lines and pauses.

Creating Files With *cat*

Now that you can list files and display the contents of text files, you undoubtedly are eager to create files of your own. After all, that's where the action is! The best way to create files is to use one of the UNIX editors that we will discuss in Chapters 5 and 6. That will take a bit of practice on your part; luckily, however, we can use **cat** again (a versatile animal) to produce files much more simply.

Suppose, for example, you wish to create a file called **poem** to contain an original composition. You can use this procedure:

```
cat > poem
A bunch of officers
Sat in their tunics
Hoping to learn
more about UNIX
<control-d>
```

When <control-d> is typed, your words are funneled into the file **poem.** To check if the procedure worked, just type **cat poem** and see the glory of your work shine again on the screen.

You now can create files, so please go ahead and create some; then you can try out this chapter's commands as you read along. Right now, however, we are going to take a brief side excursion to explain why this last procedure works. If you are eager to move ahead, you can skim through the explanation, but do pay attention to the parts on redirection.

How does this command work? There are two tricks involved. The first trick is that if you *don't* tell **cat** what file to look at (i.e., if you type **cat** and <return> without providing a filename), it will look at whatever you type in next on the terminal. Indeed, it considers *your input* to be a file. A <control-d> tells UNIX that you are done pretending to be a file; until you type that, you can put in as many lines and <return>'s as you like. Secondly, we have used the magic of "redirection," a UNIX ability we will discuss fully in Chapter 9. The > is a redirection operator; it takes information that ordinarily would be sent to the screen and channels it to the following file instead. (You can remember this easily by seeing that the > character looks like a funnel!)

Let's look at each trick separately. First, suppose you type

```
cat
```

with no filename following it. (Remember to hit <return>, however.) Then, the cursor (the white square of light) drops down to the next line, but you don't get a prompt. You, then, can type whatever text you like, hitting <return> to end the line. **cat** takes what you wrote and sends it to your screen. Now you have a copy (on the screen) of what you just typed. In other words, **cat** does what it always does; it prints a copy of the file on the screen. The only difference is that, in this case, the file was your fresh input instead of a stored file. Use a single <control-d> to leave the "cat input" mode. Be careful not to hit two <control-d>'s or you will log out. The exchange could look like this:

```
$ cat
Help! I have lost my trained fleas! <————————— original
Help! Help me, please! <————————————————— version
<control-d>
Help! I have lost my trained fleas! <————————— displayed
Help! Help me, please! <————————————————— version
$
```

The final line (the $ sign) tells you that UNIX is done.

What about the redirection part? Any command that normally sends output to the screen can be followed by the operator > and a filename. This will cause the output to be sent to file instead of to the screen. For instance,

```
who > turkeys
```

will place the list of users who are logged on into a file called **turkeys.** Where does the file come from? It is created on the spot! As soon as UNIX spots the redirection operator, it looks at the name following it and creates a file by that name.

Using *cat* to read a file.

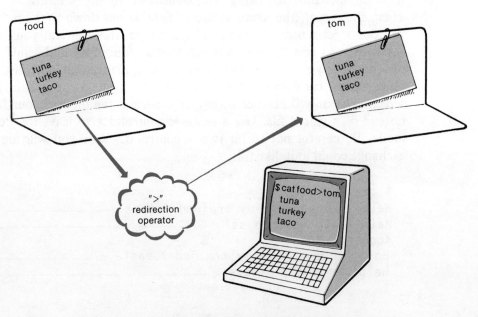

Using *cat* to read a file but redirecting the output.
***cat* being redirected.**

What if you already have a file by that name? It is *wiped out* and replaced by the new version. As you can see, this is an area in which you will want to be very careful. A careless command like the preceding example could wipe out your previous **turkeys** file of famous turkeys from history! Note, however, the box in Chapter 10 that outlines ways to protect your files.

Look back again at our example with the excellent poem. Notice how the command line (**cat > poem**) contains all the necessary instructions: where to get the material (i.e., the keyboard), what to do with it (**cat** it), and where to put the results (into the file **poem**).

Of course, this method doesn't allow you to make corrections to the file. To gain that ability, you really do need to learn about the editors.

This method of creating files involves the concepts of "input" and "output," so we will take a quick peek at just what this means.

The figure shows yet another example of redirection.

Input and Output

UNIX deals with at least three levels of input and output. First, a computer has a variety of input and output devices like terminals, printers, and disk storage units. Secondly, there is the information transmitted through these devices; it, too, is termed input and output, depending on its destination. An interactive system such as UNIX normally accepts input from the keyboard (the characters you type) and "routes" its output (the characters it produces) to the screen. The keyboard and the screen are termed the standard input and output devices.

Thirdly, a command also can have an input and output. For example, **cat** takes its input from the filename following it, and, normally, it sends its output to the output device, the screen. On the other hand, you don't have to supply **date** with an input, but it does give you an output. The redirection operators deal with the input to and the output from commands.

More on Redirection

The > operator is a very useful tool. It can be used with any command or program that normally sends output to the screen. For example,

```
cal Ø3 1984 > mar.84
```

would first create the file **mar.84,** then execute the **cal** command. The output of **cal,** which would be the calendar for March 1984, is placed in the **mar.84** file.

Note that > redirects output from a command to a file, not to other commands or programs. For example,

```
poem > cat
```

does not work because **poem** is not a command.

Let's look at one more example of redirection. Assume you have files called **bigbucks** and **morebucks.** What will the following command do?

```
cat bigbucks morebucks > laundry
```

Let's answer the question step by step.

1. What's the input? The files **bigbucks** and **morebucks.**
2. What's the operation? **cat,** or concatenate.
3. What's the output of the operation? The input files printed in succession.
4. What's the output destination? The file **laundry.**
5. What's the final result? The file **laundry** contains combined copies of the files **bigbucks** and **morebucks.**

Now for one more word of CAUTION: Do not try a command of the form:

```
cat bigbucks morebucks > bigbucks
```

While you might think this would result in adding the contents of **morebucks** to what was in **bigbucks.** However, the right-hand side of the command starts things off by erasing **bigbucks** before any **cat**ing is done. When UNIX gets to the **cat** part, **bigbucks** is already empty!

All in all, **cat** is a pretty useful command. You can use it to see the contents of a file, to create new files, and to make copies of one or more files. And, unlike the domestic variety, the UNIX "cat" obeys instructions!

We'll learn more about redirecting input and output later in Chapter 9.

Review Questions

The basic commands of this chapter will become second nature as you begin to depend on the UNIX file system to help you handle information. Here are some review questions to give you confidence in using the system and matching commands to functions.

Match the functions shown on the left to the commands shown on the right. The answers are given after the questions.

1. `cat dearsue`	**a.** Prints the contents of a file, one page at a time.
2. `pr -pl20 butter`	**b.** Lists contents of the present directory.
3. `cat story.1 story.2`	**c.** Prints the contents of **story.1** and **story.2** on the screen.
4. `ls`	**d.** Prints out the contents of the file **dearsue.**
5. `who > userlist`	**e.** Places a copy of who is presently logged into the system in the file **userlist.**

Answers:

1—d, 2—a, 3—c, 4—b, 5—e

Exercises at the Terminal

Even if you have been following the chapter while sitting at a terminal, you might like to try these exercises to illustrate the major commands and to practice their use.

1. List the contents of your home directory.

2. Use both **cat** and **pr −pl20** on each file (assuming you only have three or four files to look at).

3. After using a command that works as you expect, try the command again but with an error in it to see what happens. For example, try **lss** or **cat date** or **dates.**

4. Can you use **cat** and *redirect* to place a copy of all your files into a new file? Hint: Try **cat a b c d > e.** If this worked, try to add today's date to the top of the new file **e.** (Hint: It's all right to change filenames.)

5. Try to read the file(s) you created in Problem 4, using **cat.**

6. Send mail to yourself using the method you were shown in Chapter 3.

7. Read your mail and save any letters in a new file, perhaps calling it **letters1.**

8. Create a file using **cat** and call it **today.** Put in a list of some of the things you have to do today.

9. Try out some of the options with the **pr** and **ls** commands; for example, you might try **pr −dl20 today,** or **ls −c.**

5

Using Editors: The *ex* Family of Editors

In this chapter, you will find:

- Introduction
- Introduction to Editing
  - The Memory Buffer
  - Two Modes of Editor Operation
- Comparing the Line Editor and the Screen Editor
- The Line Editors: *ex* and *edit*
  - Calling the *ex* Editor
- The *ex* Command Format
  - Locating Lines
  - Pattern Searching
  - Stepping Through Text
- The *ex* Text Input Mode
  - The Append, Write, and Quit Commands: *a, w,* and *q*
  - Summary of Examples
- The Substitute Command: *s*
- Additional Editing Commands in *ex*
  - Making Searches and Substitutions Global: *g*
  - The Undo Command: *u*
- Reading, Writing, and Moving: *r, w,* and *m*
- Review Questions
- Exercises at the Terminal

5 USING EDITORS: THE *ex* FAMILY OF EDITORS

Introduction

These UNIX editors are the key to creative use of the computer. These editors allow you to create and alter text files that might contain love letters, form letters, sales data, programs in FORTRAN, Pascal, or BASIC, word processing, interactive programs, and much more. This chapter and the next chapter introduce the major features of the **ex** family of editors. The **ex** family of editors consists of three different editors called **ex, edit** and **vi.** In addition, an old cousin, the **ed** editor is available on most UNIX systems. The main characteristics of these editors are:

ex family of editors
>**ex** . . . . A sophisticated ''line'' editor, replaces **ed.**
>
>**edit** . . . . A slimmed down version of **ex,** useful for beginners.
>
>**vi** . . . . A ''visual'' editor, great for everyday editing.

cousin ed
>**ed** . . . . The original standard line editor.

Introduction to Editing

In the UNIX operating system, everything is stored in files, even the UNIX operating system itself. Earlier, we learned to place text, data, or programs into files by using either **mail** or redirection (>). The chief problem with those two methods is that the only way to make changes or corrections to a file is to erase the entire file and start over.

The UNIX editors overcome this problem. They let you alter files efficiently and easily, providing you with the basic support you need for most UNIX tasks. In these sections, we will give an overview of how editors and editor ''buffers'' work. Then, we will describe the major features of **ex.** We will take up **vi** in the following chapter.

The Memory Buffer

Our files are stored in the system's memory. When we set an editor to work on a file, it leaves the original file undisturbed. Instead, it creates a copy of the file for you to work with. This copy is kept in a temporary workspace called the "buffer." The changes you make are made in this copy, not in the original file. If you want to keep the changes you have made, you must then replace the original file with your worked-over copy. This is simple to do; you just give the write (or **w**) command, and the original file is replaced by the updated version. (Note: This write command is an editor command; it is not the same write that is used in sending messages to other users.)

This "buffered" approach has a big advantage. If you really botch your editing job (accidentally deleting a page, for example), you haven't damaged the original file. Just quit the editor (using the quit or **q**) command without writing, and all evidence and effects of your error(s) disappear, leaving the original file unchanged.

There is, we confess, a disadvantage to this method of operation. Your changes are not saved automatically. *You must remember to* write *your changes!* If you quit without doing so, your changes are discarded. Some versions of UNIX editors try to jog your memory if you try to quit without writing your changes, but some don't. The failure to save editing changes has led to many an anguished cry and slapped forehead across this great nation. It may even happen to you, but you have been warned.

Next, we look at how the editing process works.

Two Modes of Editor Operation

The **ex** and **vi** editors have two basic modes of operation: the Text Input Mode and the editing or Command Mode. An overview of these two modes can be seen in the following diagram.

When we first "enter" an editor, we are placed in the Command Mode. This means that any keyboard entry is interpreted to be a command like those commands shown previously. In this mode, we could delete a word or a line or change a spelling error. We can enter the Text Input Mode by using the append command, that is, by typing the <a> key. Now any key entry will be interpreted as text to be stored in the buffer, not as a command as before. We now can enter text representing FORTRAN programs, sales data, or chapters in a book. Each editor has only one way to leave (exit) the Text Input Mode; use the <esc> key to leave **vi,** or use a period <.> as the first and only character on a line by itself to leave **ex,** as shown in the preceding diagram.

If you like what you have written in the Text Input Mode or modified in the Command Mode, then it can be permanently saved in memory by using the write command. The write command is quite versatile. You can save the

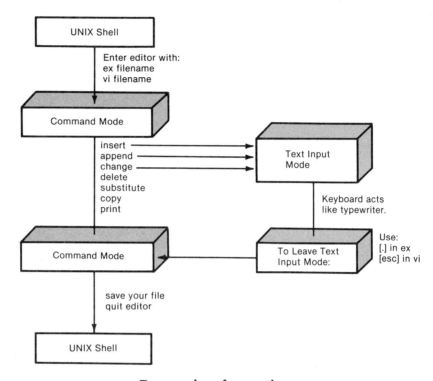

Two modes of operation.

entire buffer or a portion of the buffer using "line numbers." You can also save or write to the existing file (created when you first went into the editor) or you can write to a new file (creating the new file in the process). These "saving" techniques are almost identical in both UNIX editors. They will be discussed in detail later in the specific sections devoted to each editor.

You might be wondering which editor you should use. In the next section, we will present an overview of these two editors and how to use them.

Comparing the Line Editor and the Screen Editor

All UNIX systems running UNIX System V support the **ex** family of editors. Some UNIX systems support other editors like EMACS or INED. Which editor should you use? We recommend that you start with the screen editor, **vi,** if you generally use a crt terminal. Our experience at one college showed that the great majority of students exposed to both editors wound up using **vi.**

103

The following table gives a brief comparison of these two editors. However, many of the comments and terms might be new and will not seem important until you have tried some editing yourself.

Table 5–1. Comparing *vi* With *ex*

Function	ex	vi
Terminal	Tty, crt	Crt
Text Display	Fair. In **ex,** you display "lines" of the file but you must tell **ex** what lines you want to see.	Good. In **vi,** you always have a full page of text before you. Text can be "scrolled" or "paged."
Text Input Mode	Good. Has three commands to enter this mode.	Better. Has eleven commands to enter this mode.
Command Mode		
1. Making changes within lines.	Cumbersome, since you must type the words you replace.	Easy, since you can type over the words you replace.
2. Handling large text files.	Somewhat cumbersome.	Easy, since you can "scroll" and "page."
3. Deleting lines.	Easy.	Easy.
4. Moving lines around.	Easy.	Easy.
5. Global searching and replacing.	Easy.	Easy.
6. Saving text.	Easy.	Easy.

The last three text editing features use almost identical commands. In fact, **vi** has access to all commands in **ex** by just prefacing those commands with a colon [:].

In the next section, we will take a detailed look at the line editor, **ex.** If you plan to use **vi,** you may easily skip to the next chapter for now.

The Line Editors: *ex* and *edit*

All of the commands in this chapter apply equally well to the two line editors **ex** and **edit.** The major difference between these editors is that **edit** lacks some of the features of **ex,** which reduces the chance of surprises for new users.

We will be using **ex** throughout this chapter, but if you have a knack for getting into strange places, feel free to substitute **edit** for **ex.** The two principal advantages of **ex** over **edit** are that you can move from **ex** to **vi** and back again, and that **ex** has more abbreviations that can be used for text searches.

We will begin this section by describing how you get into and out of the editor. Then, the format for issuing commands in **ex** will be discussed. After that, we present examples of how to input and edit text. This section concludes with an **ex** command summary.

Calling the *ex* Editor

There are different expressions used for starting up an editor. We say you can "call" the editor or "invoke" the editor or "get into" the editor. No matter how you say it, the command issued from the UNIX shell is just

```
ex filename
```

The filename can be a file already in your directory. If the filename is in your directory, the file contents are placed in the **ex** temporary buffer for you to edit. If you have no file by that name, then a new file is created. When you call **ex** up with an existing file, the editor responds on the screen with the number of characters stored in the file. If the file is new, then **ex** responds with the comment [new file] and the filename. If you want to edit an existing file, but mistyped its name, this convention would alert you that **ex** was starting up a new file. (The exact responses may vary slightly from version to version.) Let's look at two examples. If you invoke **ex** with the command

```
ex poem
```

then, the editor will respond with

```
"poem" [new file] <───────────── (a new file is created and named "poem")
: <──────────────────────────────────── (the colon is the editor prompt)
or
"poem" 26 lines, 462 characters <────── (existing file has 462 characters)
: <──────────────────────────────────── (the colon is the editor prompt)
```

ex gives you the number of lines and characters in the file, but it does not print the file on the screen unless you give it the appropriate print command.

The editor is now in the Command Mode ready to accept such commands as append, move, delete, write, quit, print, and so on. The commands that you give must follow a set format, which is described next.

The *ex* Command Format

A complete **ex** command, in general, has three parts: an address, a command, and a parameter. The address tells the editor which line or lines are affected. The command tells the editor what must be done. Examples of commands are **p** (for print a line onto the screen), **d** (for delete a line), and **s** (for make a substitution). The parameter provides additional information, such as what substitution will take place. Often, however, a complete command will have just one or two of these parts.

Here are a few examples of the command format.

Table 5–2. The *ex* Command Format

Sample command	Address range	Command	Parameter
1,2p	1,2	p	
3d	3	d	
3s/The/the/	3	s	/The/the/
p	None given, thus, print current line.	p	
.,$d	Current line to end of file.	d	

In time, we will explain all these commands and more, but in case you are impatient, here is a brief rundown of what they do. The first command prints lines 1 and 2. The second command deletes line 3. The third command substitutes the word "The" for "the" in line 3. The fourth command prints the current line. The fifth command deletes everything from the current line to the end of the file.

Locating Lines

Half of the difficulty in using editors is telling the editor *where* in the text file you wish to insert text or make changes. The **ex** line editor approaches this task by using "line numbers"; text in the **ex** line temporary buffer is organized into numbered lines. A line is considered to be everything typed up to a carriage return, <return>. Each line in the buffer is numbered consecutively and renumbered whenever a new line is inserted, deleted, or moved. In addition to maintaining this list of text lines, the editor always maintains a notion of what is the "current line." You might imagine the current line to be a line pointed to by an "invisible" cursor as shown in the following sketch.

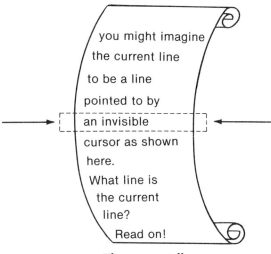

you might imagine

the current line

to be a line

pointed to by

an invisible

cursor as shown

here.

What line is

the current

line?

Read on!

The current line.

What line in the buffer is the current line? When you first invoke the editor with an existing file, the current line becomes the *last* line in the editor buffer. If you were now to type a command like print or append or insert, this command is carried out with respect to the current line. For example, if you use the print command, by typing

p

the current line is printed on the screen. On the other hand, if you type

3p

then, line 3 is printed. In this latter case, we gave the editor a specific line to work on. Now line 3 becomes the current line. In general, when you issue a command, the last line affected by that command is considered to be the new current line.

An abbreviation for the current line is the dot character (.). The current line is also called "line dot." Thus, we can speak of the line 3, or line 4, or line dot. Do not let the multiple use of the dot in **ex** confuse you. Recall that you can leave the Text Input Mode with a single dot placed alone on a line. However, in the Command Mode, a dot is an address abbreviation for the current line in the line-ending editor. Thus, you can type

.p

to print the current line, or

```
.d
```

to delete the current line.

Another useful abbreviation is $ for the last line of a file. For instance,

```
$p
```

prints the last line of the file.

You also can give relative addresses by using the + and − signs followed by a number. They work like this:

```
.+3 <─────────────────────────── (3 lines after the current line, and)
$−2 <─────────────────────────── (2 lines before the final line of the file.)
```

You can specify a range of lines by giving two line numbers separated by a comma. For example,

```
3,8d
```

deletes lines 3 through 8, while

```
1,$p
```

prints all the lines in your file onto the screen, and

```
.−9,.+9p
```

prints 19 lines altogether, with the current line in the middle.

So now we have several ways of giving line addresses. We can give a line number or a range of line numbers, we can use the special symbols "." and "$" for the current line and for the final line, respectively, and we can use plus signs and minus signs to locate lines relative to the current line or the last line. But how do we find out what the line numbers are?

If the file is short, you can use **1,$nu** to show the whole file on the screen. The second thing you can do is find the line number of the current line (line dot); you do this by typing an equal sign after the dot as follows:

```
.=
```

ex will respond by telling you the line number of the current line. (Remem-

ber that **ex** commands, like UNIX commands, should be followed by
<return>.) This command is particularly handy after you have moved
around a bit using the + and − commands described above or when using
the pattern searching described next.

Line Lengths

There is an interesting point about line lengths that may not be obvious to
you. It is this: the length of a line on the screen may not correspond to how
long the editor thinks the line is. The reason is that when you type text in, on
most systems, the screen will start a new line when you exceed 80 characters
or hit the <return> key (whichever comes first), but the editor will only start
a new line in your file when you hit the <return> key. Thus, you could type
in a line of, say, 150 characters before hitting a <return> key. This line
would be "wrapped around" on the screen and would look like two lines.
However, the editor would count it as just one line. Not only would this
throw you off if you were counting lines, but it could produce surprising
results when you send the file to a line printer. And it could really get you into
trouble if you are writing programs; FORTRAN, for example, expects commands to be in columns 7 through 72.

The most straightforward approach to this problem is to use the <return>
key as it is used on an electric typewriter. As you near the end of a line, hit
the <return> key to start a new line. You should try to make this use of the
<return> key an automatic habit when using an editor.

The **ex** editor has a "wrapmargin" command that produces automatic
<return>'s at whatever point you specify. This useful feature is discussed in
the next chapter (see box).

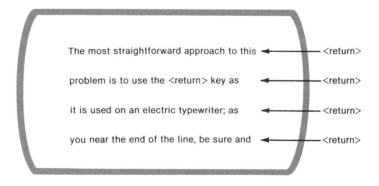

Line wrapping and the <return> key.

Pattern Searching

ex offers an interesting and useful alternative for finding lines. Instead of specifying the line number, you can give **ex** a pattern to look for. You do this by enclosing the pattern in slashes. For example, if you give the command

```
/bratwurst/
```

ex will search through your file for "bratwurst" and, then, print the line that contains the first example it finds; after that, it stops searching. The search starts after the current line and proceeds forward through the file. If **ex** doesn't find the pattern by the time it reaches the file end, it goes to the file beginning and proceeds to the original line. If it hasn't found the pattern yet, it will let you know by printing out a question mark.

ex interprets the pattern as a "character string" rather than as a word. A character string, or "string" for short, is just a series or string of characters. If you were to set **ex** looking for the string

```
/man/
```

it doesn't care whether that string is a separate word (man, in this case) or part of a longer word (the "man" in manual or command, for example). It will just find the first occurrence (either on the current line or after it) of the consecutive letters m-a-n.

A space in text is a character—the space character—and can be used as part of the search string. So the command

```
/man /
```

will find "man " and "woman ", but not "command," since there is no space after the "n" in "command."

Stepping Through Text

Here is another technique that is useful for finding lines of text. If you type

```
<return>
```

alone without any other command, **ex** will interpret that to mean

```
.+1p
```

That is, **ex** will advance one line and print it on the screen. So if you want to go slowly through your buffer looking for changes to make, the following sequence is easy to use.

```
1p
<return>
<return>
<return>
```

and so forth. When you find a line you want to change, you have two choices. You can address the current line by line number or you can use the default address, which is a line dot. That is, if you type

```
p
```

by itself, the address is the current line by default.

Here is an example of how you might read through a file called ''energy'' one line at a time.

```
ex energy
"energy" 4 lines, 320 characters
:1p
 Energy consumption during the last six months
<return>
has been brought down 17%, thus saving our
<return>
company over $6,000,000. Everyone is to be
<return>
congratulated.
<return>
: At end-of-file
```

The end-of-file at the end means there are no more lines of text in the buffer.
   You also can step backwards a line at a time by typing a minus sign

```
—
```

followed by a < return >. This is short for

```
.-1p
```

Thus, there are four approaches to locating text in the buffer. The first approach is to use specific line numbers, such as 1, 4, $, etc. The second method is to use the "current" line as a reference point and move relative to this line "dot" by using the < + > and < − > keys. Thirdly, you can let **ex** search for particular words or patterns. Finally, you can use the <return> key to step through the file line by line.

ex also has a convenient way to print a screen full of text at one time using the **z** command. The **z** command fills the screen from the current line to the bottom of the screen with text. The **z** command can also take a line number for positioning, so that a good way to view a file would be to give the following commands:

```
:  <————————————————————————————— (Command Mode prompt)
1z <————————————————————————————— (Print text on screen starting at line 1)
 z <————————————————————————————— (Print additional text as required)
```

Now that we can locate lines, we can turn our attention to creating and altering files.

The *ex* Text Input Mode

There are three commands in **ex** that will turn your keyboard into a typewriter for entering text (or data, or programs) into the editor's buffer. These commands are **a** for append, **i** for insert, and **c** for change. If no address is given, these commands affect the current line. Otherwise, **a**ppend and **i**nsert must be given a single line address and **c**hange can be given an address of one or more lines. **a**ppend will place text after the addressed line and **i**nsert will place text before the addressed line. The lines addressed using **c**hange are all deleted making way for any new text you type in. The **a**ppend command entering the Text Input Mode is illustrated in the following two examples.

The Append, Write, and Quit Commands: *a, w,* and *q*

Jack Armstrong has just received a terrific job offer and wants to draft a letter accepting the position. His first step is to invoke the editor using

```
ex jobletter
```

This creates a new empty file called **jobletter** and places Jack in the Command Mode, printing

```
"jobletter" [new file]
```

(or something similar, depending on which UNIX system is being used). Since Jack wants to use the keyboard as a typewriter, he now enters the Text Input Mode by pushing

```
: a
```

which stands for **append**.

There is no prompt to indicate the Text Input Mode. He now begins typing his letter:

```
Dear Sir:
I am delighted to accept your offer as chief trouble
shooter for the Eon Corp. for $250,000 a year.

        Sincerely,
        Jack Armstrong
```

Recall that once **ex** is in the Text Input Mode, the keyboard acts like a typewriter. The <return> key is used as a carriage return to end each line. To indent lines, Jack can use either the <spacebar> key or the <tab> key.

Satisfied with his work, Jack now leaves the Text Input Mode by typing a lone period [.] at the beginning of a new line like this,

```
    .
: <─────────────────────────────────── (command mode prompt)
```

This may seem strange at first, but remember, when we use the keyboard as a typewriter, every key we push will place characters on the screen. The good people who built the **ex** editor had to find some rare keystroke that would never be needed in the typewriter mode so that Jack and you can use it to leave that mode. While a period is not a rare keystroke, it is rare to begin a line with a period.

After leaving the Text Input Mode and reentering the Command Mode, Jack can save his text using the **write** or **w** command as follows:

```
: w
"jobletter" 9 lines, 171 characters
```

(Don't forget to follow commands with the <return> key!) If the command is successful, the editor will respond with the name of the file and number of lines and characters saved. Jack now leaves the editor with the quit command by typing

```
:q
```

which stands for **quit**.

This places him back in the UNIX shell and gives him back the shell prompt ($). He can now read and verify that his letter was properly saved with **write** by typing

```
cat jobletter
```

While rereading his letter, Jack has a new thought. He wants to add a post-script to the letter. So he "invokes" the editor with his new file by typing

```
ex jobletter
```

The editor responds with the number of lines and characters in the file as shown.

```
"jobletter" 9 lines, 171 characters
Jack types in
```

```
:a
```

which stands for **append** and adds his new message by typing

```
PS. Could you advance me $25,000? Thanks
.
:w "jobletter" 9 lines, 171 characters
:q
```

The **a** command at the beginning of an editing session appends the text at the end of the file. Every time you first invoke **ex**, the imaginary cursor is at the very end of the file. (Later, we show how the append command can add text elsewhere within the buffer file, rather than just at the end of the file.)

Summary of Examples

Here's a complete summary of these first two examples:

```
$ ex jobletter <——————————————————————— (Jack invokes ex)
```

```
"jobletter" [new file] <——————————————————— (ex prints this)
:a <———————————————————————————————————————— (append command)
Dear Sir: <————————————————————————————————— (Jack starts typing)
  I am delighted to accept your offer as chief trouble
shooter for the Eon Corp. for $250,000 a year.
        Sincerely,
        Jack Armstrong
  . <—————————————————————————————————————————— (Jack ends text entry)
:w <——————————————————————————————————————————— (writes to memory)
"jobletter" 9 lines, 176 characters <—————————— (UNIX confirms save)
:q <——————————————————————————————————————————— (Jack quits ex)
$ <———————————————————————————————————————————— (shell prompts returns)
$ ex jobletter <———————————————————————————————— (Jack invokes editor)
"jobletter" 9 lines, 176 characters <—————————— (editor responds)
:a <—————————————————————————————————————— (append after last line in file)
PS.Could you advance me $25,000. <——————————————— (Jack types this)
Thanks
  . <—————————————————————————————————————————— (Jack ends text entry)
:w <———————————————————————————————————————— (writes contents to memory)
"jobletter" 11 lines, 212 characters <—————————— (editor responds)
:q <——————————————————————————————————————————— (Jack quits editor)
$ <———————————————————————————————————————————— (shell prompt)
```

These examples illustrate the major features of the Text Input Mode using the **a** command. Later in this chapter, we will give examples of creating text using the insert command **i** and the change command **c**.

Meanwhile, a day has passed, and Jack wants to make some changes to his text. To do this, he needs the often-used "substitute" command **s**.

The Substitute Command: *s*

If you want to change the spelling of a word, or add new words to a line, you must use the substitute command **s**. Since **ex** is a line-oriented editor, our imaginary cursor can only distinguish lines. It *cannot* move within a line; this lack is the major drawback to a line editor. Thus, to tell the editor what word we want to change, we have to literally spell out the word as shown in the following entry:

```
3s/old word(s)/new word(s)/
```

Recall that the number is an address. If you leave the number off, then the substitution is made to the current line.

You can also add a print **p** parameter (a parameter is like a command) to the end of the substitute command which will cause the editor to print the line *after* making the substitution. It would look like this

```
3s/old word(s)/new word(s)/p
```

The substitution patterns are strings, just like the search patterns, so you must exercise some care when using them. For example, suppose line 3 reads

```
He commanded the next man to paint the cows blue.
```

What would the effect of the command

```
3s/man/woman/p
```

be? Since the first occurrence of the string "man" is in "command," the result would be:

```
He comwomanded the next man to paint the cows blue.
```

For this example, a better command would have been

```
3s/man /woman /p
```

It would have skipped to the first occurrence of "man" followed by a space.

Now, let's go back to our previous example and see what changes Jack wants to make and how he does it. Jack begins by typing

```
ex jobletter
```

and gets the editor's response of

```
"jobletter" 11 lines, 212 characters
:
```

The first change that Jack wants to make is to replace the word "delighted" with "happy." "It's best not to sound overeager," he thought. He can make the change by typing **p** and stepping through the letter using the <return> key until he reaches the line he wants. It's easier, though, to use the search mode; in which case, the process could look like this:

```
:/delighted/
 I am delighted to accept your offer as chief
:s/delighted/happy/p
 I am happy to accept your offer as chief
```

He could have combined his two commands into one:

```
:/delighted/s/delighted/happy/p
```

The first "/delighted/" identifies the line; the second "/delighted/" identifies the word to be changed. Too much typing for you? This command can be shortened to

```
:/delighted/s//happy/p
```

If you have a search pattern followed by a substitution command, as we just did, and the search word is the one you want to replace (again, as we just did), you can use this form. The **ex,** upon seeing the two slashes in a row (no spaces) after the **s,** will understand that it should use the preceding pattern ("delighted," in this case) for the word to be replaced.

In any case, after Jack makes the change, the affected line is the current line. He makes one more substitution as follows:

```
:s/chief/Chief/p
 I am happy to accept your offer as Chief
```

Since no new address was given, this change took place on the same line.

Finally, he wants to make a change on the next line. In order to read the next line, Jack again pushes the <return> key to get

```
 trouble shooter for the Eon Corp. for $250,000
```

Jack wants to delete the word "the" in this line so he uses the command

```
:s/the //p
```

This command reads: Take the current line and substitute for the string "the" the blank space that is between the slashes (that is, nothing) and print the results. This gives

```
trouble shooter for Eon Corp. for $250,000
```

Notice the space after the "the" in the substitution command. In the sentence, there is a space on each side of "the." If Jack just typed:

```
:s/the//p
```

two spaces would remain between "for" and "Eon." The command he used eliminated one of the spaces, thus keeping the word spacing regular.

Jack can now record these changes using the **write** command and, then, leave the editor with the **quit** command.

Although the commands we've used so far (**a**ppend, **p**rint, substitute, **w**rite, and **q**uit) are enough to get you started, there are a few more commands that can augment your editing prowess considerably.

Additional Editing Commands in *ex*

We hope you have tried out the previous editing commands on a terminal and are ready to add additional editing power to your repertoire. Here is a brief summary of the new editing commands that we will cover next.

1. Commands that operate on lines.

   A. The move command, **m**
   B. The delete command, **d**
   C. The copy command, **co**

2. Commands that enter the Text Input Mode.

   A. The insert command, **i**
   B. The change command, **c**

3. Special commands.

   A. The global parameter, **g**
   B. The undo command, **u**

We will now illustrate these commands by considering the efforts of Paul the Poet, who is trying mightily to create a short poem. So far, Paul has produced a file called **April.Rain.** He cannot use the filename **April Rain** with a space between the names because UNIX interprets this as *two* files. Paul now wants to edit what he has, so he types

```
ex April.Rain
"April.Rain" 4 lines, 113 characters
```

and, then,

```
:1z
```

to print out the entire file as follows:

```
It's not raining rain on me,
 It's raining whippoorwills
In every dimpled drop I see
 Streaming flowing hills
```

Paul wants to make some changes. Specifically, he wants to delete the last line and put in a new line. He can do this in any one of three ways. First, he could delete line 4 with

```
:4d
```

Then, he could add the new line with the **append** command, i.e., enter the new line after typing

```
:3a
```

or, if he is not changing the last line of text, he could use the insert command after the delete command by entering the line after typing

```
:4i
```

Note that the insert command inserts lines before the "addressed" line, whereas the **append** command inserts lines after the addressed line. Thus, the command **3a** will add text after line 3 and the command **4i** will add text before line 4. Command **3a** is thus equivalent to command **4i**.

The third way to make this change is to not use the delete command at all, but use the change or **c** command which deletes and replaces in one step. Paul does this by typing

```
:4c
```

```
Wildflowers on the hill
```

Now, Paul wants to start a second stanza with the same lines that started the first. That is, he wants to copy the first two lines and place them at the end of the buffer file. He does this by using the **co** command.

```
:1,2co$
```

He can check his results by printing the current line (line dot) as follows:

```
:p
```

which gives the last line copied

```
It's raining whippoorwills
```

To see if the preceding line was copied, Paul types the minus character, or − command as follows:

```
:-
```

and, the editor responds with:

```
It's not raining rain on me,
```

Now Paul thinks of some new lines to add at the end of the poem so he types:

```
:$a
Where clever busy bumblebees
  Will find their board and room.
.
```

Remember that the **$** symbol stands for the last line so **$a** means **a**ppend after the last line.

"Aha," thinks Paul, "let's change whippoorwill to daffodil!" He can do this with the substitute command, as follows:

```
:1,$s/whippoorwills/daffodils/p
```

Here the command **s** is the substitute command applied from line 1 to the end of the file ($). The last **p** prints any lines containing the substitution.

Paul now wants to step through the poem from beginning to end using the <return> key. Here is how it looks on the screen:

```
:1p
  It's not raining rain on me
<return>
   It's raining daffodils
<return>
  In every dimpled drop I see
<return>
   Wildflowers on the hill
<return>
<return>
  It's not raining rain on me
<return>
   It's raining daffodils
<return>
  Where clever busy bumblebees
<return>
   will find their board and room
<return>
:
```

In a flush of growing excitement, Paul decides to change the seventh line before continuing. To double-check that he has the right line, he types

```
:.p
```

and gets

```
   It's raining daffodils
```

He replaces that line by typing

```
:.c
But fields of clover bloom
.
```

"Aha," says Paul, "this is it!" He prints the entire poem using

```
:1z
```

The editor responds with:

```
   It's not raining rain on me
```

```
        It's raining daffodils
    In every dimpled drop I see
    Wildflowers on the hill

    It's not raining rain on me
     But fields of clover bloom
    Where clever busy bumblebees
     Will find their board and room
```

(This poem is an adaptation of "April Rain" by Robert Loveman.)

Gleefully, Paul saves his work and quits the editor using

```
:w Q
"April.Rain" 10 lines, 233 characters
```

Making Searches and Substitutions Global: *g*

The search command and the substitution command share the property that each looks for the *first* occurrence of the pattern. A search ends as soon as it finds a line containing the search pattern, and a substitution acts only on the first occurrence in the line of the pattern. Suppose, for instance that we are editing a file whose text is as follows:

```
It was a hot, blustery day. Most folks stayed indoors. Not
me. A dog came ambling down the street. He wasn't a big dog,
and he wasn't a small dog; he was just an in-between dog.
```

Suppose for this and for the following examples that the first line is the current line. Then, the command

```
:/dog/s//tiger/p
```

would produce the following result:

```
A tiger came ambling down the street. He wasn't a big dog,
```

That is, **ex** found the first line containing "dog" and replaced the first occurrence of "dog" with "tiger." We can make the command more universal or "global" by using the **g** parameter and command. There are two ways to use it in this example. First, we can put a **g** command in front of the search pattern. This will cause **ex** to find *all* lines containing "dog." The interchange would look like this:

```
:g/dog/s//tiger/p
A tiger came ambling down the street. He wasn't a big dog,
and he wasn't a small tiger; he was just an in-between dog.
```

Still, however, only the first "dog" on each line is changed to "tiger." The second way to use the **g** remedies this. By putting a **g** parameter after the substitution command, we make **ex** replace *every* occurrence of "dog" on a given line. By using a **g** in both places, we get a truly global substitution that affects all "dog" entries on all lines:

```
:g/dog/s//tiger/gp
A tiger came ambling down the street. He wasn't a big dog,
and he wasn't a small tiger; he was just an in-between dog.
```

The Undo Command: *u*

One of the truly great innovations in electronic editing is the invention of the undo command **u**. This command, given in the Command Mode, undoes the last change made to the buffer. Here are two daring demonstrations of its use on the file April.Rain.

```
$ex April.Rain
"April.Rain" 10 lines, 233 characters
:1,$d <──────────────────────────────────── (delete all lines)
10 lines <──────────────────────────── (the editor confirms deletion)
:1z <──────────────────────────────── (let's try to display buffer)
No Lines <──────────────────────────── (the editor responds)
:u <──────────────────────────────── (THIS HAD BETTER WORK)
10 more lines <──────────────────────── (the editor responds)
:1z <──────────────────────────────── (print a screen from buffer)
It's not raining rain on me,
 It's raining daffodils
In every dimpled drop I see
 wildflowers on the hills

It's not raining rain on me,
 but fields of clover bloom
where clever busy bumblebees
 will find their board and room
```

Phew!! The lines came back. Fortunately for us, the undo command works on the last change made in the buffer and not just the last command given, which, in our case, was the command **1z**.

Another demonstration of the undo command can be shown after making a rather interesting global substitution. Let's substitute two e's for every one e that now exists in the poem and print the result.

```
:g/e/s//ee/gp
It's not raining rain on mee,
 It's raining daffodils
In eeveery dimpleed drop I seeee
 wildfloweers on thee hills

It's not raining rain on mee,
 but fieelds of cloveer bloom
wheeree cleeveer busy bumbleebeeees
 will find theeir board and room
:u
```

You can have lots of fun playing with letter and word substitutions like this, just as long as you remember to give the undo command immediately after each substitution.

If you like this version of the poem and want to keep a copy, it is possible to keep both versions of the poem using the **w** command with a new filename as described in the next section.

On the other hand, if you make a mistake, and forget to use the undo command at the right time, there is an undo command of "last resort," called the **q!** command.

The command **q!** allows you to quit the editor without writing any changes to the buffer. If you feel that your current editing changes are not worth keeping, then this form of the **quit** command is what you want.

Reading, Writing, and Moving: *r*, *w*, and *m*

One of the handiest features of electronic editing is the ability to move, duplicate or insert large blocks of text, an electronic version of "cut and paste." We've already seen how to use the **co** command to copy from one part of a file to another part of the same file. Now, we'll look at three additional editing commands, read, write and move.

Suppose we want to insert an entire file into the text presently being edited. We can use the **read** command to do this. For example, the command

```
:5r Mayclouds
```

would paste a copy of the contents of the file **Mayclouds** after line 5 of our present file.

The **write** command can be used to copy excerpts from a text file for use in another file. This can be done from the editor using a command like

```
:3,7w AprilRain2
```

This command would place lines 3 through 7 in the file called **AprilRain2,** creating the file in the process.

Our last text-rearranging command is the **move** command **m.** For example, suppose that we have a file containing the lines

```
Apolexy
Bongo
Doobidoo
Cackle
```

We want to make this list alphabetical. Suppose "Cackle" is on line 4. We can have it moved to just after line 2 by commanding

```
4m2
```

which will move line 4 to a position after line 2, and all is well.

Have we been doing word processing? Or, is there more to word processing than just using the editor? Yes and yes.

Word processing involves two major functions. First, we must beg, borrow or create words or text and put them into a file. Second, we then "format" the text for displaying on the screen or printing on paper. We can use the editor for both tasks, just as we have shown in the examples in this chapter.

However, UNIX offers other ways to format text using special utilities such a **nroff.** The power of formatting utilities is that we can experiment with different formats in order to choose the style we want. For example, we can adjust margins, line lengths, paragraph indentation, or we can center, justify, number pages, create tables and much more. Instructions for formatting text are called "control lines" and are entered into a file as separate lines. Usually these lines begin with a period to distinguish them from normal text.

Here is a very simple example where we place two control lines into the file **April.Rain.**

```
$ex April.Rain
April.Rain 10 lines, 233 characters
:2a <─────────────────────────────────── (append after line 2)
.pl10 <───────────────────────────── (set page length to 10 lines)
.ce10 <───────────────────────────── (center justify 10 lines)
. <─────────────────────────────────── (leave Text Input Mode)
:w <─────────────────────────────────── (write changes)
''April.Rain'' 12 lines, 245 characters <───────── (editor responds)
:q
```

It's simple to use the **nroff** formatter. We just give the command and the name of the file to be formatted. The output appears on the screen as shown below.

```
$nroff April.Rain
It's not raining rain on me,
 Its raining daffodils
              In every dimpled drop I see
                wildflowers on the hill

              It's not raining rain on me,
               but fields of clover bloom
            where clever busy bumblebees
            will find their board and room
```

Notice that the two control lines take effect after line 2, since that is where they were inserted. If you would like to see a whole lot more **nroff** magic, or read about other word processing utilities, take a look at Chapter 11.

We have just introduced the major features of the **ex** editor. There are some aspects of **ex** that we have left out, mainly in the use of "metacharacters" and "regular expressions." You can use the manual to get more get more information about these features. We will conclude this section on **ex** with a comprehensive summary.

Summary: ex—line-oriented text editor

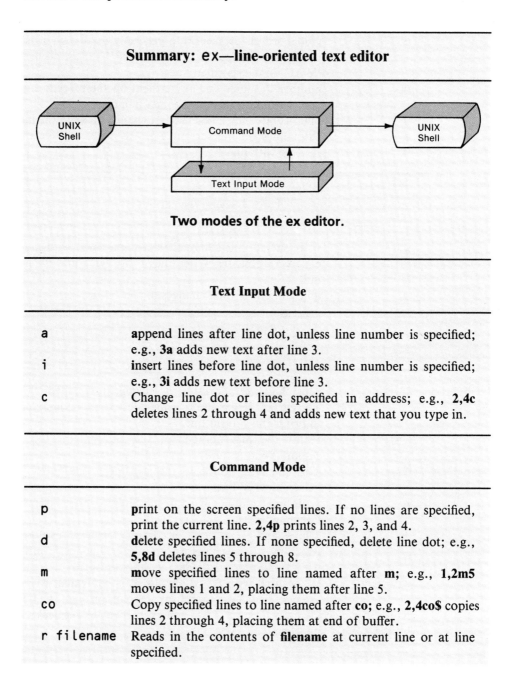

Two modes of the ex editor.

Text Input Mode

a	**a**ppend lines after line dot, unless line number is specified; e.g., **3a** adds new text after line 3.
i	**i**nsert lines before line dot, unless line number is specified; e.g., **3i** adds new text before line 3.
c	**C**hange line dot or lines specified in address; e.g., **2,4c** deletes lines 2 through 4 and adds new text that you type in.

Command Mode

p	**p**rint on the screen specified lines. If no lines are specified, print the current line. **2,4p** prints lines 2, 3, and 4.
d	**d**elete specified lines. If none specified, delete line dot; e.g., **5,8d** deletes lines 5 through 8.
m	**m**ove specified lines to line named after **m**; e.g., **1,2m5** moves lines 1 and 2, placing them after line 5.
co	**C**opy specified lines to line named after **co**; e.g., **2,4co$** copies lines 2 through 4, placing them at end of buffer.
r filename	Reads in the contents of **filename** at current line or at line specified.

s/one/two/	substitutes the word "two" for the word "one" for the first occurrence of word "one" in the specified lines.
/nice/	Searches for the next line to contain the word(s) between the slashes; in this case, the string "nice."
g	global search or substitute generally used with s or s/pat1/pat2/g substitutes "pat2" for "pat1" for all occurrences of "pat1" in the specified lines.
nu	number the lines and print them on the screen; e.g., 1,$nu numbers and prints all the lines in a file.
u	undo command. Undo the last change made in the buffer.
z	Print lines on the screen; e.g., 3z prints the file on screen starting with line 3.

Leaving the editor

w	write the specified lines that are addressed to a named file; e.g., 2,5w popcorn writes lines 2 through 5 into file popcorn.
q	quit.
q!	quit without writing changes to file

Addressing lines

.	This character addresses the current line, called "line dot." The current line is the last line affected by a command. Thus, .p prints the current line.
.=	Prints the line number of the current line; e.g., editor responds with a number like "5."
$	This character addresses the last line in the buffer; e.g., $d deletes the last line.
n	A decimal number n addresses the nth line; e.g., 3p prints line number 3.
+	The + and − are used in conjunction with a reference line which may be specified with n or $ or line dot, if unspecified; e.g., $−5,$p prints the last six lines of buffer.
<return>	When used with no command, it is equivalent to .+1, i.e., the next line. Very useful for stepping through the buffer.

Note: If you accidentally hit o or vi while in ex, the way to get back to ex is to hit the <esc> key, then the Q key.

Review Questions

Here are some questions to give you practice in applying the commands of this chapter.

A. Matching Commands to Functions

Match the commands shown on the left to the functions shown on the right. Assume all the commands are given in the Command Mode only; none are given from the Text Input Mode. The functions can be used more than once.

ex *Editor Commands*	*Functions*
1. $p	**a.** Deletes lines 2 to 4.
2. 2,4d	**b.** Prints the number of the current line.
3. 3s/fun/funny/	**c.** Copies lines 5 and 6, placing them at the end of the file.
4. 5,6m$	**d.** Moves lines 5 and 6 to end of file.
5. 5,6co$	**e.** Substitutes funny for fun.
6. 2,4/s/no/yes/g	**f.** Substitutes yes for no in all occurrences in lines 2 to 4.
7. /fun/	**g.** Prints the next line containing the string "fun".
8. .=	**h.** Appends the line "Chuckles is slow" after line 6.
9. 6a	**i.** Prints current line.
Chuckles is slow	**j.** Prints final line.

B. Questions

Here are some general questions.

1. When you invoke the editor with a file, e.g., using **ex file3**, how can you tell if it is a new file?
2. Why is the **q!** command considered dangerous?
3. When you first enter the editor with an existing file and type **a,** the append command to add text, where is that text placed?
4. What command is used to save the editor buffer contents?
5. Where does the insert command **i** place new text?
6. Write out the command that will save the first three lines only of an editor buffer containing seven lines of text.
8. Write out the command(s) to correct the following misspelled word, "sometome."
9. Write out the command(s) to delete the last five lines in ten lines of text.

Answers

A. 1—j, 2—a, 3—e, 4—d, 5—c, 6—f, 7—g, 8—i, 9—h

B. **1. ex** responds with the number of characters. **2.** It doesn't save your work. Give a **w** before **q. 3.** At the end of the file. **4 w. 5.** Before the cursor. **6. 1,3w newfile. 7.** Use a lone dot "." at the beginning of a new line. **8. s/sometome/sometime/p** will also print the line. **9. 6,1Ød.**

Exercises at the Terminal

Here are some exercises to practice your editing techniques.

1. Enter the following text into a new file called **letterrec1.**

       Dear Sir:
           This is a letter of recommendation for john doe.
           john doe is a good worker.
           john doe has a fine character.
           john doe is a-ok.
                   sincerely
                   jane doe

2. Now, do the following:
   A. Save the letter.
   B. Correct all spelling errors.
   C. Capitalize jane, john, and doe.
   D. Delete the last sentence containing a-ok.
   E. Save the corrected letter as **letterrec2.**
   F. Leave the editor.
   G. Use **cat** to print both copies on the screen at the same time.

3. Go into the shell, list your files with **ls,** and do the following:
   A. Make a copy of one of your files, e.g., **mbox,** calling it **mbox2** or something similar.
   B. Now, invoke the editor with this copy of a file and:
      (1) Insert the line, "This is a test", somewhere in the text.
      (2) Move 3 lines.
      (3) Replace all occurrences of the word "the" with "thee."
      (4) Copy 2 lines and place them in the beginning of the file.
      (5) Delete the last 4 lines.
      (6) Substitute ai for all a's, then undo the substitution.

6

The *vi* Screen Editor

In this chapter, you will find:

6 THE *vi* SCREEN EDITOR

Introduction

Welcome to the **vi** editor. If this is your initial venture with **vi,** may we suggest that you read the first five pages of the previous chapter for a quick overview of the **ex** family of editors, of which **vi** is an integral member. In addition, those pages introduce the important concepts of the editor "buffer" and the two "modes" of editor operation.

The **vi** editor is a more popular editor than **ex.** Its chief advantage is that it lets you move a cursor to any portion of the text you desire and to work on just that part. Thus, you can change a single letter or a single word in a line or you can insert new text in the middle of a line much more easily than you can with a line editor, such as **ex.**

The **vi** is an interactive text editor designed to be used with a crt terminal. It provides a "window" into the file you are editing. This window lets you see about 20 lines of the file at a time, and you can move the window up and down through the file. You can move to any part of any line on the screen and can make changes there. The additions and changes you make to the file are reflected in what you see on the screen. The **vi** stands for "visual," and experienced users refer to it as "vee-eye." A complete description of the 100 or so commands in **vi** would overwhelm the beginning **vi** user; for that reason, we have chosen to divide our presentation of **vi** commands into three parts. These three parts represent three levels of expertise.

Before we begin, here is a brief overview of **vi,** showing the three levels of commands we have chosen to describe. A beginning user should read Part 1 which lists the basic commands to start using **vi** and, if possible, should practice them before seriously studying the next levels. The **vi** startup card in the front of the book serves as a helpful reference card.

1. Basic commands to start using **vi.**
   A. Commands to position the cursor—**h, j, k, l** and <return>
   B. Commands to enter the Text Input Mode—**a, i, o, O**
   C. Commands to leave the Text Input Mode—<esc>
   D. Commands that delete or replace—**x, dd, r**
   E. Commands that undo changes—**u, U**
   F. Commands to save and quit the editor—**ZZ, :w, :q!, :wq**
   G. Commands from the "shell" for erasing—<del>, or <control-h>, or [#]

133

2. Advanced **vi** commands to enhance your skill.
   A. Commands to position the cursor including "scrolling," "paging," and "searching"—<control-d>, <control-f>, <control-b>, <control-u>, **e, b, G, nG**, <control-g>, /**pattern, $, Ø**
   B. Commands that will operate on words, sentences, lines, or paragraphs—**c, d, y**
   C. Abbreviations for words, sentences, lines, or paragraphs—**w, b, e, >, <, Ø, $, {, }**
   D. Commands to print storage buffers—**p, P**
   E. Joining lines—**J**

3. Additional **vi** Commands.
   A. There are 60 or so additional commands to do more of the same kinds of editing as described above. In addition to these commands, there are "special" features of **vi**, such as "mapping" and adjusting **vi** to fit your terminal type.

In this introduction to **vi,** we will present five examples demonstrating the following ideas.

    1 . . . . Getting into **vi**
           getting out of **vi**

    2 . . . . getting into **vi**
           moving the cursor in an existing file
           getting out of **vi**

    3 . . . . getting into **vi**
           creating the text in a new file
           saving the text and getting out of **vi**

    4 . . . . getting into **vi**
           adding text to an existing file
           saving the changes and getting out of **vi**

    5 . . . . getting into **vi**
           making deletions and other changes
           saving the changes and getting out of **vi**

As with many UNIX programs and utilities, we can see that it is just as important to know how to "get out" of the utility as how to "get in" and use the utility or editor.

Starting *vi*

Although **vi** is a very sophisticated editor with an enormous number of commands, the basic structure of **vi** is very simple. There are two modes of operation, the Command Mode and the Text Input Mode, as shown in the following diagram.

```
        ┌──────────────┐
        │  UNIX Shell  │
        └──────┬───────┘
               │ vi filename
               ▼
        ╔══════════════╗
        ║ Command Mode ║
        ╚══════╦═══════╝
          append ───────────►  ╔══════════════╗
          insert ───────────►  ║  Text Input  ║
          open   ───────────►  ║     Mode     ║
          delete                ╚══════════════╝
          undo                        │   Keyboard acts
          position cursor             │   like typewriter
               │                      │
               ▼                      ▼
        ╔══════════════╗  ◄──  ╔══════════════╗
        ║ Command Mode ║       ║    <esc>     ║
        ╚══════╦═══════╝       ╚══════════════╝
          save your file              Use "escape"
          quit editor                 key to leave
               │                      text mode.
               ▼
        ┌──────────────┐
        │  UNIX Shell  │
        └──────────────┘
```

The *vi* modes of operation.

In this section, we will limit ourselves to the minimum number of commands that you will need to start using **vi.** Even though these commands are just a few of the total commands in **vi,** they cover the four major features of editing:

> cursor positioning
> text insertion
> deletions and changes
> permanently storing information

Our first example shows us how to get into and out of the **vi** editor.

The method of starting **vi** is identical to the way we started the **ex** editor. We must be in the UNIX shell as indicated by a shell prompt ($). The command given is

```
vi filename
```

135

In order to get out of **vi,** we use the command sequence

```
<esc> ZZ
```

Remember that <esc> means to push the key marked ESC or esc or ESCAPE, depending on your terminal, then push the capital zee key <shift-3> twice.

Just as in **ex,** the "filename" may be a file already in your directory; in which case, the file contents are copied into a temporary buffer for editing. If you do *not* have a file by that name, then a new file is created. When you call the **vi** editor, it responds on the screen with the contents of the file, followed by a series of tilde (~) marks—only if the file is less than a screen in length—and, at the bottom of the screen, the name of the file. The editor is now in the Command Mode and the cursor is positioned in the upper left-hand corner of the screen.

Any changes, deletions, or additions that we wish to make are made with reference to the cursor position. So the next question is, "How do we move the cursor?"

Moving the Cursor

More than 40 commands in **vi** help you position the cursor in the buffer file. In this section we will show you how to get anywhere on the screen (and, therefore, in a text file) using the five basic keys shown in the following sketch. In the section "Cursor Positioning Commands," we will demonstrate many more cursor moving commands.

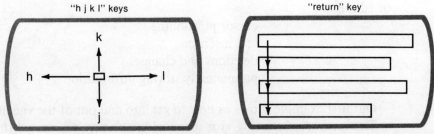

Basic cursor positioning keys.

Some terminals have "arrow" keys to move the cursor. However, most experienced typists prefer the <h, j, k, l> keys since they are close at hand. (At least they should be.) The <return> key is similar to the <j> key in that it moves the cursor down one line. However, the <return> key always positions the cursor at the *beginning* of the next line down, whereas, the <j> key moves the cursor straight down from its present position, which could be in the middle of a line.

If you have never tried moving the cursor, you should try it out at your earliest convenience. It's fun and easy to do. Make sure to practice cursor positioning on an existing file, since the cursor cannot be moved in a new file that doesn't contain any text. That is, these keys will only move the cursor over lines or characters of text that already exist in a file. This situation is shown in the drawing titled "Positioning the cursor."

Here is one way to practice moving the cursor. First, we'll list the contents of our directory in order to find a file to practice on, then we'll make some suggestions on what to do. Let's assume that we're logged in and showing the prompt. Our second example looks like this.

```
$ls <————————————————————————————————— (list your files)
mbox notes today <——————————————————————————— (typical listing)
$vi mbox <————————————————————————————— (we'll edit this file)
```

(the screen now fills up with the contents of your **mbox** file and/or with tildes "~".

Suggestion . . . . Use the <j> and <k> keys several times to move the cursor up and down the file.

Now use the <h> and <l> (ell) keys to go left and right on the same line.

Suggestion . . . . Use all four keys to move the cursor to the first 10 e's that appear in the text

```
<esc> ZZ <————————————————————————————— (to leave the editor)
```

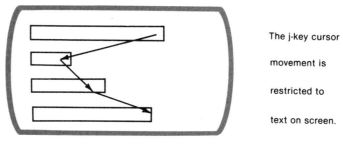

The j-key cursor

movement is

restricted to

text on screen.

Positioning the cursor.

The Text Input Mode

We will show you four commands that let you use your keyboard to type text into a file. These commands are

a for **a**ppend
i for **i**nsert
o and **O** for **O**pen

Each of these commands is referenced to the cursor location.

If you start **vi** on a new file, the cursor is restricted to the upper-leftmost position on the screen. The cursor cannot be moved by any of the cursor moving keys. However, if you use the append **a,** insert **i,** or open **O** commands, then text can be entered starting in the upper left-hand corner of the screen, just as you normally start writing on a piece of paper. You might wonder, "How can you place text in the middle of the line; for example, a title?" The answer is that you use the <space bar> key *after* entering the Text Input Mode.

If you start **vi** on a new file and use the open command **o** or **O,** then the cursor is moved one line up **(O)** or one line down **(o),** and is ready to receive text from the keyboard.

The usual way to start a new file is to type **vi** and follow it with a space and the filename that you want to use. When the editor is ready, type **a.** Then, start typing away as if you were using an electric typewriter. Hit the <return> key to start a new line. If you make a typing error, you can use <control-h> or your regular erase key to back up and correct yourself. On some terminals, the erased letters don't disappear from the screen until you type over them, but they are erased from the buffer regardless.

An example of beginning a new file and using the **a**ppend command to insert text in it would look like this:

```
$vi ohio <————————————————————————— (invoking the editor)
a <————————————————— (to get into append mode—this doesn't show on screen)
What is the capital of Ohio?
Columbus.
<esc> <————————————————————————— (to leave the Text Input Mode)
<esc> ZZ <————————————————————————— (to leave the editor)
```

Adding Text to an Existing File

Now that we have a file called **ohio,** let's look at ways we can add text to it. Our next example assumes that we have gone into **vi** and have moved the cursor to the position shown with the arrow.

```
What is the capital of Ohio?
Columbus              ↑
```

The cursor is assumed to be on the letter "o" in the word "of." What happens when we use the four text input commands?

Each command puts us in the Text Input Mode for entering text. We can enter one letter or dozens of lines of text. The major difference between the commands is *where* the new text is entered. For example,

a enters whatever we type after the cursor, "pushing" the rest of the line to the right. (On many terminals, you don't see the words pushed over until after you hit the <esc> key to leave the text mode. The new text will appear to obliterate the old text while you type, but the old text reappears when you hit <esc>.)

i enters whatever we type *before* the cursor, again pushing the rest of the line to the right.

o opens up a line *below* the cursor, places the cursor at the beginning of the new line, and enters whatever you type.

O is like **o** except that it opens a line *above* the present cursor position.

Suppose we try out each of the commands just described and enter 33333 from the keyboard (typewriter). Here is what each command would do to the text:

```
What is the capital of Ohio? <———————————— (cursor on "o" in of)
Columbus
```

```
What is the capital o33333f Ohio? <———————————— (append a)
Columbus
```

```
What is the capital 33333of Ohio? <———————————— (insert i)
Columbus
```

```
What is the capital of Ohio? <———————————— (open o)
33333
Columbus
```

```
33333
What is the capital of Ohio? <———————————— (open O)
Columbus
```

Push the <esc> key to end each of these Text Input Modes. This places you back in the Command Mode.

You might be wondering what happens to the original text if we type in more than just five 3's. Suppose we insert several sentences before the letter "o". Where does "Ohio" go to? It just moves to the right of the screen as far as possible, and if more text is introduced, "Ohio" drops down to the next line. This is called "wraparound" and is shown by the following sketches.

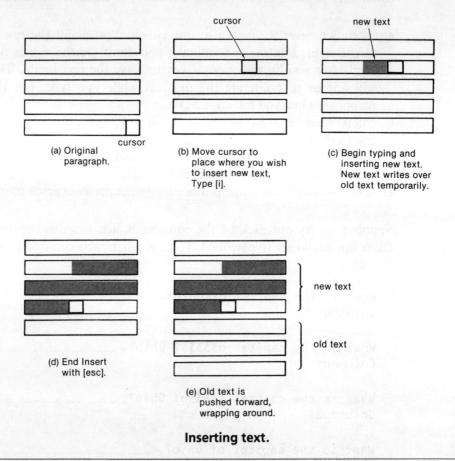

(a) Original paragraph.

(b) Move cursor to place where you wish to insert new text, Type [i].

(c) Begin typing and inserting new text. New text writes over old text temporarily.

(d) End Insert with [esc].

(e) Old text is pushed forward, wrapping around.

Inserting text.

Adjusting Your vi Environment

In the preceding chapter, we told you about the distinction between the length of a line on the screen and the length of a line in the file, and we stressed the importance of using the <return> key to start new lines. In **vi** and in **ex,** you can have the right margin set and can have new lines started automatically. Suppose, for example, you want the right margin set 15 spaces from the end of the screen. Then, while in the Command Mode, give this command:

```
:set wrapmargin=15
```

There should be no spaces in **wrapmargin=15.** Now, enter the Text Mode and try typing some text. When you reach the sixty-fifth column (that's 80 − 15), the editor will start a new line, just as if you had hit the <return> key. Actually, the editor is even cleverer than that; if you are in the middle of a word that would take you past the sixty-fifth column, **vi** will move the whole word to the next line. This means your right margin may not be even, but your lines won't end with broken-off words.

The **wrapmargin** command will stay in effect until you quit the editor. It is just one of several such commands available. Others do such things as adjust the tab widths, cause a new line to start with the same left margin as the preceding line, and tell the editor to check for matching parentheses. You can see a list of these options by typing **:set all.**

Redraw: Improving Screen Performance

Just as the **wrapmargin** option can ease the problem of wraparound, the **redraw** option can ease the anxiety of watching new text get inserted (temporarily) over old text. The **redraw** option displays the correct location of every character on the screen at all times. This option can be set with the command

:set redraw

redraw does cost a considerable amount of computer time. So, if your system is heavily loaded and acting sluggish, then it would be considerate of you to turn off the **redraw** option with the command

:set noredraw

The **redraw** option, like the other options mentioned above can be set semi-permanently in a file called .exrc (or as an EXINT variable as described in Chapter 11).

We can use the **vi** editor to create a file called .exrc with these changes in it as shown next.

```
$vi .exrc
a
```

```
set wrapmargin=15
set redraw
<esc> ZZ
$
```

In order to make these changes take effect immediately, type in the line

```
$source .exrc
$
```

Otherwise, the changes will not take effect until the next time you log in. These **set** options also can be used with **ex.**

Now that we have these four versions of "Ohio," how can we "clean" them up? To "clean up" text or a program is a commonly used expression in a computer environment. It means to make it right; to remove all unnecessary garbage. Unfortunately, there always seems to be a lot of "cleaning up" of files to do. This leads to our next set of commands for deleting and changing words and lines.

Deleting and Changing Text

There are three oft used commands for making small changes to the contents of a file. These are the **x** command for erasing one character, the **r** command for replacing one character, and the **dd** command for deleting one line. All three commands are made while in the Command Mode and all three leave you in the Command Mode after using them. Of course, all three commands use the cursor on the screen as the reference point for making changes.

Let's use the following example to illustrate the use of these commands. Suppose we have an existing file called **ohio**; begin by typing:

```
vi ohio
```

The editor responds by displaying

```
What is the capital o33333f Ohio?
33333
Columbus
~
```

```
~ <————————————————————————— (the left column is filled with tildes ~ ~ ~)
~
~
~
~
~
~
"ohio" 3 lines, 49 characters
```

The cursor starts out in the upper left-hand corner on the letter W.

To eliminate the 3's in the word "o33333f", we first use the <l> key (ell key) to move the cursor to the first number 3. Then, type:

```
x
```

This deletes the first 3 and very conveniently moves the rest of the line to the left. We can repeat the process four times more. That is, type:

```
xxxx
```

to delete the remaining 3's. The screen should look like this:

```
What is the capital of Ohio?
33333
Columbus
```

The cursor is left on the letter "f" in the word "of." Now, to get rid of the remaining 3's, we must move the cursor down one line. There are two ways to do this. We can use the <j> or the <return> key. The <j> key moves the cursor straight down. However, since there is no text below the "f," the closest point is the last number 3 in the next line.

The <return> key would position the cursor at the beginning of the line, on the first number 3. Actually, when we want to delete a line, it doesn't matter where in the line the cursor is located; we just type

```
dd
```

and the line is deleted. On some terminals, the editor places an @ symbol on the deleted line and moves the cursor down to the next line. It looks like this

```
What is the capital of Ohio?
```

```
@
Columbus
```

The @ symbol means that the line does not exist in the buffer even though we still see the space it left behind on the screen. Some terminals are "smart" enough to actually remove the line on the screen right after you delete it; the screen is redrawn with the remaining text moved up line by line to replace the deleted line.

Suppose that we wanted to make one last change. We wanted to capitalize each letter in the word "Ohio." First, we move the cursor up to the letter "h" by pushing the <k> key to move up one line, and then the <l> key to move to the right. Once we are on the letter "h," we type the following sequence:

```
rH
```

The first letter we type is **r**, the **r**eplace command. We replace whatever is under the cursor with the next keystroke, which in this case is a capital H <shift-h>. The cursor remains on the letter H.

In order to replace "i" with "I," we move the cursor one letter to the right using the <l> key and now type

```
rI
```

We can repeat the process and type

```
rO
```

to complete the change. Now to leave the editor, saving these changes, we type

```
ZZ
```

You may think that there ought to be a better way to make these changes. There is. In fact, there are two slightly easier ways, but in order to keep this introduction to **vi** simple, we have postponed discussion of these until later in the chapter.

Undoing Changes: *u* and *U*

Sometimes you may make a change and suddenly wish you hadn't done so. When that time comes, you will bless the "undo" commands. As the name implies, these commands undo what you have just done. The **u** command, which can only be given in the Command Mode, negates the preceding command. If you delete a line with a **dd**, then typing **u** will restore it. If you use the **i** command to insert the word "mush" in a line, then **u** will remove it. (You must go back to the Command Mode to undo.)

The **U** command is more general. It will undo *all* the changes you've made on the current line. For instance, consider the example where we used the **r** command to change "Ohio" to "OHIO". Hitting the **u** key would undo the last command (which was replacing "o" with "O") so that command would restore "OHIO" to "OHIo". But the **U** key would undo all the changes, restoring "OHIO" to "Ohio".

The undo command is unduly nice to have around. It gives you a way to practice changing a line, then restoring the line to its original pristine condition.

How To Leave the *vi* Editor

Probably the single most frustrating experience you can have with a computer is to *lose* several hours worth of work. It is possible to do this in an editor with one or two careless commands. When considering leaving the editor, you might ask yourself this basic question: "Do I want to save the changes made during this editing session?" There are three possible answers: Yes, No, and Maybe.

The different ways you can save information and leave the **vi** editor are summarized as follows:

Command	*What it Does*
`<ESC> ZZ <return>`	Writes contents of temporary buffer onto disk for permanent storage. Uses the file name that you used to enter **vi**. Puts you in the shell.
`<ESC> :wq <return>`	The same as ZZ. **w** stands for **w**rite, **q** stands for **q**uit.
`<ESC> :w <return>`	Writes the buffer contents to the memory,
`<ESC> :q <return>`	then quits the editor. A two-step version of **:wq**.
`<ESC> :q! <return>`	Quits the editor and abandons the temporary buffer contents. No changes are made.

All of these commands must be made from the Command Mode and they will all place you back into the shell as indicated by the prompt ($). We have shown you use of the <return> key once more to clarify these important commands.

To leave the **vi** editor and save any changes made, it is best to use **ZZ** while in the command mode. You could also leave the editor with either **:wq** or **:w** <return> **:q**. However, you run the risk of absent-mindedly typing **:q!** instead. (This may not sound very likely to you. Of course, it didn't sound very likely either to the many people who have made this error.)

To leave the editor *without* saving changes, the normal way is to use **:q!**. You might use this command if you started to edit a file and did not like the way the changes were shaping up. The **:q!** leaves the original file unchanged and lets you abandon the editor's temporary buffer.

If you're not sure about saving changes, the best step is to save both versions of the file, the original and the changed version. This is done by using the **w**rite command with a new filename. For example, it might look like this:

```
:w ohio.new
```

or

```
:w ohio2
```

Thus, if you are editing **ohio** and make some changes, this command creates a new file under the new name. Here we show two common ways to create similar names; by adding a ".new" or a "2" to the existing name. After creating this new file, the **vi** editor will provide you with a confirmation as follows

```
"ohio.new" [New file] 2 lines, 39 characters
```

You can now safely leave the editor with **:q** or with **:q!**.

The difference between the commands **:q!** and **:q** is that **:q** will only leave the editor if there have been no changes since the last **w** command. Thus, it provides some protection against accidentally quitting the editor. The command **:q!** leaves the editor in one step.

Actually, when you are involved in long editing sessions, it is advisable to use the **w**rite command every 15 to 20 minutes, or so, to update your permanent file copy. Some users use **cp** to make a copy of a file before editing. Thus, they can update their copy every 15 to 20 minutes and can still retain the original version. All of these comments pertaining to saving text will apply equally to all types of files, no matter whether they are programs, data, or text files.

If you have been trying out these commands, you now have the basic skills needed to edit a file. You can create a file with the **vi** command, insert text with the **a, i, o,** and **O** commands. You can delete letters and lines with **x** and **dd.** You can replace letters with **r.** You can undo rash changes with **u** and **U.** You can save your results and exit the editor. This structure of **vi** is summarized on pages 148 and 149, and on the tearout card earlier in the book.

These **vi** commands should be enough to allow you to easily edit or create short files. You should practice them, if at all possible, before going on to the next section. You may find these commands are good enough for all your needs. However, if you seek greater variety and control, read on.

Additional *vi* Commands

If you need to edit or create short text files once or twice a week, you will usually find that the basic **vi** command list, discussed in the previous section, will be satisfactory for most work. However, if you must edit long texts, you may begin to long for greater editing power; **vi** has plenty of editing horsepower. In this section, we will shift into high gear to further explore the magic of the **vi** editor.

Since cursor positioning in the text buffer is so important, especially in medium-size and long files, we will show you how to place the cursor anywhere in the file with just a few keystrokes. Then we will explore three commands known as "operators" that can make changes to words, lines, sentences, or paragraphs. Two of these operators actually provide you with temporary storage buffers that make relocating lines and paragraphs within a text file very easy to do.

Cursor Positioning Commands

We have already used five basic keys to position the cursor—the h, j, k, l, and <return> keys. Now we will add nine more keys and a searching function that will position the cursor easily over any size text file. We will start by considering four keys [b, e, $, Ø] that are useful in short text files. Then we add four keystrokes, <control-d>, <control-u>, <control-f> and <control-b>, that are handy for medium (2-10 screen pages) text files. At

UNIX STARTUP CARD

TO LOGIN
login:
password:

login: don
password: fun2run (not shown)

Welcome to UNIX

TO LIST YOUR FILES
ls

$ ls
mbox notes today wantlist

TO READ A FILE
cat filename

$ cat today
Here is a reminder!
dentist 4:00
haircut: 4:30
meeting 5:00
keep movin'

TO SEND MAIL
mail loginname

(text here)

. (lone period)

$ mail dick
Hi Dick
Could we hold our meeting
at 5:30 today?
don

TO RECEIVE MAIL
mail

(text here)

<RETURN>

$ mail
 >dick Fri Apr 1 12:39 1984
?<RETURN>
From: dick
To: don
Subject: meeting
That's fine. Meeting at 5:30
dick
?s dickstuff
<RETURN>

TO MAIL A FILE
mail loginname < filename

$ mail dick < today

 IN CASE OF DIFFICULTY
Try to get the "prompt" back.
First, try the <RETURN> key, then try
the "interrupt" key, usually <RUB> or <DEL>
or sometimes <CONTROL·C>

TO GET A PRINTOUT OF A FILE
lp filename

$ lp notes

TO LOGOUT
<CONTROL·D>

$ <CONTROL·D>

VI STARTUP CARD

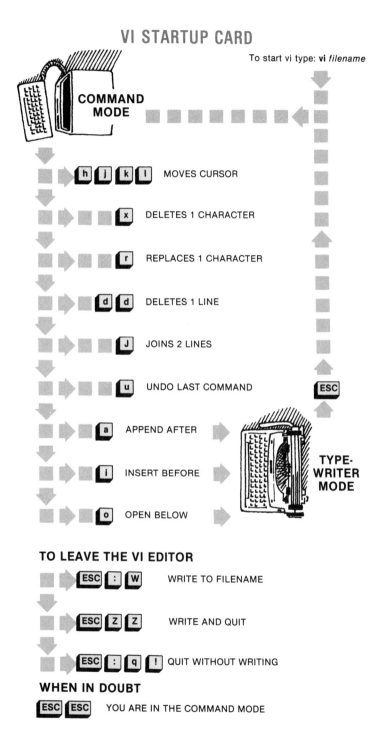

To start vi type: **vi** *filename*

COMMAND MODE

h j k l — MOVES CURSOR

x — DELETES 1 CHARACTER

r — REPLACES 1 CHARACTER

d d — DELETES 1 LINE

J — JOINS 2 LINES

u — UNDO LAST COMMAND

ESC

a — APPEND AFTER

i — INSERT BEFORE

o — OPEN BELOW

TYPE-WRITER MODE

TO LEAVE THE VI EDITOR

ESC : W — WRITE TO FILENAME

ESC Z Z — WRITE AND QUIT

ESC : q ! — QUIT WITHOUT WRITING

WHEN IN DOUBT

ESC ESC — YOU ARE IN THE COMMAND MODE

this point, we will also explain "scrolling" and "paging." Then, we will complete our cursor positioning repertoire by looking at two commands used to position the cursor in large (10-100 or more screen pages) text files. These are the nG and /pattern commands.

The four keys <b, e, $, Ø> have a certain symmetry in their operation. Here is what they do:

<b>   Moves the cursor to the beginning of a word. Each time you push the <b> key, the cursor moves to the *left* to the beginning letter of the preceding word.

<e>   Moves the cursor to the *end* of a word. Each time you push the <e> key, the cursor moves to the *right* to the end letter of the next word.

Both the <b> and <e> keys will move to the next line, unlike the <h> and <l> keys which can only move the cursor back and forth to the end of the line. The <b> and <e> key operations are shown in the following drawing.

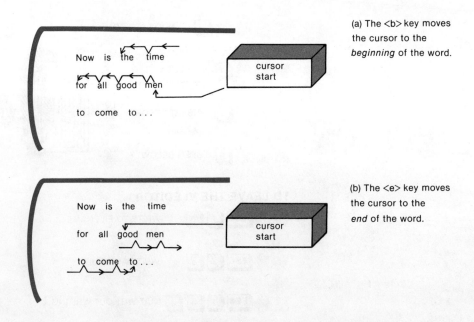

(a) The <b> key moves the cursor to the *beginning* of the word.

(b) The <e> key moves the cursor to the *end* of the word.

Using the <b> and <e> keys to move the cursor.

In a similar way, the <∅> and <$> keys move the cursor to the beginning and end of a *line* (rather than a word) as follows:

<∅>   This is the number zero key. It moves the cursor to the *beginning* of the line.

<$>   Moves the cursor to the *end* of the line.

These two keys can only be used on the line containing the cursor. The cursor does not jump to the next line as it does with the <b> and <e> key commands. Recall that the <return> key will jump lines and is similar to the sequence <j> <∅>. The <∅> and <$> operations are shown in the following drawing.

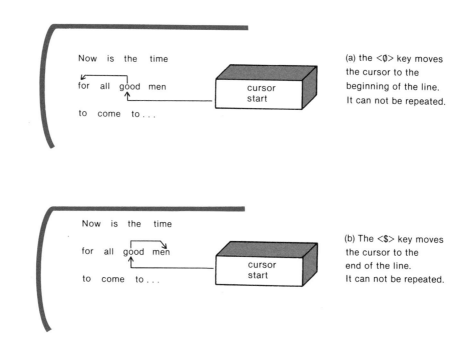

Using the <∅> and <$> keys to move the cursor.

Now, let's take a closer look at how text moves on the screen.

Screen Scrolling and Paging

Sometimes, there is more text in the buffer than can fit on the screen at one time. You may have noticed that if this happens, you can bring more text into view by trying to move the cursor past the bottom (or top) of the screen. The cursor stays put, but a new line moves up (or down) into view. This is called "scrolling." So far, the <j>, <k>, and <return> keys, discussed in the previous section, as well as the <b> and <e> keys, will cause the screen to scroll. To visualize scrolling, imagine that the text is arranged on one long continuous page (like a scroll) and that only a portion of it appears on the screen at any particular time. Your crt screen, then, is like a window into the text, usually showing 24 text lines with 80 characters per line. See the following sketch. Imagine that the window moves while the text remains fixed.

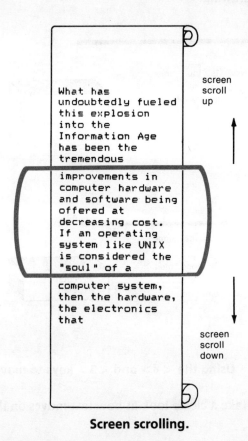

Screen scrolling.

The direction of scrolling usually refers to the direction the window moves past the text. For example, when we give the command to scroll down, the window moves downward and the text below the original window comes into view. When we scroll up, we "push" the window up and reveal portions of the text that precede the text in the original window location.

Different terminals will behave differently, even though the same **vi** commands are used. Some terminals can scroll down but will not scroll up. If a terminal cannot "scroll" up, then it must "page" up.

"Paging" means that the screen is completely erased and redrawn in a new position. Paging has the same end effect as scrolling 24 lines, but the process is different.

The cursor positioning keys <b>, <e>, <j>, <k>, and <return> will generally "page" or "scroll" the screen one line at a time. However, since a screen usually contains 24 lines, moving the text one line at a time in a large text file is unnecessary and time consuming. **vi** has four handy "scrolling" (or "paging") commands that solve this problem. They are the commands <control-u>, <control-f>, <control-b>, and <control-d>. Recall that to get a <control-d>, you hold down the <control> key and hit the <d> key smartly.

Here is a summary of these four cursor positioning keys.

<control-d>   Scrolls or pages the cursor *down,* usually 12 lines at a time.
<control-f>   Scrolls or pages the cursor *forward,* usually 24 lines at a time.
<control-u>   Scrolls or pages the cursor *up,* usually 12 lines at a time.
<control-b>   Scrolls or pages the cursor *back,* usually 24 lines at a time.

Generally, most users prefer scrolling to paging since it is easier to follow the positioning of the cursor in the text file as the file moves up or down. Recall that paging erases the screen and redraws it, so you cannot follow the cursor to its final position.

If you have really *long* text files, even several <control-f> keyings can take too long. For example, this chapter contains about 1400 lines of text. This would require over 50 <control-f> keyings to reach the end of the file. Fortunately, there is an easier way. The command

    nG

where "n" is an integer number will place the cursor on the line number "n". Thus, we could type

    1400G

to move to line 1400. A similar command is the lonesome **G** command (capital G), which moves the cursor to the end of the file. Thus, if you type

G

while in the Command Mode, the cursor is positioned at the end of the file. To get to the beginning of the file, tell the editor that you want the first line; that is, type

1G

One very useful command related to the **nG** command is the <control-g> command, which tells you the line number the cursor is currently on. This is valuable in two ways. First, if you remember the number or write it down, you can come back to the spot later. Secondly, if you want to copy a portion of a file, <control-g> can be used to get the beginning and ending line numbers of the section. You can then save the section by using the **write** command with line numbers. The **write** command would look like this:

```
:120,230w chapter4.2b
```

This command would copy lines 120 and 230 and place them in a newly created file called **chapter4.2b.** If a file already existed with that name, the **w** command either destroys the file or does not work, depending on your particular version of **vi.**

Pattern Searches

Another way to position yourself in the file is by giving the editor a word or string of characters to search for. If you are in the **vi** command mode, you can type the character, /, followed by a string of characters that are terminated by a <return>. The editor will position the cursor at the first occurrence, in the text, of this string that comes after the cursor. For example, if you want to find the words, "happy day", just give the command

```
/happy day
```

If the first occurrence of "happy day" was not the one you wanted, you can move to the next occurrence by typing **n** for **n**ext. These searches will "wrap around" the end of the file and go back to the beginning to continue the process for as long as you type **n.**

If you prefer to search backward through the file instead of forward, the ? will do that for you. Thus, the command

```
?malodorous
```

will start from the current cursor location and search backwards through your file for the word "malodorous." Again, the ? will continue the search for the next preceding example. The search will wrap around to the end of the file when you reach the top.

Once you have the cursor where you want it, you are again in a position to make changes, move text around, or add new text to the file. We will look at these activities next.

Operators that Delete, Duplicate, Change, and Rearrange Text

We learned, in the section of basic **vi,** how to delete a line using the command **dd.** This delete command is actually made up of two parts; the delete "operator" **d** and the operator's "scope," the *line* symbolized by "d" again. The command **dw** uses the delete operator **d** but has as its scope a "word" as defined by the cursor and symbolized by "w." We can represent these types of commands as follows:

$$\text{Operator} + \text{Scope} = \text{Command}$$

In this section, we will discuss three operators and nine scopes. The operators are the "**d**elete," "**c**hange," and "**y**ank" operators. They can operate with the following scopes: words, lines, sentences, and paragraphs. We will then use the commands formed by these operators to delete, duplicate, change, and rearrange text. Sometimes, these kinds of changes are referred to as "cut and paste," describing the old-fashioned changes made with scissors and glue. This electronic version of "cut and paste" is more powerful, however, since we can "cut" more precisely and can make multiple copies for pasting.

The three operators and their scopes are summarized in the following lists. (We also include a description of the "put" command, for it teams up with the "yank" and the "delete" commands.)

155

Command	Operator
d	*Delete* operator. Deletes text, but stores a copy in a temporary memory buffer. The copy can be recovered using the "put" command, **p.**
y	*Yank* operator. Places a copy of text (word, sentence, line, etc.) into a temporary memory storage buffer for positioning elsewhere. The original text is left unchanged. The copy is "pasted" relative to the cursor position using the "put" command, **p.**
p	*Put* command. Works with the *yank* and the *delete* commands. Puts whatever was last deleted or yanked in place after or below the cursor.
c	*Change* operator. This is equivalent to a **d**elete operation and an **i**nsert command. It deletes a word, sentence, etc., and enters the Text Input Mode to allow the typing in of changes. Must be ended with an <esc>.

These operators act with the following scopes, which are summarized as shown.

Scope	Operation
e	The scope is from the cursor to the *end* of the current word; e.g., if the cursor is on the "u" in "current" and you type **de,** then "urrent" is deleted.
w	The scope is from the cursor to the beginning of the next *word* including the space.
b	The scope is from the letter before the cursor backwards to the *beginning* of the word.
$	The scope is from the cursor to the end of the line.
Ø	The scope is from just before the cursor to the beginning of the line.
)	The scope is from the cursor to the beginning of the next sentence. A sentence is ended by ".", "!", or "?" followed by either an "end of line" (provided by the <return> key) or 2 spaces.
(	The scope is from just before the cursor back to the beginning of the sentence containing the cursor.
}	The scope is from the cursor to the end of a paragraph. A paragraph begins after an empty line.
{	The scope is from just before the cursor back to the beginning of a paragraph.

You might notice that there is no symbol for a *whole line*. The creators of **vi** decided that since an operation on a whole line is done so often, the easiest way to do it would be to hit the operator key twice. Thus, **dd** and **cc** and **yy** are commands affecting the whole line.

Of course, the commands formed by these operations and their scopes need to be practiced to be appreciated. The following paragraphs give a few examples to illustrate their format and action.

The Delete Operator

The delete operator is easiest to visualize since it is a one-step process. Consider the short line.

123 456 789. ABC.

Assume the cursor is on the 5, then

de deletes to the *end* of the word, thus deleting 56 and leaving   123 4 789. ABC.

dw deletes to next *word,* thus deleting 56 and leaving   123 4789. ABC.

db deletes to *beginning* of word, thus deleting 4 and leaving   123 56 789. ABC.

d∅ deletes to *beginning* of line, thus deleting 123 4 and leaving   56 789. ABC.

d) deletes to end of *sentence,* thus deleting 56 789. and leaving   123 4ABC.
    (Since there were two spaces after the decimal point in 4789., **vi** interpreted the decimal point to be a period at the end of a sentence.)

dd deletes the whole line.

A really neat way to practice these deletions is to use the "undo" command **u.** Since the **u** command *undoes* the last command, you can easily try out one of the deletions just described and, then, use the **u** command to get back to the starting point. Here is an example. Assume you have the text

123 4<u>5</u>6 789. ABC.

with the cursor on the "5".

Just type **dw** to see the 56 and one space deleted, and then type **u** to get back to the original text. It would look like this:

```
123 456 789. ABC. <————————————————————————— type dw to get
123 4789. ABC. <————————————————————————————— type u to get
123 456 789. ABC.
```

For fun, you can hit **u** again, and undo your undo!

All of the **d**elete operations and the **u**ndo commands are used in the Command Mode and they keep you in that mode. Now, let's consider the "change" operator.

The Change Operator *c*

The **c**hange operator **c** can use the same scopes as the delete operator *d*. In fact, the **c**hange operator deletes the exact same characters as the delete operator. The difference between the two operators is that the **c**hange operator places you in the Text Input Mode. You then can use the keyboard as a typewriter and can enter as much text as you like. Existing text moves to the right and "wraps around" as necessary to make room for your text insertion. You leave the Text Input Mode just as always by using the <esc> key. Some versions of **vi** include a marker with the **c**hange operation in order to mark the last character to be deleted using the $ symbol. Here is an example of a small change being made. Suppose you are in the **vi** command mode and have the following text on the screen with the cursor on the "6".

```
1234. 5678. 90.
```

You now type

```
cw
```

and the editor deletes to the end of the *word* leaving

```
1234. 567$. 90.
```

on display. Notice that the final character scheduled for replacement, the number 8, is replaced by the "$" symbol. The cursor is still on the 6, the first character scheduled for replacement. Now, if you type

```
Helloooo!<esc>
```

you get

```
1234. 5Helloooo!. 90.
```

The **cw** command lets you change everything from the cursor to the end of the *word*. The other change commands, **c)** and **c}**, etc., operate in a similar way, but with different scopes. If you don't want to change or delete text but just want to make a copy elsewhere, then the **yank** operator and the **put** command are just what you need.

Using the "yank" and "delete" Operators With the "put" Command

You can use **delete** and **put** commands to move text around in a file. **Y**ank and **put** commands, on the other hand, are ideal for *copying* and moving text around. The nine "scopes" allow you to mark precisely various parts of words, lines, sentences, and paragraphs. The **y**ank and **d**elete commands store these pieces of text in a temporary buffer that can be copied onto the screen with a **put** command. As usual, the commands are made with respect to the position of the cursor. As far as the **put** command is concerned, **y**ank and **d**elete work identically. The difference to you is that **y**ank leaves the original text unchanged, while **d**elete removes it.

Here is an example using **y**. Assume you are in the **vi** Command Mode with the following text on the screen and the cursor on the 6.

```
1234. 56789.
```

If you now type

```
y$
```

you will have stored a copy of 6789. in the temporary buffer. You can now move the cursor to another position (for example, at the end of the line) and type

p

This *puts* a copy of the buffer contents immediately after the cursor as in an append command. It would look like:

1234. 56789. 6789.

You might be wondering if the **p** command empties the buffer or if the buffer contents can be used again. You can, in fact, use it repeatedly to *put* down as many copies as you like. The only way to change the buffer's contents is to yank or to delete something else. The new text then replaces the old yank contents.

It seems too bad that the delete command and the yank command have to share the same buffer. Also, what if you wanted to save some text for longer periods of time in an editing session. You might think that there should be more buffers for temporary storage! In fact, there are, and this is the subject of our next section.

Deleting, Duplicating, and Rearranging Text Using Temporary Buffers

As we explained earlier in the chapter, when you wish to edit an existing file, a copy of that file is brought from memory to the editor buffer. The use of memory buffers is so convenient that the **vi** editor actually has over 30 such temporary memory areas that are used for duplicating, rearranging, and temporarily storing text. In addition, if you accidentally delete lines of text, you can recover not only the last deletion made but the eight previous ones as well. These deletions are stored in a set of temporary buffers numbered 1 to 9. You can get the **n**th previous block of deleted text back into your file by using the command "**np**. (The double quote mark alerts the editor that you are about to give the name of a buffer.) This command will place text after the cursor. A similar **p**ut command is **P**, which places the buffer contents before the cursor. Thus, the command

"1p

will recover the last deletion made and put it *after* the cursor, and the command

"1P

would place the last deletion *before* the cursor.

The **undo** command **u** is especially helpful if you want to search through deletion buffers 1 through 9. For example, you can display the contents of buffer number 4 by commanding

"4p

and if you don't want to keep it, type

u

You could repeat this to take a quick look at several buffers.

There is a better way to save, duplicate, and rearrange text than to use buffers 1 through 9 as described above. The problem with buffers 1 through 9 is that buffer No. 1 always has the last deletion made. Thus, if you move some text, and then make a deletion, the contents of the buffers change. If you plan to move or copy text, it is better to use a set of buffers that are unchanged by the ordinary delete operations. There is such a set, and the members are named with alphabetic letters from "a" to "z." To use these buffers, you precede the **d**elete operation with the name of the buffer in which the text is to be stored. Again, you need to use the quote symbol (") to inform the editor that you are using a buffer name. For example, the command

```
"c5dd
```

will delete 5 lines and store them in buffer c. These lines can be put back in their same place or in several places in the file by using the **p**ut commands, **p** and **P,** as follows:

```
"cp
```

This will put the contents of buffer c after the cursor. You can move the cursor and repeat the command to place additional copies of buffer c anywhere in the file.

These alphabetically labeled buffers will also store your **y**ank contents if you wish to just *copy* and store information. The commands are used identically. Consider the following example. Assume you have the following text on the screen for editing purposes.

```
Ancient Adages
Bountiful Beauties
Credulous Cretins
Diabolic Dingos
```

and the cursor is on the "Bountiful Beauties" line. Now you type

```
"fdd
```

The editor deletes the line containing the cursor and stores the contents in a buffer labeled "f," leaving on the screen

```
Ancient Adages
Credulous Cretins
Diabolic Dingos
```

If you now move the cursor to the bottom line and type

```
"fp
```

you will get

```
Ancient Adages
Credulous Cretins
Diabolic Dingos
Bountiful Beauties
```

The contents that are stored in buffer "f" are printed.

Now, if you were to start with the same original text, but substitute **yy** for **dd,** then the screen would display

```
Ancient Adages
Bountiful Beauties
Credulous Cretins
Diabolic Dingos
Bountiful Beauties
```

Here we see that the **yank** command leaves the original text (the second line) in its place, while letting us place a copy elsewhere.

Just as before, the **d**elete and **y**ank commands "share" storage buffers for saving deleted or copied text. The text stored in buffer f ("f) will remain in the buffer until new text is placed there or until you leave the **vi** editor. Thus, these buffers are extremely helpful for rearranging text.

These **d**elete and **y**ank commands may be repeated using commands like

```
"g7yy
```

which copies seven lines of text and stores them in a buffer named g.

Moving Larger Blocks

You can extend the range of these operator-scope combinations by prefixing the command with a number. The number indicates the *number* of lines, words, sentences, etc., that you wish affected. For example,

```
20dd
```

would delete twenty lines, and the command

    5cw

would let you change 5 words. If you use this last command, a $ will appear in place of the last character of the fifth word, so that you can see which words would be replaced. You are free, of course, to replace the 5 words with 1, 2, or 7 words, if you want.

If you want to move rather large blocks of material, you probably will find it more convenient to use the **co** and the **m** commands of the **ex** editor. You don't have to change editors to do this, for these commands are available from **vi,** too. We will show you how to get to **ex** commands shortly.

Joining and Breaking Up Lines

All of these "cutting and pasting" operations can leave the text on the screen somewhat messy looking. A paragraph might look something like that shown in the following illustration.

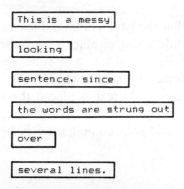

A messy looking paragraph.

How can we "clean" it up? (That is, how can we get the line lengths to be more equal?) There are three major ways to join sentences together. The *slowest* way is to retype the lines leaving out the blanks. A much easier way is to use the **J** command in **vi** which joins the next line down to the current line. For example, if you are in **vi** and have four short sentences, each on a line by itself, then you can place the cursor on the top line and type

    J

three times. This would join the sentences on the same line and wrap them around, if necessary, as shown in the next sketch.

START	FINISH
1. The tall man strolls away.	The tall man strolls away. An alarm
2. An alarm sounds.	sounds. RUN! A dead end.
3. RUN!	*Sentences joined and wrapped around.*
4. A dead end.	

Four short sentences.

Joining sentences.

If you wind up with lines that are too long, just insert a <return> where you wish to break the line. You can do this most easily by placing the cursor on the space where you wish to make the break, and then use the **r** command to replace the space with a <return>. You can reshape your line lengths as you see fit by using this and the **J** command.

Another way to clean up text is to use one of the text-formatting utilities discussed briefly in the section on ''Word Processing'' in Chapter 5 and more fully in Chapter 11. We will conclude this long chapter by mentioning some additional commands that are available in **vi** and by giving the **vi** summary.

Additional Commands and Features of *vi*

We hope that the commands you have learned so far will meet most of your editing needs. In order to keep this chapter fairly simple, we have omitted about 60 additional commands that are available in most versions of **vi.**

The **vi** editor has several features in addition to its commands, and you may wish to learn about them. These additional features let you do many things, including

* specifying your terminal type
* adjusting the screen size
* adjusting indentation, tabs, and wrap margin settings

* using macros and abbreviations to simplify a complex operation or a long keystroke entry
* editing two or more files at the same time
* using **ex**-like commands

The last feature deserves further mention, especially since we have already used it several times without telling you. To use an **ex** command, enter the Command Mode, then hit the [:] key. This will give you a :-prompt at the bottom of the screen. Now you can give any of the commands listed in the **ex** chapter. As soon as the command is executed, you are returned to the standard **vi** command mode.

If you prefer a longer stay in line editor **ex,** you can give the **Q** command while in the **vi** command mode. This, too, will give you a :-prompt at the screen bottom, but you will stay in the **ex** mode until you type **vi** to return.

The examples that we have used so far have involved the **write commands** (such as **:w** and **:120,230w chapter4.2b**) and the **quit commands** (**:q, :wq,** and **:q!**).

Of the other **ex** commands available, the most useful are those that let you deal with large blocks of material. Two important examples are the copy command **co** and the move command **m.** These perform the same tasks as delete-and-put and yank-and-put, respectively, but they work only on entire lines. Briefly, the command:

```
:20,300m500
```

will move lines 20 through 300 to just after line 500. The command:

```
:20,300co500
```

places a copy of the lines 20 through 300 just after line 500, but leaves the original lines 20 through 300 in place.

Another **ex** command that is very useful is the global search-and-replace command. For example, the command:

```
:g/e/s//#/g
```

will find every "e" in the file and replace it by a "#". Try it, it is visually stimulating. Just remember that you can undo this change with the **u** command. For more detail on the preceding commands, see the chapter on **ex.**

The **vi** editor also has a read-only option that is called up by typing **view** instead of **vi.** This is useful if you want to use the cursor-positioning keys to *read* text without worrying about accidentally adding or changing the file. Of course, you can do the same thing by leaving **vi** with a **:q!.** This command quits **vi** without writing any changes made.

More information about using the **vi** features and commands is presented in the manual.

A Summary of the Screen Editor *vi*

The screen editor **vi** has an abundant set of commands that rivals the best word processing systems in terms of flexibility and power. It can also be used by the beginning user who limits his or her commands to a few basic commands, such as those discussed in the section on basic **vi** commands. It is very important to remember that **vi** has two modes of operation—the Command Mode and the Text Input Mode. One important point to consider about the Command Mode is that most of the commands are used to position the cursor or to find text. The rest of the commands either delete something or place you in the Text Input Mode.

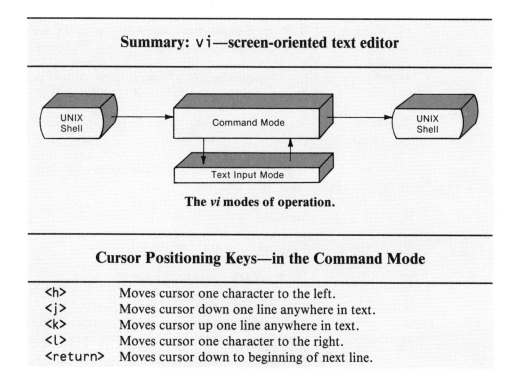

Summary: vi—screen-oriented text editor

The *vi* modes of operation.

Cursor Positioning Keys—in the Command Mode

`<h>`	Moves cursor one character to the left.
`<j>`	Moves cursor down one line anywhere in text.
`<k>`	Moves cursor up one line anywhere in text.
`<l>`	Moves cursor one character to the right.
`<return>`	Moves cursor down to beginning of next line.

Entering Text Input Mode—End this mode with an \<esc\>

a	Appends text after the cursor. You can type as many lines and \<return\>'s as you wish.
i	Inserts text before the cursor. You can insert as many lines of text and \<return\>'s as you wish.
o	Opens a new line below cursor. Ready for your text input.
0	Opens a new line above cursor. Ready for your text input.
R	Replaces characters on the screen, starting at the cursor, with any characters you type.

Command Mode—These commands, after execution, return you to the Command Mode

r	Replaces a single character under the cursor with a single character that you type.
/happy	Search sequence; looks for next occurrence of pattern following /; in this case, the word "happy."
?Lark	Search sequence; like /, but searches backwards from the cursor.
n	Used after / or ? to advance to the next occurrence in the buffer of the pattern.
u	Undo the last command.
U	Undo all the changes on the current line.
x	Deletes character under the cursor.
\<del\> or #, or \<control-h\> or \<rub\>	This backspace feature of the shell also works in the editor. These commands move the cursor character by character leftward within a line, erasing each character from the buffer.

\<control-f\> \<control-b\>	Scrolls or pages the screen forward or back, one page at a time.
\<control-d\>, \<control-u\>	Scrolls or pages the screen down or up, one-half page at a time.
nG	Positions the cursor at line **n** in the files.
\<control-g\>	Identifies the line where the cursor is located by line number.

Operators in the Command Mode (see following scopes)

---

d	Deletes indicated text starting at the cursor. For example, use **dw** to delete a word and **dd** to delete a line; **3dd** deletes 3 lines. Deleted text is stored temporarily in a buffer whose contents can be printed out with the **p** command. Also, **d** can be used with named buffers in the manner described for **y** below.
c	Deletes indicated text starting at the cursor and enters the Text Input Mode. Thus, **cw** deletes from the cursor to the *end* of the word, allowing you to add text between those positions.
y	Copies indicated text, starting at the cursor, and stores it in a buffer. There are nine unnamed buffers (1–9) that store the last nine **d**elete or **y**ank operations and 26 named buffers (a–z) that can be used for storage. The double quote mark (") is used to tell the editor the name of the buffer. Thus, **"cy$** will store text from the cursor to the end of the line in a buffer named c.
p	The **p**ut command, used to put down "delete" and "yank" buffer contents after the cursor or on the next line. Command **p** puts the last item yanked or deleted back into the file just after the cursor, and **"cp** will put the contents of buffer c after the cursor.
P	The "put" command. Identical to **p**, except it places the buffer contents before the cursor.

Scopes for Use With Operators

e	The scope from the cursor to the *end* of the current word; e.g., if the cursor is on the "u" in "current," and you type **de,** then "urrent" is deleted.
w	The scope is from the cursor to the beginning of the next *word,* including the space.
b	The scope is from the letter before the cursor, backwards, to the *beginning* of the word.
$	The scope is from the cursor to the end of the line.
Ø	The scope is from just before the cursor to the beginning of the line.
)	The scope is from the cursor to the beginning of the next sentence. A sentence is ended by ".", "!", or "?" and followed by an "end of line" (provided by the < return > key) or by 2 spaces.
(	The scope is from just before the cursor back to the beginning of the sentence containing the cursor.
}	The scope is from the cursor to the end of a paragraph. A paragraph begins after an empty line.
{	The scope is from just before the cursor back to the beginning of a paragraph.

Leaving the Editor

<esc>:w	Writes the contents of the buffer into the current file of the same name. Can be given a new filename to write to. Also, can send partial buffer contents using line numbers, such as **:3,1Øw popcorn.**
<esc>:q	Quits buffer after a :w command.

`<esc>:wq`	Write and quit, placing buffer contents in file.
`<esc>:q!`	Quits buffer without making changes in file. Dangerous.
`<esc>ZZ`	Write and quit, placing buffer contents in file.

Using the ex Editor While in `vi`

:	Gives a colon (:) prompt at the bottom of the screen and lets you make one **ex** command. You are returned to the **vi** mode when the command finishes execution.
Q	Quits **vi** and places you in the **ex** editor, giving you a Command Mode prompt, the colon [:], at the bottom of the screen. You can get back to **vi** just by typing the command **vi** while in the Command Mode.

When in Doubt

`<esc>`	Puts you in the command mode.

Review Questions

A. Match the commands shown on the left to the functions shown on the right. Assume all the commands are given in the Command Mode only, none are given from the Text Input Mode.

vi Editor Commands   *Functions*

1. `35G`   **a.** Scrolls screen down 1/2 page

2. `3yw`   **b.** Moves cursor down 1 line

3. `r2`   **c.** Stores 4 lines in buffer c

4. `/fun`   **d.** Prints line number of the current line

5. `<control-g>`   **e.** Moves cursor to left one character

6. `2dd`   **f.** Replaces character under cursor with number 2

7. `j`   **g.** Yanks out 3 words

8. `"c4dd`   **h.** Substitutes funny for fun

9. `<control-d>`   **i.** Deletes 2 lines

10. h

j. Puts cursor on line 35

k. Finds the word "fun"

B. General Questions

1. When you invoke the editor with a file, that is, type **vi file3,** how can you tell if it is a new file?

2. Why is the **:q**! command considered dangerous?

3. When you first enter the editor with an existing file and type **a,** the append command to add text, where is that text placed?

4. What command is used to save the editor buffer contents?

5. Where does the insert command **i** place new text?

6. Write out the command that will save the first three lines only of an editor buffer containing seven lines of text.

7. How do you exit the Text Input Mode?

8. Write out the command(s) to correct the following misspelled word, "sometome."

9. Write out the command(s) to delete the last five lines in ten lines of text.

Answers

A. 1—j, 2—g, 3—f, 4—k, 5—d, 6—i, 7—b, 8—c, 9—a, 10—e

B. **1.** The left column of the screen fills with tildes (~) **2.** None of the changes you've made are saved **3.** After the cursor **4.** :w, ZZ **5.** Before the cursor **6.** :1,3w filename **7.** Use [esc] **8.** Position cursor over "o", type ri **9.** Position cursor on first line to be deleted and type **5dd**

Exercises at the Terminal

Here are some exercises to practice your editing techniques. You can use either editor.

1. Enter the following text into a new file called **letterrec1.**

> Dear Sir:
> This is a letter of recommendation for john doe.
> john doe is a good worker.
> john doe has a find character.
> john doe is a-ok.
> sincerely
> jane doe

2. Now, do the following:

    A. Save the letter.

    B. Correct all spelling errors.

    C. Capitalize jane, john, and doe.

    D. Delete the last sentence containing a-ok.

    E. Save the corrected letter as **letterrec2**. (Use the **w** command.)

    F. Leave the editor.

    G. Use **cat** to print both copies on the screen at the same time.

3. Go into the shell, list your files with ls, and do the following:

    A. Make a copy of one of your files, e.g., **mbox,** calling it **mbox2** or something similar.

    B. Now, invoke the editor with this copy of a file and:

        (1) Insert somewhere the line, ''This is a test.''

        (2) Move 3 lines.

        (3) Replace all occurrences of the word ''the'' with ''thee.''

        (4) Copy 2 lines and place them in the beginning of the file.

        (5) Delete the last 4 lines.

7

Manipulating Files and Directories:
mv, cp, and *mkdir*

In this chapter, you will find:

7 MANIPULATING FILES AND DIRECTORIES: *mv, cp,* and *mkdir*

Introduction

Now that you have the basic file *reading* commands from Chapter 4, you can get into the real fun of directory and file manipulation. However, before we do that, we will take a brief look at how UNIX names files so that they don't get mixed up. We will then conclude this chapter by showing you some typing shortcuts that you can use with metacharacters (abbreviations).

Filenames, Pathnames, Heads, And Tails

What happens if Bob, Lola, and Nerkie (each of whom has his or her own UNIX account on the same system) each decide to create a file called **whiz**? Does UNIX become confused? Does Lola find Bob's work in her file? Of course not! UNIX is much too clever for that. To understand what happens, you first should review the tree structure of the UNIX directory system. The full name of Lola's **whiz** file includes the name of the directory it is in. The full names of all three **whiz** files would be

```
/usr/bob/whiz
/usr/lola/whiz
/usr/nerkie/whiz
```

These are called the ''pathnames'' of the files because they give the path through the directory system to the file. The very last part of the pathname (the part after the last /) is called the **tail,** and the rest of the pathname is called the **head.**

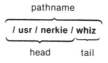

A pathname, a head, and a tail.

The head of the first file tells us that the **bob** directory branches off the

usr directory and that the **usr** directory branches off the / directory (our old friend, **root**). For this example, all three pathnames have the same tail; i.e., **whiz.** On the other hand, they all have different heads (**/usr/bob/**, **/usr/ lola/**, and **/usr/nerkie/**), so UNIX has no problem distinguishing between them.

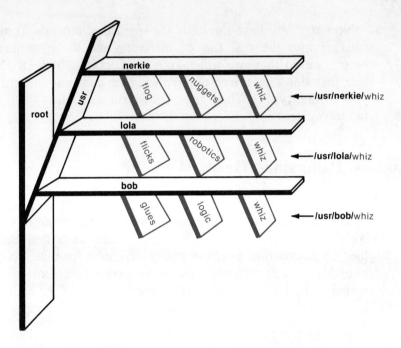

Pathnames and the directory tree.

The slash (/) takes on two roles in a pathname. The slash at the very beginning stands for the **root** directory. The other slashes serve to separate the name of a directory from the name of the following directory or file.

When a file is in your working directory, you can be casual and call it by its tail name. When the file is in a different directory, however, you need to tell UNIX which directory the file is in. One foolproof method is to use the pathname. For example, if Nerkie wishes to read Bob's **whiz** file, he can enter the command

```
cat /usr/bob/whiz
```

There are other ways, using abbreviations and conventions, to identify files but, if you are in doubt, use the pathname!

Let's look at one more example. Lola has created a directory called **bigstuff** and, in it, she has placed the file **walrus**. The pathname of this file is

```
/usr/lola/bigstuff/walrus
```

The tail name is

```
walrus
```

The head is

```
/usr/lola/bigstuff/
```

If Lola is in the directory **/usr/lola/bigstuff** and wants to read the files, she can simply call the file **walrus**.

However, if she is in her home directory **(/usr/lola),** she can refer to the file as **/usr/lola/bigstuff/walrus,** or, more simply, as **bigstuff/walrus.**

This illustrates an important special case. If a file is in a subdirectory of the one you are in, the only part of the pathname you need to use is the subdirectory name and the tail.

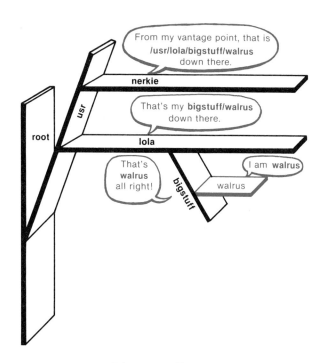

What to call a *walrus.*

179

Basic File and Directory Manipulation Commands

As a walrus once said, "The time has come to talk of many things." We now will look at the following commands:

```
rm, cp, mv, ln, mkdir, rmdir, cd, pwd
```

These commands will let you manipulate your files and directories with ease and versatility. Their basic use is rather simple, but many of them can be used in more than one way. We will show you all you need to know soon enough, but first let's run through a sample session to highlight some of the most common uses.

Mimi has some files called **roses** and **daisies.** She would like to create a new directory called **Flowers** and move those files into it. So she types

```
mkdir Flowers <——————————————————— makes the new directory
mv roses daisies Flowers <————————— moves files to the directory
```

Next, she wants to change to the **Flowers** directory to do some work there. She types

```
cd Flowers <——————————————————— changes to new directory
vi violets <——————————————————— works on a new file there
```

The **violets** file joins the other files in that directory. When she finishes, she wants to return to her home directory, so she types a simple

```
cd <————————————————————————— return to home directory
```

Her friend Rudolpho has written a poem for her in his directory, and she wants to have a copy. She types

```
cp /usr/Rudolpho/for.mimi moonlight
```

where the first pathname identifies the original file, and **moonlight** is the name of the copy in her directory.

As you can see, these are useful, simple commands. Now we will take a more detailed look at each. Again, we urge you to try the commands as you read along. Use one of the editors or the redirected **cat** command to create some files to work with.

Directory Commands: *mkdir, rmdir, cd,* and *pwd*

Directories give you a place to keep your files. The first three commands let you create, remove, and move through directories. The last command tells you where you are.

The Make Directory Command: *mkdir*

This is the command that lets you build your own directory subsystem. If you are on a UNIX system, you should have a ''home'' directory; this is the directory you are placed in when you log on. We will assume that your directory is a subdirectory of **/usr** so that the full pathname of your directory is **/usr/yourname** (i.e., **/usr/roscoe** if your name is Roscoe). The procedure is simple and quick; to create a subdirectory called, say, **formletters,** you enter

```
mkdir formletters
```

The general form of the **mkdir** command is

```
mkdir name1 name2 . . .
```

where **name1,** etc., are the names of the directories you wish to create. You can make directories only within your own directory system (unless, of course, you have special privileges on the system). If **name1** is a tail and not a pathname, then the new directory is attached to the directory you are in when making the command. For example, if Bob is in his home directory and issues the command

```
mkdir foibles
```

the result is a new directory whose pathname is **/usr/bob/foibles.** After doing this, Bob could switch from his home directory to the **foible** directory (see **cd**) and make the command

```
mkdir gambling
```

to create the directory **/usr/bob/foibles/gambling**

It's easy to make directories. The challenge is to design the directory system that's the most helpful to you. Again, experience is a great teacher.

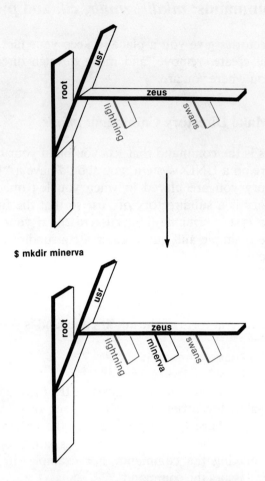

$ mkdir minerva

The *mkdir* command: before and after.

Summary: mkdir—makes a new directory		
Name	**options**	**arguments**
mkdir		[directoryname . . .]

Description: This command creates a new subdirectory in the present directory.

Example: **mkdir Chapter4**
This command creates a new subdirectory called **Chapter4** that exists in the directory where you entered the command. Note that you should not use a blank space in your directory names.

The Change Directory Command: *cd*

Once you've created a new directory, you would like to use it. The **cd** command lets you change from one directory to another. The general form of the command is:

```
cd directoryname
```

The change directory command was once called **chdir,** but it is used so often that newer versions of UNIX have shortened the name to **cd.** Once it is executed, the named directory becomes your "working directory." For example, if you enter the commands

```
cd /usr/lola/quarkdata
ls
```

The result will be a list of files in the directory **/usr/lola/quarkdata.** Of course, there is a question of "permissions." If Lola gave this command, she would have the power to alter the files in this directory. If Bob gave the command, normally he could look but not touch. (The standard setup allows you to look at someone else's files but not alter them. However, you can copy the file and alter the copy.) The **chmod** command, discussed in Chapter 10, lets you change the permissions governing your files.
The command

```
cd
```

with nothing following it will place you in your home directory.

Summary: cd—change directory

name	options	arguments
cd		[directoryname]

Description: This command makes the named directory your current working directory. If no directory is given, the command takes you to your home directory.

Example: **cd /usr/reggie/foods/carbo**
This command would place you in the **/usr/reggie/foods/ carbo** directory.

The Print Working Directory Command: *pwd*

Once you have the power to change working directories, you have the possibility of forgetting which directory you are in. The command **pwd** causes UNIX to print the full pathname of your current working directory. If, when you try to copy or move a file, UNIX claims that the file doesn't exist and you know it does, try **pwd.** You may find that you are in a different directory than you thought and that you need to use a full pathname for a file. The use is simple. If you type

pwd

and if UNIX replies

/usr/src/cmd

then you are currently in the **/usr/src/cmd** directory.

Summary: pwd—print working directory

name	options	arguments

pwd

Description:	This command prints out the pathname of the current working directory.

The Remove Directory Command: *rmdir*

Sometimes you find you have no more use for a directory; the **rmdir** command lets you get rid of it. The standard form of the command is:

```
rmdir dir1 . . .
```

The command removes the one or more directories listed after the command. The command will not remove nonempty directories or, normally, directories belonging to others.

UNIX gives you the tools to organize your files efficiently and easily. We have given you the rules governing several useful commands, but it is up to you to make good use of them. The first step is to practice with them, creating new directories, populating them with files, and then copying and moving files. Get comfortable with the procedures.

Next, give thought to your own needs. Don't hesitate to create new directories. It's a good idea to use different directories to house different projects or different types of material. Give your directories and files names that tell you what the contents are; use names like **chapter3** and **unixbook** rather than **file1** and **directory2.** UNIX gives you the opportunity to make your directory system a model of clarity and convenience—take advantage of it!

Summary: `rmdir`—remove directories

name	options	arguments
rmdir		directoryname(s) . . .

Description:	**rmdir** removes the named directories, providing that they are empty.

185

Example: **rmdir budget65 budget66**
This command removes the directories **budget65** and **budget66**
if they do not contain any files.

File Commands: *rm, cp, mv,* and *ln*

Handling old-fashioned files involved much paper shuffling. These four UNIX commands let you do the modern equivalent—electron shuffling—with much greater ease.

The Remove Command: *rm*

This command removes files. If you don't use it, your directories can become a jungle choked with unused and superceded files. The command is simple to use; you just follow **rm** with a list of the files you wish gone. Each filename should be separated by a space from the others. Thus,

```
rm dearjohn dearjoe dearfred dearigor
```

removes four files.

As you can see, it is very easy to remove files; in fact, it is so easy and so irreversible that you should stop and ask the following questions:

1. Am I sure I no longer want this file?
2. Is this the file I think it is?
3. Am I really sure about my answers to Questions 1 and 2?

Summary: rm—remove files		
name	option	argument
rm	−i, −r	filename(s) . . .

Description: **rm** removes each file in the argument list.

Options: **−i** asks, for each file on the list, whether or not to delete it; the

user responds with **y** or **n** for yes or no.
−**r** deletes a directory and every file or directory in it.

Example: **rm −i Rodgers**
This will cause UNIX to query **rm:** remove Rodgers? And you reply with a **y** or **n.**

Special caution is needed when using **rm** with the "wildcard" substitutions discussed later in this chapter. We'll remind you again when you reach that section. You may want to use the −**i** option described in the summary.

Ordinarily, you can't remove directories with **rm;** use **rmdir** if that's what you want to do. The −**r** option given in the summary *does* let you remove directories, but you had better be certain that you really do want to remove *everything.* **rmdir** is safer because it only removes empty directories.

Normally, you are not allowed to remove files from someone else's directory. To make things fair, someone else can't remove yours.

The Copy Command: *cp*

The **cp** command is used to create a copy of a file. There are several reasons you should have a copy command. One is to create backup copies of files. A file you are working on can be wiped out by a system problem or (believe it or not!) by slips on your part, so "backups" are a good idea. (A backup is a second copy of a file.)

A second reason is that you may wish to develop a second, slightly different version of a file, and you can use a copy as a convenient starting point. Another need may develop from the fact that UNIX is a shared system. A colleague may write a program or collect some data you can use, and a copy function gives you an easy way to place it in your own directory. The simplest form of the copy command is:

```
cp file1 file2
```

The command works from left to right; **file1** is the original and **file2** is the copy. This is the way the command functions. First, it creates a file called **file2.** If you already have a file by that name, it is *eliminated* and replaced by the new empty file. Then, the contents of **file1** are copied into **file2.** You, of course, would use whatever names you want for the files; you aren't limited to **file1** and **file2.** For example, Sam Softsell might use the command:

```
cp buypasta buytacos
```

to copy the contents of his **buypasta** file into a **buytacos** file.

Sam should be careful that he doesn't already have a valuable file called **buytacos,** for it would have been wiped out by the last instruction. This is one of the less friendly aspects of UNIX, but you can use **chmod** (Chapter 10) to protect your valuables.

To copy a file from another directory into your own, you need to know the full directory name of the file. If you enter

```
cp bigthought idea
```

UNIX will search only your directory for a file called **bigthought**. If the **bigthought** file is in, say, Bob's directory (assumed to be **/usr/bob**), then the proper command is:

```
cp /usr/bob/bigthought idea
```

Here **/usr/bob/bigthought** is the pathname of the original file. (At the end of this chapter, we will show some abbreviations that will let you reduce the amount of typing you need do when dealing with long pathnames.) Incidentally, Bob can use **chmod** (Chapter 10) to keep others from copying his files.

A second form of the copy command is:

```
cp file1 file2 . . . directory2
```

This copies the list of files given into the named directory, which must already exist. This instruction will become more useful to you once you begin establishing additional directories. The new files retain the tail name of the originals. For example, suppose Sam Softsell has a subdirectory called **backup** in his home directory of **/usr/sam.** The command:

```
cp pasta backup
```

creates a file named **pasta** in the **backup** directory. There are two points to note here.

First, although both files are named **pasta,** they exist in different directories and, thus, have different pathnames. For the preceding example, the pathname of the original file is **/usr/sam/pasta** and the pathname of the copy is **/usr/sam/backup/pasta.**

Secondly, if the directory named **backup** didn't exist, UNIX would assume that this command was in the first form we described. In other words, it would just copy the file **pasta** into a file called **backup**, all in the original directory.

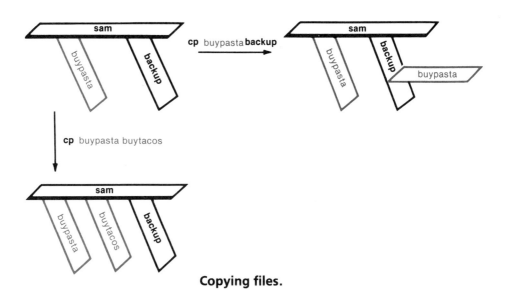

Copying files.

Sometimes, UNIX may give you messages like "cp: cannot create file2" or "cp: cannot open file1." This is UNIX's way of confessing bafflement at your instructions. Check to make sure that you typed the names correctly, that you're not trying to place files in someone else's directory, or that, perhaps, you need to use a full pathname.

Summary: cp—makes copies of files

name	options	arguments
cp		file1 file2 file(s) . . . directory

Description: The command **cp file1 file2** creates a copy of the first file (**file1**) and gives it the name **file2**. If a file named **file2** already

> exists, it will be replaced by the new one. The second form of the command **(cp file(s) . . . directory)** makes copies of all the files listed and places them in the named directory.
>
> Examples: **cp flim flam**
> This command makes a copy of the file **flim** and calls the copy **flam.**
>
> **cp /usr/snoopy/storm /usr/ruff**
> This command makes a copy of the file **stormy** (from the **/usr/ snoopy** directory) and places the copy in the **/usr/ruff** direc- tory; the pathname of the copy is **/usr/ruff/stormy.**

The Move Command: *mv*

This command lets you change the name of a file and lets you move a file from one directory to another. The simplest form of this command is:

```
mv file1 file2
```

The effect of this command is to change the name of **file1** to **file2.** The file is left unchanged, but a new name is moved in. Suppose Lola LaLulu wants to change the name of a file from **a.out** to **findanswer.** She could solve her problem with the command:

```
mv a.out findanswer
```

Suppose, however, she already had a file called **findanswer? Mv** is as ruth- less as **cp;** it would wipe out the old file in order to make the name available for the contents of **a.out.**

You can use the **mv** command to change the name of a directory, too. The form is

```
mv oldname newname
```

and is the same as that for changing a file name. In other words, **mv** doesn't care whether **oldname** is a file or a directory, it will just proceed and give it the new name.

The final use of **mv** is to move files to an existing directory. The form is:

```
mv file1 file2 . . . directory
```

We can think of this command as moving one or more files to the specified directory. This is a very handy housekeeping command. For example, if Lola, an exotic physicist studying those exotic subatomic particles called quarks, has accumulated four files of quark data, she can create a directory called **quarkdata** (using **mkdir**) and, then, could type:

```
mv quark1 quark2 quark3 quark4 quarkdata
```

to gather the four files together in the new directory. This form of the command leaves the tail of the pathname unchanged. For example, the preceding command would change the pathname of **/usr/lola/quark1** to **/usr/lola/quarkdata/quark1**. (At the end of the chapter, we will see a much quicker way to make the same move!)

Of course, this use of **mv** won't work if the destination directory doesn't exist or if you don't have permission to "write" in that directory.

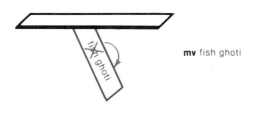

mv fish ghoti

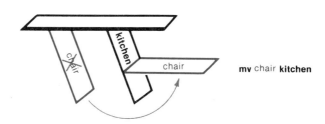

mv chair **kitchen**

Two smooth moves.

If you give a command like

```
mv chair kitchen
```

how does the UNIX know whether you want **kitchen** to be a file or to be a directory? Well, UNIX may be clever, but it isn't psychic; it doesn't know which you want. It *does* know, however, whether or not you already have a directory called **kitchen.** If you do have such a directory, UNIX puts the **chair** file there. If you don't have a directory called **kitchen,** UNIX assumes you want **kitchen** to be a filename.

Summary: mv—move or rename files

name	options	arguments
mv		filename1 filename2 or filename(s) directoryname

Description: **mv** allows the user to change the name of a file. The first form of the command shown above changes the name of "filename1" to "filename2."

However, since filenames can include the full pathname, it is possible to use the command to move a file to a new directory as shown in the second form of the command.

Examples: (We assume here that the user is in the **/usr/flisk** directory and that **hobo** is a subdirectory of that directory.)

mv mrak mark
This changes the name of the file **mrak** to **mark.**

mv mark hobo
This changes the name of the file **mark** (pathname **/usr/flisk/mark**) to **/usr/flisk/hobo/mark,** thus moving the file to the **hobo** directory.

mv mray hobo/mary
This changes the name of the file **mray** (pathname **/usr/flisk/mray** to **/usr/flisk/hobo/mary),** thus changing the directory and the tail of the pathname.

The Link Command: *ln*

This command allows you to assign multiple names to a single file. This allows you to refer to the same file by different pathnames. This can be handy when you have many subdirectories, for it lets you "link" one file to several different directories. (The names you assign are the links between the file and the directories.)

A general form of this command is:

```
ln file1 name2
```

name2 can be either a new name you wish to give to the file or it can be an existing directory name. If it is a proposed filename, the result of executing this command is that **file1** will now have two names: **file1** and **name2.** If **name2** is the name of a directory, then **file1** will also be known by the tail of its old name **(file1)** in the directory **name2.** Let's clarify these two cases with two examples.

Suppose Tana the Wonder Dog is in her home directory **(/usr/tana)** and gives the command:

```
ln soupbone chews
```

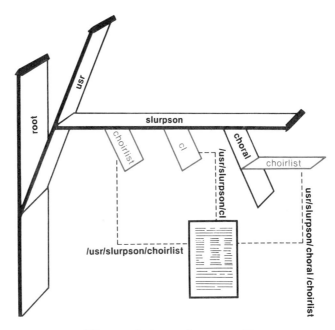

Different links to the same file.

UNIX checks to see if the name **chews** has been used yet. If it hasn't, then UNIX gives the new name to the file while still keeping the old one. (A **ls** command, for example, would show both; and a **ls −l** command would show that each had two links.) Tana then could call up the file by either name. What if there had already been a file called **chews** in the home directory? Then, **ln,** being more polite than **cp** or **mv,** would tell you so and would not make the new link. What if **chews** already was a subdirectory? Then, the situation would be like the next example.

Now suppose Tana has a subdirectory called **tidbit.** The command

```
ln soupbone tidbit
```

adds the **soupbone** name to the **tidbit** directory, but leaves the original name undisturbed. Thus, the same file is now in two directories and has two pathnames: **/usr/tana/soupbone** and **/usr/tana/tidbit/soupbone.** These are the same file, not copies. When Tana is in her home directory and wants to see the file, she can type (after all, she is a wonder dog):

```
cat soupbone
```

(short for **cat /usr/tana/soupbone**).

If she switches to the **tidbit** directory (see **cd),** she can see the contents of the file by typing:

```
cat soupbone
```

(short for **cat /usr/tana/tidbit/soupbone**).

Without the **ln** command, she would have had to type:

```
cat /usr/tana/soupbone
```

to see the **soupbone** file when in the **tidbit** directory. When you have paws and have to type, you appreciate all the shortcuts you can get.

Suppose Tana, while in her home directory, now issues the command:

```
rm soupbone
```

Soupbone, of course, disappears from her home directory. Does this mean that the contents of the file disappear? No. The file still exists in the **tidbit** directory! Only when all of the names or links to the file have been removed will the file itself be erased.

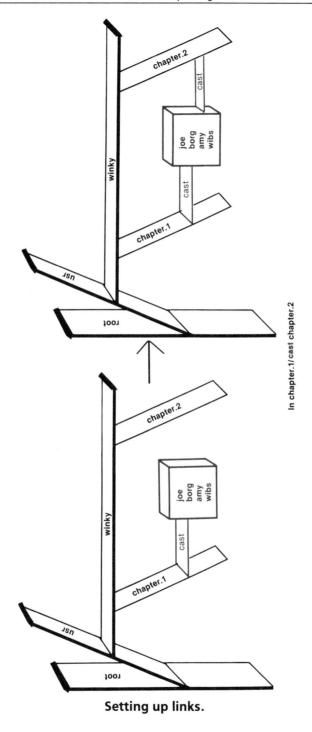

ln chapter.1/cast chapter.2

Setting up links.

Summary: ln—make file links

name	options	arguments
ln		filename1 [filename 2] or filename(s) directoryname

Description: This command lets you add one or more names to an existing file providing a cross-reference system. Each name located in your directory has equal priority for reading or writing to the file. However, if a file is linked to another user, generally only the originator of the file can write in it (see the chmod command in Chapter 10).

The form "**ln** filename" creates a link between the current working directory and filename1. Filename1 can include a full pathname, therefore, it is linked to a file in another directory.

The form "**ln** filename1 filename2" is like the preceding action, except the name of the new file is filename2.

The form "**ln** filename(s) directoryname" lets you put new filenames or links into other directories.

Examples: (We will suppose the current working directory is **/usr/francie/spring** and there is a file called **math** in the **/usr/francie** directory.)

ln /usr/francie/math
This command creates the filename **math** in the current directory (**/usr/francie/spring**) and links that name to the file called **math** in the **francie directory**. The full pathname of the new link is **/usr/francie/spring/math**.

ln /usr/francie/math trig
This command does the same as above except that the newly created filename is **trig** instead of **math**. The full pathname of the new filename is **/usr/francie/spring/trig**.

> **ln hist eng /usr/francie**
> This command puts the two filenames **hist** and **eng** from the current directory into the **/usr/francie** directory.

Suppose you have established several subdirectories and you want them to have access to the same mailing list. You could, of course, place a copy of the mailing list in each directory, but that would use up too much disk space. By using the **ln** command, you can link the file containing the list to a name in each of the directories. In effect, the same file will exist in each directory. An additional advantage is that if you update the file from one directory, you've updated it for all the directories.

There are limitations to **ln**. One is that you can't use **ln** to assign two names to the same directory.

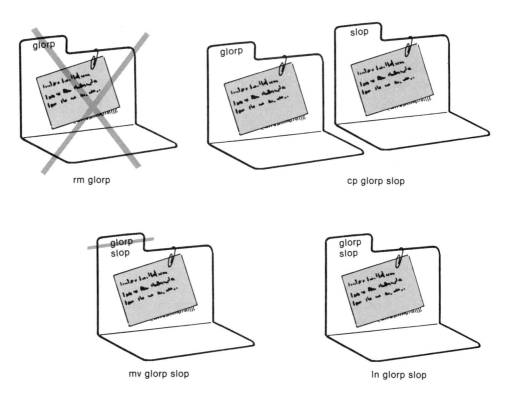

A comparison of *rm, mv, cp,* and *ln.*

The File Commands *cp, mv,* and *ln*

These three commands form a family. All affect filenames, and they are used in similar fashion. This similarity occasionally can create confusion in the new user. We think a closer look at their workings can help prevent this, so let's take that look.

Suppose you have a file called **jazz** in your home directory. To you the file is called **jazz,** but to the *computer,* the file is known by an identification number. Normally, you don't need to know this number but you can find it by using the −**i** option of **ls.** For example, the command

```
ls −i jazz
```

could yield as output

```
2312 jazz
```

where 2312 is the ID number. This ID number is the true, permanent name for the file. If, for instance, you change the name by typing

```
mv jazz cool
```

the ID number remains the same. (Try it and see!)

In the UNIX way of things, the name you choose (**jazz, cool,** or whatever) acts as a "link" between the file and your directory system. These links tie the files to the directories. This gives us a way to visualize the effects of the three file manipulation commands:

1. The **ln** command establishes a new link between the file and a directory. All the old links (i.e., names) continue to exist. No new files are created. Linking one file to different directories makes it appear as if several different files exist, but, in fact, there is just one file with multiple names. This is very useful when you want a particular file to be easily accessed from several directories without typing out pathnames.
2. The **mv** command establishes a new link while removing an old link. If the the link is to be a different directory, it makes it appear as if the file has been moved. However, only the link (or name) has been changed, and the file has the same ID number as before.
3. The **cp** command actually creates a new file with a new ID number and with its own link (name) to a directory. The old file continues to exist.

In summary, the **cp** command creates *new files* that are copies of the originals. The **mv** command creates *new names* for existing files and dumps the old names. The **ln** command creates new names for existing files and simultaneously maintains the old names. Neither **mv** nor **ln** create new files.

Searching Through Files: *grep*

grep is a command whose beauty of function far exceeds its beauty of name. **grep** performs the invaluable service of searching your files for a key word or phrase and telling you what it finds. Suppose, for example, you have several inventory files (**infile1, infile2, infile3,** and **infile4**) and want to find out which one contains the description of your widget. The following command will serve that high purpose:

```
grep widget infile1 infile2 infile3 infile4
```

grep will search each file in turn and will print out those lines that contain the string of characters "widget."

The form of this command is:

```
grep pattern file(s)
```

In Chapter 11, we explore **grep**'s abilities much more fully. For the moment, we will point out just two more aspects.

First, if the pattern has a space in it, enclose the pattern in single quotes so that **grep** will know that the second word is part of the pattern and not a file to be searched. For example, if you were interested only in a glaxon widget, you could type:

```
grep 'glaxon widget' infile1 infile2 infile3 infile4
```

Secondly, the wildcard substitutions described in the next section can make it easier to specify filenames. For instance, as you will soon learn, the first example could have been typed:

```
grep widget infile?
```

grep is one of the most heavily used UNIX commands. As you become more involved with the system, you will find **grep** growing on you. Don't worry if it does; it's just a sign of a healthy relationship.

One of the pleasures of UNIX is the freedom it gives you in creating files and directories and in manipulating them. Whether you are a collector keeping an inventory, a businessman dealing with accounts, mailing lists, and sales records, a researcher working with experimental data and computer programs, or a homeowner monitoring your budget and your energy usage, easy file handling is a key to happy computing.

Marvelous Metacharacters!! Wildcards—Character Substitutions

You can get tired and bored punching in filenames and directory names, especially when you have to use the full pathnames. UNIX provides some tricky ways to save time. We'll look here at some alternative ways to identify filenames.

One of the cleverer abilities of UNIX is pattern searching. That is, it can find filenames that match a "pattern" which you supply. You can have it list all your files that start with **chubby,** or have it remove all your files that end with **old,** or have it **cat** all your files having names with exactly four characters. The secret is in the use of special characters that can be used to stand for one or more characters in a file name. The special characters are "**?**" and "*****". The rules are these:

1. A **?** matches any one character.
2. An ***** matches any grouping of zero or more characters, except that it will not match a period that is the first character of a name. This protects the **.profile** file (Chapter 6) and your current working directory (see next section).

Some examples should make the workings of these rules clear.

First, suppose that your directory contains the following files:

```
co.5      coward     hog      huge      part2.2   thug
cow       coy        hug      part2.1   start2.3
```

The command **ls** alone will list all these files, while the command **ls cow** will list only the **cow** file. The command:

```
ls co?
```

however, will list **cow** and **coy,** but not **co.5** or **coward.** We can describe the process this way. You provide the pattern of "co?"; this means a **co** followed by exactly one character (which can be any character). UNIX searches for filenames that match this pattern, and it finds **cow** and **coy.** It doesn't list **co.5** or **coward** because they both have *more* than one character after the **co.** Here are other examples of using **ls** and **?** with the sample directory above.

1. command: `ls hu?`
   response: hug

2. command: `ls hu??`
   response: `huge`
3. command: `ls ???`
   response: `cow coy hog hug`
4. command: `ls ?o?`
   response: `cow coy hog`

The process of finding out which of your files match the pattern you give is called "filename expansion." For instance, in the last example, we could say that the pattern **?o?** was expanded to match **cow, coy,** and **hog.** Note that you use two **?**'s to represent two characters, etc.

The ***** character is more general yet. As promised, it will represent any number of characters. Here are some sample commands and the responses using it.

1. command: `ls h*`
   response: `hog hug huge`
2. command: `ls *g`
   response: `hog hug thug`
3. command: `ls hug*`
   response: `hug huge`
4. command: `ls *hug`
   response: `hug thug`
5. command: `ls *.*`
   response: `co.5 part2.1 part2.2 start2.3`

Let's take a closer look at how these examples work. The first example lists all files beginning with **h.** The second command lists all files ending in **g.** The third command lists all files starting with **hug.** Note that in this case, the ***** even matches the "null character" (i.e., no character at all). (The pattern **hug?** matches **huge** but not **hug** because **hug?** has exactly four characters. However, **hug*** matches both **hug** and **huge.**) The fourth command matches all names ending with **hug;** again, the null character is matched. The final example matches all names containing a period in them, except for files whose name begins with a period. (Recall that **ls** doesn't show such files unless you use the **−a** option.)

The "*****" and "**?**" characters, as well as the "**>**" character, belong to a group of characters having special meanings and uses in UNIX. They are called "metacharacters," an imposing term that hints at their latent power. Besides metacharacters, UNIX also possesses metasequences. An example is the pattern-matching sequence [ ]. Like **?**, this sequence matches one character, but more restrictively. The trick is to place between the brackets a list of characters to be matched. Here are some examples:

1. command: `ls co [xyz]`
   response: `coy`
2. command: `ls [cdeghr]o[gtw]`
   response: `cow hog`

The first example matches all 3-character names beginning with **co** and ending in **x, y,** or **z**. The second example would also have matched **cog** and **how,** among others, if you had had them in your directory. Note that the [ ] sequence matches one character and *only* one character. For example, **[nice]** matches an **n**, or an **i**, or a **c**, or an **e**; it does not match **ice** or **nice.**

You can specify a range of characters using the [ ] notation. For instance, **[2–8]** represents the digits 2, 3, 4, 5, 6, 7, and 8, while **[A–Z]** represents all the capital letters. Thus,

`ls [A-Z]`

would match all filenames consisting of a single capital letter, and

`ls [A-Z]*`

would match all filenames starting with a capital letter and ending in anything. The last example points out that you can combine the different pattern-matching operations into one command.

Very interesting, you say, but of what use is this? In part, the usefulness depends on what sort of names you give your files. Consider the earlier example that we gave of the **mv** command:

`mv quark1 quark2 quark3 quark4 quarkdata`

Lola could have accomplished the same result with

`mv quark? quarkdata`

or

`mv quark[1-4] quarkdata`

Of course, the first instruction would also move any other files matching that pattern, such as **quarky** or **quarkQ.**

Here's another example. Suppose you created a directory called **backup** and you wanted to place copies in there of *all* the files in your home directory. The following entry would do the job.

```
cp * backup
```

In general, one should be cautious using a solo *. Consider, for example, what the command

```
rm *
```

does. Since * matches anything, the command removes all of the files in your current working directory. Well, you're hardly likely to give that command unless you mean it, but it can crop up accidentally. Suppose that Lothario wishes to get rid of 20 files called **Hortense1, Hortense2,** etc. He could type:

```
rm Hortense*
```

and all would be well. But, if he accidentally hit the space bar and typed:

```
rm Hortense *
```

UNIX would first look for a file called **Hortense,** remove it if found, and then proceed to * and remove all files. Here is another example. You wish to *cat* the file **Fourtney.Bell.** If you have no other files starting with **F,** you can type

```
cat F*
```

If you have other files starting with **F,** perhaps

```
cat Fo*
```

or

```
cat F*l
```

will work, depending on the names of the other files.

The wild cards are great time-savers. The more you work and play with UNIX, the more often and the more naturally you will use their help.

Directory Abbreviations: "." and ".."

UNIX also offers you some useful abbreviations for directory names. We now will unveil them.

If Nerkie wants to copy two files called **tillie** and **max** from Bob's subdirectory **gossip** into his own subdirectory **lowdown,** he could type, as we have seen,

```
cp usr/bob/gossip/tillie /usr/bob/gossip/max /usr/nerkie/lowdown
```

UNIX offers some shortcuts to those of you who desire less typing. They are abbreviations for particular directories. Here they are:

Your current working directory: .   (a simple period)

The directory from which yours branches: ..   (two periods)

Here are some abbreviations and what they stand for, assuming Nerkie uses them while in the **user/nerkie** directory.

```
.            /usr/nerkie
..           /usr
./lowdown    /usr/nerkie/lowdown
```

If Nerkie uses **cd** to switch to the **/usr/nerkie/lowdown** directory, the meanings of the first two become:

```
.   /usr/nerkie/lowdown
..  /usr/nerkie
```

The directory abbreviations often come in handy when you decide to make wholesale revisions in your directory system. They give you a convenient way to shift large blocks of file about.

Suppose, for example, that Nerkie is working in his **/usr/nerkie/programs/fortnerkie** directory and that he wishes to copy several files, all of whose names end in **.f**, from **/usr/nerkie/programs** to his current directory. If he didn't know about these directory abbreviations, he could use

```
cp /usr/nerkie/programs/*.f /usr/nerkie/programs/fortnerkie.
```

But now that he knows better, he can just type

```
?cp ../*.f .
```

i.e. copy everything from the directory above that ends in **.f** into the current directory. Not only is this quicker to type, but it also offers many few opportunities to make typing errors. Ah, how lucky Nerkie is to have a UNIX system at his service!

Review Questions

The hierarchical structure of the file system is one of the major features of the UNIX operating system. Here are some review questions to give you confidence in using the system.

A. Matching Commands

Match the functions shown on the left to the commands shown on the right. The answers are given at the end of the chapter.

1. **cd ..**
2. **pwd**
3. **mv dearsue dearann**
4. **mail sue**
5. **cat part.? > final**
6. **ls**

a. Makes a new subdirectory named D2.
b. Lists contents of working directory.
c. Changes the name of **dearsue** to **dearann**.
d. Initiates sending mail to sue.
e. Prints all lines containing the word "sue" in the file **dearann**.

7. **mkdir D2**

8. **grep sue dearann**

9. **rm fig***

10. **cp /usr/hoppy/stats .**

f. Copies the file **stats** in hoppy's home directory into a file called **stats** in the current working directory.

g. Gives your current working directory.

h. Concatenates all files whose names consist of **part.** followed by one character, and places the result in the file **final.**

i. Moves your working directory up one level.

j. Removes all files whose names start in **fig.**

B. Creating Commands

Use the hypothetical file structure shown in the following figure to create the commands that will accomplish the following actions (in some cases, there is more than one way).

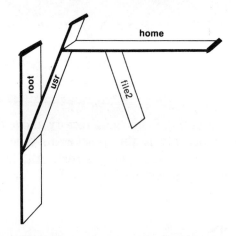

Your hypothetical working directory.

Assume that you are in the directory called *home.*

1. List all files and directories in your account.

2. Read the file name **file2.**

3. Make a copy of **file2** and call it **file5.**

4. Make a subdirectory called **D2.**

5. Put yourself in subdirectory **D2.**

6. Move **file2** into **D2.**

7. While in directory **D2,** list all files in directory **home.**

8. Create a subdirectory **D3** at the same level as **D2;** i.e., not a subdirectory of **D2.** (Hint: This is a 2-step sequence.)

9. Place today's date in a file in **D3,** calling it **f8.**

10. Remove subdirectory **D3.**

Answers:

A. 1—i, 2—g, 3—c, 4—d, 5—h, 6—b, 7—a, 8—e, 9—j, 10—f

B. **1.** ls **2.** cat file2 **3.** cp file2 file5 **4.** mkdir D2 **5.** cd D2 **6.** mv ../file2 . or cd home and mv file2 /D2/file2 **7.** ls ../ **8.** cd to go to your home directory, then mkdir D3 **9.** date > D3/f8 or cd D3 and date > f8 **10.** First, cd D3, second pwd to make sure you're there, then rm * (a powerful command!), then cd to get back home and, finally, rmdir D3.

Exercises at the Terminal

Even if you have been following the chapter while sitting at a terminal, you might like to try these exercises to illustrate the major commands and to practice their use.

1. Find your full pathname.

2. List the contents of your home directory.

3. Some UNIX systems have games on them. Can you find the directory that they are stored in and list them?

4. Create a new subdirectory called **D7.** Put yourself in **D7** and try to copy any two files into the directory. You should use full pathnames for the experience.

5. Can you place a backup copy of your **D7** files into a new subdirectory called **D8** using metacharacters?

6. Try creating a new file name using **ln.**

7. Use **grep** on your mailbox file **mbox** to find the occurrence of a word such as ''dear'' or ''hello.''

8. Clean up your file system by removing the files from **D8** and, then, removing **D8** itself.

8

Using Programming Languages: FORTRAN, Pascal, and C

In this chapter, you will find:

8   USING PROGRAMMING LANGUAGES: FORTRAN, Pascal, and C

New UNIX user Wendell Turnbull Krumpnose rushed to the computer room clutching the magnetic tape that he had just received in the mail (ordinary mail, this time, not electronic mail). The tape contained a FORTRAN program that made home solar energy calculations.

"Here, guys, please load this on the system for me."

Since Wendell was such a nice guy, the technicians gladly dropped what they were doing, loaded the tape on a tape drive, and read the contents of the tape into a file called **solcalc** in Wendell's directory. Wendell sat down at his terminal, eager to use the new program.

But how? Wendell thought for a moment (that being the usual unit of time he devoted to thought). "Commands like **cat** and **ls** really are programs, and I run them just by typing their names. So maybe all I have to do is type **solcalc**." He did so, and UNIX replied with

```
solcalc: Permission denied.
```

Hmm. Maybe he should try typing the FORTRAN commands himself. He picked a line at random (**real rval**) from the program listing and typed it to see what would happen. UNIX responded with

```
real: not found.
```

Hmm. Perhaps a different approach was needed. "Help!" he cried, and the technicians hurried in with concerned looks upon their faces. "What can we do to assist you?" they choroused.

Wendell explained his problem, and they quickly set him straight. The computer has its own private language, and it isn't FORTRAN. UNIX systems, however, have a special program called **f77** that translates FORTRAN into the simple instructions that the host computer can understand; this process is called "compiling." Soon, under the benevolent tutelage of the staff, Wendell was able to master the needed skills. He changed the name of his file to **solcalc.f** so that **f77** would recognize that it was a FORTRAN file. Next, he typed

```
f77 solcalc.f
```

and waited while **f77** labored mightily for him. Finally, **f77** produced a ready-to-go program and placed it in a file called **a.out** (a favorite UNIX name for such files). Now to use it! All Wendell had to do now was type the word **a.out,** and the program ran. His original idea had not been that bad, he had just applied it to the wrong file.

Eventually, Wendell thought of modifications he wanted to make in the program. The program had many subsections called subroutines, and it seemed a shame to have to recompile the whole program when his changes were made to just one subroutine; compilation uses a lot of computer time. Again, his friends helped him out and showed him how to use the UNIX editors to place each subroutine in a file of its own. Now, when he submitted the collection of files to **f77**, the compiler not only gave him a ready-to-run program (**a.out**), it also gave him a compiled version of each subroutine. From now on, if Wendell needed to change a subroutine, he needed just to recompile that one subroutine and let **f77** combine it with his compiled versions of the rest of the program. With support like this, Wendell could not avoid fame and riches.

* * * *

Running a Program

How do you run a program on a computer? This is a pretty important question for many people. Perhaps you know a computer language or two yourself; perhaps you have purchased, borrowed, or otherwise acquired a program from elsewhere; perhaps you are just learning to program. Once you get a program, it is a simple matter to run it using UNIX. In this chapter, we will outline some of the basic concepts that concern programs, discuss some of the languages with which you can work, and explain how to run programs in C, FORTRAN, and Pascal. We won't tell you how to write programs, but this chapter will get you started in the process of using programs.

Languages, Compilers, and Interpreters

Once upon a time, not so long ago and not so far away, you needed to have mastered much terminal lore and have great skill to run a computer. Now, it is getting easier and easier every day to use them. People haven't gotten any smarter, and neither have the computers. (But computers have gotten faster, cheaper, more compact, more powerful, and are capable of storing more information, so they are not doing too badly!) What has changed is that clever people have written clever programs to make it easier for the nonspecialist to deal with computers. In particular, the development of programming languages, of compilers and interpreters, and of operating systems makes programming much simpler. What do all these terms mean? To clarify these points, we will survey how a computer is used.

Computers are machines that follow instructions. If you devise a set of instructions to accomplish some particular task, that is a program. Thus, the trick to use to get a computer to work for you is to give it the right instructions. This is not that easy to do, for the computer, itself, understands only a limited set of rather basic instructions called the "instruction set." Furthermore, it knows these instructions not by name but by a code (binary code) that uses only ones and zeros. The most basic way to program a computer, then, is to feed a string of these binary-coded instructions to the computer. This is called working in "machine language." Programming in machine language is tedious and exacting; it certainly is not going to capture the imagination of the general public. Also, each type of computer would, in general, have its own machine language, so every time a new machine was acquired, the users would have to learn the new language and rework their old programs. Thus, users were driven by their own laziness to develop a universal language that could be used on many different machines.

Now, that is an interesting problem. How do you create programs to run on any machine when each machine has its own primitive machine language? One way is to do it in two steps. The first step is to create a more universal language that humans can understand easily, and, perhaps, even love. Such a language, of course, is incomprehensible to a computer. The second step is to write a translation program that translates the new language into the machine's own language. This translation program is called a "compiler." Each kind of computer, then, would have its compiler written in its own machine language; the compiler, then, lets the computer understand the universal language.

What universal language resulted from this plan of attack? By now, hundreds of languages have been created along these lines, but none is regarded as universal (except, perhaps, by its creator). Several, however, do have a widespread popularity, including such stalwarts as FORTRAN, COBOL, BASIC, Pascal, APL, PL/M, LISP, Logo, and C. UNIX systems usually are supplied with most of these languages and can have the others installed.

This means that UNIX-compatible compilers or interpreters exist for these languages. (An "interpreter" is a particular kind of compiler used for interactive languages such as Logo and BASIC. See the following box.)

Compiled Languages and Interpreted Languages

Compiled languages and interpreted languages represent two approaches to using languages on a computer. The compiling approach was developed in the days when the usual way of using a computer was to feed it punched cards, punched tape, or magnetic tape. This meant that the user had to prepare the entire program in advance and then submit the whole thing to the computer. A compiler would then take this entire block of programming and work it into a language acceptable to the computer. Thus, the end result of the compiler's toil was a complete program arranged in machine language. You could save this program and, next time, use it instead of the original. Hence, once your program was successfully compiled, you didn't have to compile it again unless you needed to change it. Since compilation is a slow process, you will save much time when you avoid compiling programs.

The development and rapid spread of the video keyboard terminal opened up a much more exciting way of communicating with a computer—direct interaction. Now we have an electronic "Simon says" machine. You tell the computer to do this, and it does; you tell it to do that, and it does. But, compiled languages don't fit into this scheme very easily; nothing gets done until after you type in the entire program and, then, have it compiled and run. Interactive languages, such as BASIC and Logo, get around this by translating each line *as you type it in*. For example, suppose you type the following three lines in BASIC:

```
LET X = 6
LET Y = 2 + X
PRINT Y
```

Immediately after you enter the first line, the computer creates a storage area, names it "X," and stores the value 6 in it. Immediately after you enter the second line, the computer creates a storage area, names it "Y," adds 2 to 6, and stores the value of 8 in Y. Immediately after you enter the third line, the computer prints the value 8 on your terminal screen, letting you see how clever it is. The program that does the work of translating your instructions into machine actions is called an "interpreter."

Suppose, though, you want to collect a few instructions together into a program before having them acted upon. BASIC and Logo allow you to do this. However, when you do finally run the program, it is still interpreted line by line rather than as a block. That is, the interpreter looks at one line of instructions, converts it to the proper code, executes the translated instruction, and only then looks at the next line.

The chief difference, then, between a compiler and an interpreter is that the compiler translates entire program chunks at a time while an interpreter translates single lines at a time. Each method has its advantages and disadvantages. The main advantage of the interactive approach is the direct and rapid feedback you get. Do it right, and you see your success immediately. Do it wrong, and you find out right away. Also, you get to correct it right away. The main disadvantage is that interactive systems are relatively slow. For example, if a program cycles through the same instruction several times, that instruction has to go through the translation process each time. Compilers more or less reverse the situation. You don't get any feedback until you complete the program and try to compile and run it. On the other hand, once the program works properly, you have an efficient machine-language version. Compilers are fairly intelligent programs and, by looking at program segments larger than a line, they can put together a more efficient translation than an interpreter does.

We've indicated the role of languages and of compilers and of interpreters. What about operating systems? Operating systems, such as UNIX, handle such tasks as feeding a program to a compiler, loading the resulting machine-language program into the computer, and running the program. Thus, modern computers are set up so that you can have them attend to all the grungy details while you act as the master planner.

Let's take a brief look at some of the more common languages.

FORTRAN

FORTRAN is an acronym for "FORmula TRANslation." This language was developed in the 1950s to deal with scientific and engineering programming. As the name suggests, FORTRAN is particularly suited to working with equations and formulas. Since then, of course, computers have been used for a wider and wider range of problems, and FORTRAN has been modified to meet these new needs. The latest version, FORTRAN 77 (so named because its standards were defined in 1977), is a general-purpose language, capable of dealing with numeric and nonnumeric problems. Many people in computer science feel that FORTRAN is dated and is not state-of-the-art, but there is a tremendous body of programs and software available in FORTRAN. FORTRAN still is used widely in engineering, science, and education. Thus, the language will continue to be an important one for a long time.

COBOL

COBOL (for COmmon Business-Oriented Language) was developed a little after FORTRAN and was intended to meet the needs of business programming. At that time, computers were huge and expensive so it was mainly only the giant companies that had them. Thus, much of the business programming for the major corporations has been done using COBOL. Small businesses, on the other hand, acquired computers when computers became smaller and cheaper. Business programming, on this smaller scale, more typically has been done in BASIC, for this language is better suited for small computers.

BASIC

BASIC (for Beginners All-purpose Symbolic Instruction Code) was developed in the 1960s at Dartmouth College to help students with no computer background to learn to use a computer. It is an easy language to learn and to use, and its simplicity and small memory requirements have made it a natural choice for microcomputers. It's probably the most widely used language in the world. It is used for business applications, educational purposes, research, and computer games. It is an interactive language with all the advantages and disadvantages that that implies. The original version had severe limitations in such things as highly restricted variable names, so now several enhanced versions are available. These versions are more powerful, but the existence of more than one version can cause problems when you try to shift a program from one machine to another.

Pascal

Pascal (named after the 18th Century mathematician Blaise Pascal) was developed in the 1970s by Niklaus Wirth, a Swiss mathematician. By that time, people had been programming long enough to evolve a feeling for good programming principles. Wirth developed Pascal to embody these ideas. His main intent was to provide a language that would help, even compel, computer science students to develop a good programming style. However, the use of Pascal has grown beyond education and, today, Pascal is a very popular general-purpose language. Its use is being promoted in industry, where experience has shown it to produce programs that are more reliable and understandable than the older FORTRAN, BASIC, and COBOL programs.

C

C was developed by D. M. Ritchie at the Bell labs in the 1970s. In many ways, it is based on the same ideas as Pascal, but it was developed with an eye to systems programming, that is, the writing of programs to be used in running a computer system. For example, most of UNIX is written in the C language, including the FORTRAN and Pascal compilers. Although that is the orientation of the language, it can be used as a general language. On UNIX systems, programs written in C generally use less computer space than similar programs written in other languages.

Logo

Logo was developed in 1966 with the design goals of being simple to use, yet extremely powerful. It grew from work in Artificial Intelligence and is used in educational research. It is an interactive language that integrates in a uniform manner the facilities for graphics, calculation, and list processing. It is not yet widely available on UNIX, but its use is expected to grow rapidly in the next few years.

Compiling and Using Programs

Writing a program involves several major steps. The first is deciding what you want the program to accomplish. The second is working out a logical approach to accomplish the goal. The third step, called ''coding,'' is used to express that approach in a programming language. We aren't going to tell you how to do any of these things (we'd like to, but that would take another book or two), but we will show you what to do once you get that far.

Each language has its own compiler. They are all used in much the same fashion, so we will go through two examples in C and then outline the use of the FORTRAN compiler.

Compiling a C Program

To get the feel of UNIX compilers, you may want to run through this example at a terminal. We begin with a very simple example of a program in C. It's simple enough that you don't really have to know C to work through this example.

```
# include <stdio.h>


main()
{



char name [72];



printf("Hi! What's your first name?\n");
scanf(" %s", name);
printf("Hello, %s!\n", name);
printf("You have a very nice, intelligent-sounding name.\n");


}
```

To use this program, your first step is to use an editor to create a file. If you've been good and have read the preceding chapters, you know how to do that. The name of the file should end in **.c**; this will identify the file as a C program to the C compiler. For example, you could call the file **lets.c.** If you copy this program into a file, be sure to type it exactly as it appears here. Don't substitute ('s for {'s or ['s and don't omit the semicolons. The indentations and blank lines are used to clarify the organization of the program to a human reader; they are ignored by the compiler. The "# include" statement tells the compiler where to find some standard input/output information.

Suppose, now, that you have this program in the file **lets.c.** Your next step is to feed the program to the C compiler. The UNIX C compiler is called **cc** (clever name, eh?), and the feeding consists of typing **cc** and following it with the name of the file you wish to compile. In this case, you would type


```
cc lets.c
```

There will be a brief wait while **cc** does its work. If you made a detectable error in typing the program, **cc** will tell you so. It even will tell you exactly what it thinks is wrong; whether you can make sense out of the message depends on what you know about C. Of course, you may never make errors and, so, will need not worry about error messages.

Once **cc** is finished, the standard UNIX prompt will return. If you list your files, you will find a new one called **a.out.** This is the name **cc** gives to the file in which it places the machine-language version of your program. The program is ready to work; just type

```
a.out
```

to run it. If you want to save the program, it is a good idea to rename **a.out** so that you don't clobber your old program the next time you compile another program!

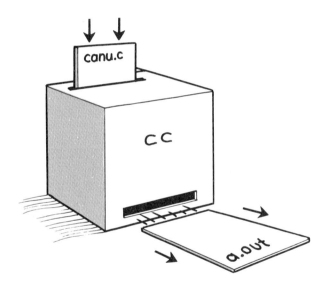

Feeding a program to *cc*.

Now let's extend the example a little. First, use an editor to add a new line to **lets.c** so that it now looks like this:

```
# include <stdio.h>


main()
{
```

```
    char name [72];

printf("Hi! What's your first name?\n");
scanf(" %s", name);
printf("Hello, %s!\n", name);
printf("You have a very nice, intelligent-sounding name.\n");
addsome();



}
```

We've added the line with **addsome()** in it. Now, create a new file called **addsome.c** and enter the following text in it:

```
addsome()
{
   printf("I am happy to have felt your fingers on me.\n");
}
```

Now we have two files. One **(lets.c)** contains the main program, and one **(addsome.c)** contains a subordinate program (called a "function" in C) that is used by the main program. To get this combination to work, we compile both files simultaneously:

```
cc lets.c addsome.c
```

Once this is done, you can **ls** your files and see that you have three new files: **lets.o, addsome.o,** and **a.out.** When you type **a.out,** your new program will run. What about **lets.o** and **addsome.o**? They contain the object code (see next box) for **lets.c** and **addsome.c,** respectively. They, too, can be fed to the **cc** compiler. Because they already are in machine code, they will be processed faster than the original files. Thus, if you lose your **a.out** file, you can reconstruct it with any one of the following instructions:

```
cc lets.c addsome.c
cc lets.c addsome.o
cc lets.o addsome.c
cc lets.o addsome.o
```

The last choice would be the fastest, since both programs already are in object code. Note, too, that you could use the **addsome.o** file with any other program that you devised that would call the **addsome()** function.

Normally, **cc** produces object files only when two or more files are compiled, but you can request an object file even if you compile only one file. The on-line manual will give you a complete outline of your options.

Summary: cc—C compiler

name	options	arguments
cc	[−c, −o]	file(s)

Description: **cc** compiles programs in the C language. If the input file is in C, its name should end in **.c;** if it is an object code file, its name should end in **.o.** The submitted files are compiled (if necessary) to create an executable program file called **a.out.** An object code file is created for each C file and is stored in a file whose name is the same as the original, except that **.c** is replaced by **.o.** (This step is skipped if only one program is submitted.)

Options: −c
    Suppresses the loading phase (creating **a.out**) and forces an object file to be produced.
−o **filename**
    Causes the executable program to be given the name **filename** instead of **a.out.**

Example: **cc −o poker straight.c flush.o**
    This command takes a C program from the file **straight.c** and the object code of a previously compiled C program from the file **flush.o.** The C program from **straight.c** is compiled and the object code is placed in a file called **straight.o.** The two object codes are combined along with required C routines to form an executable program called **poker.** Typing **poker** will run the program.

Object Files and *a.out*

When you submit a program to one of the UNIX compilers, it generally produces two types of output files: object files (identified by ending in **.o**) and a loaded and executable file (called **a.out** by default). Both contain machine-language versions of your programs, so you may wonder what the difference is. (If you don't wonder, you have our permission to skip this box.)

An object file contains the machine-language code for your program. It is, however, an incomplete file. First, your program will probably use one or more system functions. By that, we mean programs provided by the system. Examples would be print or write statements, trig functions, and the like. Your object file will not contain the code for these functions; it just has the code for the part of the program that you wrote. Secondly, you may have spread your program over two or more files. The object files wouldn't contain the instructions needed to tie the files together. Thirdly, an object file is not set up to run; it is just a passive storehouse of information.

The **a.out** file, on the other hand, *is* ready to run. It includes the code for system functions, it combines your files together if you have more than one, and it is set up to execute when you type its name. It contains the same sort of code as the **.o** files; it is just more complete.

Well, you may wonder, why bother with object code files if **a.out** is all you need to run a program? The answer is that object files become very handy if you modularize your programs. In FORTRAN, you should give each subroutine its own file. In C, you should give individual functions their own files. In this manner, you can build up your personal library of little task-solvers and construct programs from various combinations of files. Even if you don't have such ambitions, this approach of separating programs into several files allows you to update individual files without having to recompile the entire program. Object files compile much more quickly than does the original code.

Can you mix together object code files from different compilers? You can to some extent, but not in a casual manner. It takes a special blend of information to do so; a blend that is beyond the scope of this modest book. The pamphlet, *A Portable FORTRAN 77 Compiler,* by S. I. Feldman and P. J. Weinberger (a Bell Labs publication) provides information on how to make C and FORTRAN programs compatible.

The FORTRAN Compiler: *f77*

The UNIX FORTRAN compiler is called **f77** to remind us that it can handle the latest version of FORTRAN (FORTRAN 77). A great mass of FORTRAN programming is in the preceding version (called FORTRAN IV or FORTRAN 66), and **f77** accepts programs in that version, too. In fact, it accepts all sorts of files; the on-line manual will document the limits of its appetite. We'll assume here that you are interested in running a standard FORTRAN program (either 77 or 66). (The **f77** compiler replaces the **fc** compiler, which just did FORTRAN 66.)

The first step, once you have a FORTRAN program, is to place it in a file whose name ends on **.f.** This identifies the file as a FORTRAN file to the **f77** compiler. (Incidentally, the column spacing in the files should be set up the same way that they are on punched cards; i.e., columns 2–5 for line numbers, column 6 for the continuation mark, and columns 7–72 for statements.) Then, submit the file to the compiler by typing **f77** and the filename. For example, if your program is in a file called **sun.f,** you would type

```
f77 sun.f
```

If your program is acceptable, **f77** then produces two files. The first is called **a.out** and the second, **sun.o.** The **sun.o** file contains the object code for your program, and **a.out** has the executable version. (See the preceding box if you have forgotten the difference.) To run your program, just type

```
a.out
```

If your program is spread over more than one file (in subroutine files, for example), just enter all the file names after the **f77** command. These files can be FORTRAN files, object code files, or a mixture of the two. For example, suppose you had already compiled the three files **sun.f, moon.f,** and **earth.f,** and had saved the corresponding object code files. If you then changed **moon.f** and needed all three files for a complete program, you could type

```
f77 sun.o moon.f earth.o
```

to get a new **a.out** file. As we've mentioned earlier, it's a good idea to change the name of the **a.out** file if you plan to use the program again.

Summary: f77—compiles FORTRAN programs

name	options	arguments
f77	[−o, −c]	file(s)

Description: **f77** compiles programs written in FORTRAN. If the program is written in FORTRAN, it should be placed in a file whose name ends in **.f.** If the program is in object code form, it should be in a file whose name ends in **.o.** The compiler takes **.f** files, compiles them, and stores the object code in files of the same name, but with the **.f** replaced by a **.o.** The object code, along with required support routines, are loaded into an executable file called **a.out.**

Option: **−o filename**
This option causes the executable program to be called **filename** instead of **a.out.**
−c
This suppresses loading but still produces object files for each source.

Example: **f77 −o porker slop.f**
This command takes the FORTRAN program in the file **slop.f,** compiles it, and places the object code for it in a file named **slop.o.** It then takes the object code, combines it with the required FORTRAN support programs, and loads them into an executable file named **porker.** The program can be run by typing **porker.**

A PASCAL COMPILER

The **cc** and **f77** are standard components of the UNIX system, but there is no standard Pascal compiler. However, there are Pascal compilers available. We will look at a representative one that is available on Motorola 68000-based System V.

As UNIX becomes more widespread, successful software running under other operating systems is being adapted to run under the UNIX operating system. This Pascal compiler is one example of this trend. Because of its history, the compiler is used somewhat differently from the other compilers we have discussed, particularly in the use of options. Let's begin, however, with a bare-bones compilation.

Here are the steps to go through:

1. Write a Pascal program and store it in a file whose name ends in **.p.** Let's assume the program resides in the file **rascal.p.** This is called the source file.

2. Feed the source file to **pascal,** phase 1 of the compiler:
   ```
   pascal rascal.p
   ```
   This produces an intermediate code, called "pcode," and places it in a file for which the **.p** in the **name** is replaced by **.pc.** Thus, **rascal.pc** is the name of the new file in this case.

3. Feed the pcode file to **pascal2,** phase 2 of the compiler:
   ```
   pascal2 rascal.pc
   ```
   This produces object code and places it in a file for which the **.pc** is replaced by **.ro.** Thus, **rascal.ro** is the new file in this case.

4. Feed the object code to **link,** a program that brings in code from the Pascal library to complete your program:
   ```
   link rascal.ro
   ```
   This produces an executable file called **a.out.** To run the program, just type **a.out.** Again, we suggest that if you wish to keep the program, that you **mv a.out** to a new name.

That's the basic approach. A bit of explanation is in order. First, why a two-part compiler producing an intermediate pcode? The idea here is a common one. The first phase condenses your program to a "universal" code that is closer to machine language instructions than the original Pascal code. By universal, we mean that the *same* pcode would be produced by any brand of computer. The second phase then converts this universal pcode to the particular machine language of the system you are using. This approach has several advantages. One is that if the compiler is transferred to a new machine, only phase 2 needs to be rewritten. Another advantage is that if you move your Pascal programs to a new machine, you just need to go through phase 2 of the compilation, providing you have the pcode files.

A second matter is the use of **link.** The Pascal object code files (the **.ro** files) have a different format from the usual UNIX **.o** files. Thus a new-to-UNIX program **(link)** has been brought in for the purpose of producing the standard **a.out** files we have come to expect from UNIX. (Incidentally, **cc** and **f77** actually call upon the **ld** program to perform a similar service on the **.o** programs that they produce.)

We mentioned that options are handled differently. The **pascal** system uses a plus sign to turn an option on and a minus sign to turn it off. Thus, in the command

```
pascal -c +w rascal.p
```

The **c** option (generate pcode file) is turned off and the **w** option (generate warnings of nonstandard Pascal usage) is turned on. The **pascal** program has 13 such options. Fortunately, you don't have to set them all, for each has a default value. Thus, if you don't mention the **c** option, it is assumed to be on.

The compiler also features an optional optimizer program. Once you find that a program works to your satisfaction, you may wish to optimize the code for efficiency. To do this, start with the pcode file, and feed it to **poptim:**

```
poptim rascal.pc
```

This produces optimized pcode, which is forwarded to a file in whose name the **.pc** is replaced by **.po.** Then feed this file to phase 3:

```
pascal2 rascal.po
```

Then pass the resulting **.ro** file on to **link.**

Once you learn about shell scripts (Chapters 9 and 12), you should be able to construct a shell script that lets you run through the **pascal, pascal2,** and **link** steps with one command.

Summary: `pascal`—compiles Pascal programs		
name	**options**	**argument**
`pascal` (phase 1)	several	file.p
`pascal2` (phase 2)	some	file.pc or file.po
`poptim` (optimizer)	some	file.pc

Description: **pascal** is a two-phase compiler for Pascal. It has an optional optimizer. **link** links the compiler code to library code to produce an executable program.

Phase 1, **pascal,** takes as input a Pascal program in a file whose name ends in **.p.** It produces pcode, which is placed in a file with the **.p** replaced by a **.pc.**

The optional optimizer, **poptim,** takes a **.pc** file as input and produces optimized pcode, placing it in a file in which the **.pc** is replaced by **.po.**

Phase 2, **pascal2,** takes a pcode file (**.pc** or **.po**) as input and produces relocatable object code stored in a file in which the suffix is **.ro**

link takes a **.ro** file as input and produces an executable program, which is placed in the file **a.out.**

Options: Options are turned on with a plus sign and turned off with a minus sign. Default values are assumed if an option is not mentioned:

Example:
```
pascal zorro.p
pascal2 zorro.pc
link zorro.ro
a.out
```

Compilers: Summing Up

As you probably noticed, the compilers **cc** and **f77** are all used much the same way. Each accepts language files (whose names should end in **.c** and **.f,** respectively) and object code files (whose names should end in **.o**). Each will accept several files simultaneously and will combine them into a complete program. Each can generate object code files from the language source files. Each loads the assembled program into a file called **a.out** which can then be run by typing its name. About the only point of caution that we might raise is that you cannot routinely feed object code files produced by one compiler to a compiler for a different language. (This task is not impossible, but it is definitely beyond the scope of this book.)

The compilers are easy to use and will produce efficient programs, so if you know one of these languages, get in there and write a great program!

Compiler	Accepts* files names end with	Produces[†] .o files	Executable program[†] placed in file
cc	.c, .o	If more than one file is submitted.	a.out
f77	.f, .o	Yes	a.out

* partial list
† assuming no options specified

Compilers and files.

Running a Program in Background

Has this happened to you? You start a program running at a terminal. Then you think of something else you want to do on the computer, but the program seems to take forever (i.e., more than 60 seconds) and you have to sit twiddling your thumbs until the program is done. If you enjoy that sort of situation, read no further. But if you think you deserve better, UNIX agrees. That's why UNIX offers the background job option, which lets the system work on a problem out of view, freeing the terminal for other tasks or games.

The way to run a program in background in simple. Suppose, for example, you have a program called **a.out** that reads information from one file, does a bunch of amazing things, and then prints brilliant results into a second file. To run this program in background, type:

```
a.out &
```

The **&** symbol following the command is the instruction that tells UNIX to run the program in background. Once you enter this command, you'll get a number back:

```
6784
$
```

The 6784 is a job identification number assigned by the system to this particular job. The actual number assigned will depend on what the computer is doing just then. (Every job running on the system, background or not, is assigned its individual job identification number.) Do these numbers have any uses? Yes, and we will tell you one of them before this chapter is done.

The second line, the usual UNIX prompt, tells you that UNIX is ready for your next command. Now you can continue your work while your program works away unseen by you. Neat!

There are some things you should know before doing background jobs. First, if the system is heavily loaded with tasks, background jobs will just bog it down further. Secondly, you can't give a background job any input from the terminal. If your job needs terminal input, it will just get stuck and stop when it reaches that point. Thirdly, if your program normally sends output to the screen, it still will when in background. This means that you could find yourself inundated by a string of numbers while you are editing one of your sensitive poems. There are remedies for these situations. If the system is heavily loaded, don't run background jobs. If your job normally takes input from the terminal, you can use redirection (see the next chapter) to get the program to take its input from a file. Just remember to put the right data in the file. Finally, you can use redirection to channel the output to a file instead of to the screen.

Sometimes, it can happen that your job gets stuck or is taking too long and you want to terminate it. Here's where we get to use the identification numbers. For example, to end the job we mentioned previously, you can type:

```
kill 6784
```

and the job is "killed." Don't worry, the job doesn't feel a thing.

Additional Programming Features

UNIX has much more language support than we have described so far. Here, we would like to point out some additional options just so that you will know what's there.

Many UNIX systems carry one or more interactive languages such as BASIC or Logo. Several versions are available. One usually initiates an interactive language by typing in a key word, such as:

```
basic
bas
```

or

Logo

The key word calls up the interpreter and changes the user prompt (perhaps to > or *) to remind you that you are working in that language now. Once this happens, you can then communicate with the computer in that language. When you are finished, typing another keyword (perhaps **goodbye** or **bye**) takes you back to the usual UNIX mode and returns the usual UNIX prompt.

Many UNIX systems carry a Pascal load-and-run interpreter (called **pix**) in addition to a Pascal compiler. This interpreter does not make Pascal an interactive language; you still have to submit a complete Pascal program in a file to it. The interpreter translates the program into an intermediate code line by line but without taking the overview of the program that the compiler does. The result is that the interpreter is quicker to produce a program, but the compiler gives a program that runs faster. This makes the interpreter good for developing programs and the compiler good for putting together the finished product.

Other programming aids include **lint** (which checks out C programs), **cb** (which beautifies C programs with proper indentations and the like), **sdb** (a symbolic debugger for C and FORTRAN), and **make** (which helps you maintain large programs). If you revise a subroutine, **make** puts together the whole program with minimum recompilation.

Two other languages commonly found on UNIX systems are APL and LISP. The former is handled by the interpreter **apl** while the latter is handled by the compiler **liszt** and the interpreter **lisp.**

There is one other language that you may wish to program in. UNIX, itself. Not only does UNIX have a large number of commands, but it also has some control statements that allow you to use UNIX programs to perform loops and make logical decisions. You can construct a program from a series of such commands, store them in a file, and, then, use the **chmod** command to make that file into a program that you can run just by typing the filename. We will discuss such "shell scripts" in Chapters 9 and 12.

A Final Word

Actually, there is no final word. UNIX is an open-ended system, and you can go as far as your knowledge and imagination can take you. If you obtain a compiler or interpreter (written in C) for some other language, you

can install it in your directory and use it. If you want to create your own computer language, go ahead. Not only can you install it in your own directory, but UNIX supplies **yacc** (Yet Another Compiler Compiler) to help you put together a compiler for it!

Review Questions

A. Matching functions.

(This will be a tough one.) Match the compiler with the language it compiles:

1. cc	**a.** Pascal
2. f77	**b.** French
3. pascal	**c.** FORTRAN
	d. C

B. Questions

1. Which of the following is a proper name to give a file containing a C program?
   a. blaise.c

   b. `blaise.p`
   c. `blaise.o`
   d. `blaise`

2. What two files are produced by the following command: **f77 henry.f**?

3. You have the object code of a C program stored in a file named **red.o.** Will typing the filename cause this program to run?

Answers:

A. **1**—d, **2**—c

B. **1.** a; **2. a.out** and **henry.o; 3.** No; you type the name of the executable file (**a.out** by default), not the object code file, to run a program.

Exercises at the Terminal

If you know how to use **FORTRAN**, or **C**, write a simple program in one of those languages. Then, try the following:

1. Make a programming error deliberately and see what the compiler says about it.

2. Correct the error and compile the program.

3. Run the program.

4. Obtain the object code file for the program.

5. Feed the object code to the compiler and see how that works.

The UNIX Shell: Command Lines, Redirection, and Shell Scripts

In this chapter, you will find:

9 The Unix Shell: Command Lines, Redirection, and Shell Scripts

Introduction

Much of UNIX's awesome strength comes from its shell, the program that handles your interactions with the computer system. The UNIX shell plays two roles. First, it acts as a "command interpreter." Second, it is a programming language. Sounds good, but what do these terms mean? By calling it a command interpreter, we mean (what else?) that it interprets your commands. If, for example, you type the **date** command, the shell tracks down where the **date** program is kept and then runs it. By calling it a programming language, we mean that you can string together a series of basic commands to perform some larger task. The pipelines and the shell scripts we will discuss in this chapter are examples of that ability.

Clearly, if you want to know UNIX, you should get to know the shell. We hope to help you do that in this chapter. First we will discuss the usual form for commands to the shell. Then we will discuss redirection again and introduce pipes. Then we will talk about job control. Even the more casual UNIX user will want to pick up on these topics. If you wish to get deeper into the shell, read on and be introduced to shell scripts, shell variables, shell metacharacters, and to your **.profile** file. Okay, let's begin by looking at the command line.

The Shell Command Line

When you sit down to a UNIX system, you have hundreds of UNIX commands at your call. Many will become indispensable to you, some you will use occasionally, and some you may never see. There are some basic commands that almost every user needs to know, and frequent use will burn them into your brain. The more you use the system, the more commands you'll know by heart, but with so many commands available, remembering the details can be a problem. Fortunately, most UNIX commands are used in a similar fashion. Unfortunately, there are many exceptions, but we can view this as a sign of the vibrant vitality of the UNIX system.

We've seen the main elements of a command in Chapter 3, but you probably would enjoy seeing them again. The elements are the command name, the options, and the arguments. (Technically, anything following the command name is an argument, but we will use the term "argument" to mean the file, the directory, or whatever it is that the command acts upon, and we will use the term "option" to indicate a modification of the command.) When put together on one line, these elements constitute the "command line." An example of a command line is:

```
ls -l /usr
```

Here the command name is **ls**, the option is **-l** (i.e., the *long* form), and the argument is the directory name **/usr.**

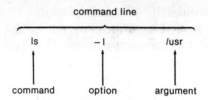

Command line structure.

Computers, being the simple-minded machines they are, require that you follow rules when typing in a command line. Here are some of them.

1. Each element should be separated from the others by at least one space. UNIX uses the spaces to tell when one element ends and another begins, so if you type:

```
ls-l /usr
```

UNIX will think you are looking for a command called **ls-l,** and if you type:

```
ls -l/usr
```

UNIX will think you are looking for an option called **-l/usr.** In either case, you will leave UNIX dumbfounded. Why can't UNIX figure out what you really meant? After all, there aren't any other command names beginning with **ls,** so UNIX should have known that **ls-l** must have been intended to be **ls -l.** Ah, but UNIX is so flexible that you *could* have *created* a new command called **ls-l,** so UNIX takes the safe route and doesn't try to second guess what you meant. Since many users forget to put a space between a command name and the option flag, we remind you once again: *put a space after the command name.* On the other hand, *don't* put spaces within an element.

RIGHT	WRONG
ls -l /usr	ls - l /usr
ls -s /bin	ls-s /bin

2. The proper order of elements is command name, options, and arguments. Often, you don't need any options and, sometimes, you don't need an argument; just omit the elements you don't need. Here are some examples of right and wrong command line orders.

RIGHT	WRONG
cat -n hobo	cat hobo -n
cat hobo	hobo cat
ls -a	-a ls

A few commands may violate this sequence.

3. Options usually are indicated with the "flag" notation, where one or more characters follow a hyphen. Typical examples are the **-n, -a,** and **-l** flags that we just saw. More than one option can be used at a time (unless they contradict each other) and the order usually is not important. Multiple option flags may be separated from each other by spaces or, if they require no further input, may be strung together on the same hyphen. (In some instances, only one of these two approaches may work, depending on the particular command.) For example, if we wished to get a long listing **(-l)** of all files **(-a)** in reverse order **(-r),** we could type any of the following left-hand examples:

RIGHT	WRONG
ls -l -a -r	ls -l-a-r
ls -lar	ls -l a r
ls -r -al	
ls -r -la	

What's meant by "requiring no further input"? We mean an option that is called up just by giving a letter or symbol alone. For example,

the **-l** and the **-a** options of **ls** need no further input. On the other
hand, the **-o** option of **cc** (see Chapter 8) needs a file name to be supplied with it.

4. Some commands take, or can take, more than one argument. These
should be separated from each other by spaces.

RIGHT   *WRONG*

```
cat cabbage king walrus    cat cabbagekingwalrus
                           cat cabbage, king, walrus
```

5. You can combine several commands on one line by separating them
by semicolons. For example, if you wanted to compile the FOR-
TRAN program in the file **lulu.f** and, then, run the resulting **a.out**
program, you could type:

```
f77 lulu.f; a.out
```

6. You can spread a command over more than one line by typing a
backslash (\ ) just before hitting the <return> key. The shell will
switch from using the **$** prompt to using a > prompt to let you know
it thinks the command is not finished. Once you type a <return>
without a backslash, it executes the command and returns to the
usual prompt. Here we **cat** the file **dolphin,** splitting the command
line:

```
$cat   \
> dolphins
Dolphins can use their sonar to observe the heart and
lungs of a human swimmer. Thus, to a dolphin, a human
looks more like a dolphin (albeit a sickly one) than
does a fish.
$
```

A command can be your own creation. For example, we saw in the last
chapter that you can run a computer program simply by typing the name of
the file in which the executable program is stored. Later in this chapter we
will see how to use shell scripts to produce your own commands. First,
though, let's take a fuller look at redirection.

Redirection

Redirection is one of those features that makes UNIX a joy to use. We've
already seen one type of redirection in Chapter 4 when we discussed the >

operator. Now we will trot out a full stable of redirection operators for your appreciation. They are >, > >, <, and |. (For good measure, we will throw in the **tee** command.) As you can see, they are fine looking operators, but what do they do? Read on, and see.

Redirecting Output to a File: >

This operator we have seen before. It allows us to redirect the output of a command or program to a file. An example is:

```
cat list1 list2 > list3
```

In this case, the output of **cat** is the joined contents of the files **list1** and **list2.** The file **list3** is created, and this file then is filled with the joined contents of **list1** and **list2.** For instance, if the contents of **file1** are:

```
milk 2 qt
bread 1 loaf
hamburger 2 lb
```

and, if **file2** contains

```
lettuce 1 hd
spaghetti 1 lb
garlic
basil
butter
```

then, the newly created **file3** will contain

```
milk 2 qt
bread 1 loaf
hamburger 2 lb
lettuce 1 hd
spaghetti 1 lb
garlic
basil
butter
```

The general form for using > is

```
COMMAND > filename
```

The command (which can include options and arguments and which can be an executable program of your own) should be one that produces some sort of output normally routed to the screen. It could be something like **ls**, but not something like **rm list1**, for this second command performs an action but doesn't produce an output to the screen.

Perhaps the most important point to remember is that the right-hand side of the command should be a file. (However, UNIX treats I/O devices as files, so the right-hand side of the command could represent a printer or another terminal. See the following box.) Using this command automatically causes a file to be created and be given the name you choose. If you already have a file by that name, it will be wiped out and replaced by the new one, so be careful.

I/O Devices and Files

UNIX's marvelous redirection operators are made possible by the fact that UNIX treats I/O devices (input and output devices) as files. This means that each device is given a filename. These files usually are kept in the directory **/dev.** This directory contains a separate file for each terminal, printer, phone hook-up, tape drive, floppy disk, etc. For example, this is being typed on a terminal named **/dev/tty06.** (How can you tell what your terminal's file name is? Type in the command **tty** and UNIX will return you the device name.) If you **ls** the contents of **/dev,** you'll get to see all of the device filenames.

How can you make use of these names? Normally, you don't have to. For instance, remember how we got the **cat** command to use the terminal for input? We typed:

```
cat
```

and UNIX interpreted the lack of a filename to mean that it would use the terminal as an input. However, we could also have used:

```
cat /dev/tty06
```

if we were using tty06. This would be using the filename directly, but omitting a filename is simpler in this case.

When we give a command like **ls**, this is really the same as

```
ls > /dev/tty06
```

---

if we are using tty06. Thus, when we use a command like

```
ls > save
```

we are just substituting one file for another as far as UNIX is concerned. This equivalence is what makes it simple to include the redirection feature.

When you use the redirection operators, you don't need to make use of device filenames. UNIX, itself, takes care of the bookkeeping, but it is the file system that makes redirection convenient.

Redirecting and Appending Output to a File: >>

Suppose you want to add information to an existing file. The >> operator was designed to do just that. To add the contents of file **newpigs** to the file **pigs,** just type:

```
cat newpigs >> pigs
```

The new material is appended to the end of the **pigs** file. Suppose there was no **pigs** file? Then the file named **pigs** would be created to receive the contents of **newpigs.**

The general format for using >> is

```
COMMAND >> filename
```

where COMMAND is a command or sequence of commands that produces an output, and **filename** is the name of a file.

Redirecting Input From a File: <

The last two operators send data to file; this operator gets data out of files. You can use it with commands or programs that normally take input from the terminal. For example, you could use one of the editors to write a letter and store it in a file called **letter.** You could then mail it to another user (let's assume a login name of "hoppy") with the following command:

```
mail hoppy < letter
```

The < operator tells **mail** to take input from the file **letter** instead of from the terminal.

The general form for using this command is:

```
COMMAND < filename
```

The command should be one that would normally take input from the keyboard.

This form of redirection is particularly useful if you are running a program originally designed for punched cards. In FORTRAN, for example, a READ statement normally causes a punched card system to look for data on punched cards. (Where else!) The same program run on a UNIX system causes the system to expect *you* to type in that data from the keyboard when the program is run. You can get around this with the < operator. Suppose, for instance, that the executable program is in a file called **analyze.** You could place the data in a file called, say, **datafile,** and run the program this way:

```
analyze < datafile
```

When the program reaches the part where it reads data, it will read the data in **datafile.** The data should be entered in **datafile** in the same format used for the punched cards.

Combined Redirects

Suppose the program **analyze** produces some output that you want to save in a file called **results.** At the same time, you want **analyze** to get its inputs from the **datafile** file. You can do that with the command sequence:

```
analyze < datafile > results
```

This command causes the program **analyze** to look for input in the file **datafile** and to place its output into the file **results.** The redirection instructions can be in either order. The next example would work also:

```
analyze > results < datafile
```

Don't use two or more inputs (or outputs) in the same command.

```
analyze < data1 < data2 <─────────────────────── WRONG
```

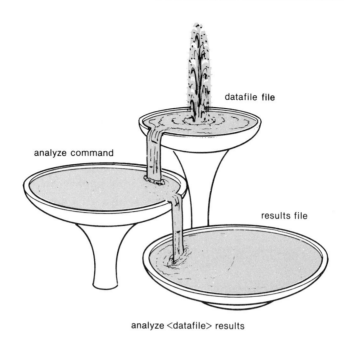

analyze <datafile> results

Combined Redirects using a hypothetical command **analyze** .

Combined redirects.

The Pipeline: |

Sam Nifty has lots of files in his directory. He wants to know how many, but he feels (rightly so) that the computer, not he, should do the counting. The **ls** command, he knows, lists the names of his files, and the **wc** command (see Chapter 10) counts words. Can he use the > and < operators to somehow link these commands together? Not really, for these operators always link a command to a file, never a command to a command. He could create a temporary file and do it this way:

```
$  ls > temp <─────────────────────────────── list files, store in temp
$  wc -w temp <────────────────────────────── count words in temp
$  rm temp <───────────────────────────────── remove temp
```

However, this is a little awkward, and there is a real need for an operator that links a command to a command.

If there is a need, UNIX tries to fill it; for this particular need, UNIX provides the "pipeline" operator, which is represented by the symbol "|".

(On some keyboards, this is a solid vertical line; on others, it is a vertical line with a small gap in the middle.) This operator **pipes** the output of one command into a second command. For example, Sam can solve his problem with this combined command:

```
ls | wc -w
```

In this case, the *output* of **ls** (i.e., a list of filenames) is accepted as the *input* of **wc -w,** which then counts the number of words. Because the list of filenames is shunted to **wc,** it does not appear on the screen; all that Sam will see is the final output of **wc.** Thus, this simple command that uses a pipe replaces three commands and counts the number of files that you have in your directory.

The general form for using the pipe is:

```
COMMAND | COMMAND
```

The output of the first command becomes the input of the second command. You can string together as many pipes as you need and you can use > and <, too. Suppose, for example, that you have written a program called **bigword** that selects words longer than 8 letters from its input and prints them out. What will the following compound command do?

```
bigword < MyLife | wc -w
```

This command causes **bigword** to search through the file **MyLife** for words longer than 8 letters; these words are then counted by **wc -w,** and the end result is the number of big words that you have in the file **MyLife.**

Here's an example with two pipes. Suppose you have a program **randomword** that chooses a hundred words at random from its input. (Perhaps you are an author who needs a few extra words to sprinkle through your work.) You want to sort these words alphabetically and process the list with a program of your own called **caps.** Here's how to do it.

```
randomword < MyLife | sort | caps
```

In this example, the output of **randomword** is sent to **sort** (Chapter 10), and the output of sort is then sent to **caps.** Only the output of **caps** is sent to the terminal, so the rest of the process is invisible to the user.

Split Output: *tee*

Suppose you are running a program and want to see the output as it is produced and want also to save the output in a file. One way is to run the program twice; once without using > and once using it. This is a bit wasteful and, thanks to **tee,** is unnecessary. Actually, **tee** is not an operator like > or | but is a command. It takes its input and routes it to two places: the terminal and the file of your choice. You can think of it as a tee-fitting to the pipeline. It is used this way:

```
ls | tee savels
```

The pipe relays the output of **ls** to **tee; tee** then sends the output to the terminal and to **savels,** the file that you choose for saving the output.

The output to the terminal can be piped further without affecting the contents of the file. For example, you can try this command:

```
ls | tee savels | sort -r
```

The file **savels** will contain a list of your files in alphabetical order (since that is what **ls** produces), but your terminal screen will show your files in reverse alphabetical order, for the other output of **tee** has been routed to **sort -r,** which sorts in reverse order.

The general form for using the **tee** command is this:

```
COMMAND | tee filename
```

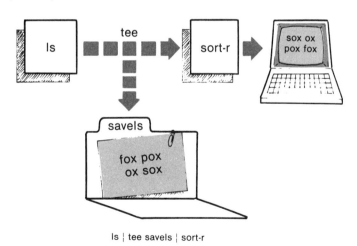

ls ¦ tee savels ¦ sort-r

Using the *tee* command.

Here the output of COMMAND is piped to **tee,** which routes copies of COMMAND's output to the terminal and to the file, **filename.** Actually, **tee** has a couple of options, which are described in the following summary.

<table>
<tr><td colspan="3" align="center">Summary: <code>tee</code>—splits output</td></tr>
<tr><td align="center">name</td><td align="center">options</td><td align="center">argument</td></tr>
<tr><td align="center"><code>tee</code></td><td align="center"><code>[−i, −a]</code></td><td align="center">filename(s)</td></tr>
</table>

Description: **tee** routes its input to the terminal and also to the named file or files.

Options: **−i**
This option ignores interrupts.
−a
This option causes the output to be added to the end of the named file.

Example: **ls −l /usr | tee −a clutter**
This command produces the long listing of the contents of the **/usr** directory. This listing is sent to the terminal screen and it also is added to the end of the file, **clutter.**

As you have seen, the redirection operators give you some very flexible means for routing data through the system. They are an important component of the design of UNIX, so make yourself familiar with them.

UNIX redirection offers one form of controlling how your tasks are performed. The UNIX job control system offers another way with different possibilities. We will look at it next.

Job Control: *&, nohup, ps,* and *kill*

UNIX gives you control over the jobs you ask it to do. For instance, in Chapter 8 we discussed how we can use the **&** command to run a job in background. Here we will review that command, then see how to have a job run after you sign off the system, how to check the status of your jobs, and how to terminate jobs that get out of hand.

Background Jobs: &

To run a job in background, just follow the command with the & symbol:

```
$ sort biglist > newlist &
 4242
$
```

The *sort* command (Chapter 10) can take time for a very large file. Placing it in background means that your terminal is freed so that you can do other tasks while the sorting process goes on. The **4242** is the particular process identification number assigned to this background job. Every job running on the system has its own unique ID number, and we will check out some uses for these numbers in a moment.

Keep in mind that a job running in background still normally sends its output to the screen, where it can surprise you amidst some other activity. Just use redirection (as we did previously) to avoid that problem.

Suppose your background job is a long one and that you don't feel like waiting around for it to finish. But if you just log out or hang up, the job will be arrested and killed when you do. UNIX has a way out of that difficulty: the **nohup** command.

No Hangups: *nohup*

The **nohup** command tells UNIX to ignore the terminating signals generated when you log out or hang up. Thus a job started under the protection of this command will keep running even after you sign off. If you are using a phone line to communicate with the computer, this can save you money. To use this feature, just precede the desired command with **nohup:**

```
nohup sort biglist > newlist &
```

Notice that we use **nohup** in conjunction with **&.** If you run a **nohup** job in foreground, you won't be able to start the logout procedure until the job is finished, so you save nothing.

What if you forget to use redirection to collect the output of the job? Then UNIX will send you a message like this:

```
output sent to 'nohup.out'
```

When you next log back on, just check for a file called **nohup.out;** it should hold the output. Even if you do use redirection, UNIX will create and use the **nohup.out** file if any error messages were generated by your job.

Summary: nohup—run a program after hanging up

name	options	arguments
nohup		command

Description: **nohup** lets you initiate a command that will continue running even if you hang up your phone connection or otherwise log off the system. It should be run as a background process. Unless you use redirection, output will be placed in a file called **nohup.out.** Error messages also are sent to that file.

Example: **nohup spell ch23 > sp.ch23 &**
The **spell** command checks the spelling of the file **ch23** in background. Misspelled words are redirected to the **sp.ch23** file. If the program generates any error messages, they are sent to a file called **nohup.out.**

Okay, we can now get background programs to run even when we sign off. Another useful skill would be to stop a background program that was turning out badly. That's the next topic.

Terminating Unruly Jobs: *kill*

Into every computer user's life comes the program that just won't quit. The computer insists on taking some trivial error seriously and expends considerable time doing useless things with great speed and accuracy. Ordinarily you can use an interrupt (a <control-c> or <break> key) to stop such a program, but that won't work for a program running in background. You need a special tool, and that tool is **kill.** To use **kill,** type the command and follow it with the process ID number. For instance, earlier we gave the example

```
$ sort biglist > newlist &
 4242
$
```

To stop this background program, just type

```
kill 4242
```

and your program will terminate. Or, at least, it usually will. Some resistant processes may ignore the ordinary **kill** signal, and you may have to use the potent "sure kill" option:

```
kill -9 3452
```

Here we invoke the -9 option, which brooks no opposition.

Summary: `kill`—terminating jobs

name	options	argument
`kill`	[−9]	process ID number

Description: **kill** terminates the specified job. You can obtain the process identification number by using the **ps** command. The form is **kill** number

Option: **−9**
This is a "sure kill" which can be used if an ordinary kill fails. (This is a special case of a more general option that you can study in the manual.)

Example: Suppose the job **spell essay > err &** has a PID of 3492. Terminate the job with **kill 3492**

But what if you have forgotten the process I.D.? Then you can use the **ps** command to find it.

Process Status: *ps*

The **ps** command reports on the processes currently going on in the computer. Let's see what happens when we give the command:

```
$ ps
  PID TT TIME COMMAND
5863 30 0:11 sh
5922 30 0:01 ps
$
```

Aha! Two processes! The **ps** command, of course, is the one we just ran. But what's this **sh?** It's the shell program itself! When you log in, UNIX starts up a shell process to handle your needs. This reminds us that to the computer, the shell is just another program. For each process there is a process ID (PID), the terminal number (TT) of 30, the time used so far, and the name of the process. Now let's put a process into background and repeat the command:

```
$ sort bigfile > newfile &
 6234
$ ps
  PID TT TIME COMMAND
5863 30 0:11 sh
6234 30 0:03 sort bigfile
6235 30 0:01 ps
$
```

Here we have used a file big enough so that the sorting is still going on when we invoke **ps.** Now we get the PID for the sorting process as well as for the **ps** process itself. Wait a bit and repeat the command:

```
$ ps
  PID TT TIME COMMAND
5863 30 0:11 sh
6258 30 0:01 ps
$
```

Since this is a new invocation of **ps,** it has a new process number. It is still the same shell, so that PID is unchanged. In the meantime our sorting job has finished, and other users have created processes 6236 through 6257.

What about those other users? We can learn what they are up to by using the **-a** option:

```
$ ps -a
  PID TT TIME COMMAND
 4347 03 0:53 sh
 5288 03 0:22 sh
 6321 03 0:00 lpd
 6238 07 0:11 sh
 6514 07 0:01 vi .remind
 5553 08 0:23 sh
 6494 08 0:08 vi mbox
 5698 28 0:13 sh
 6405 28 0:13 vi menu5.c
 5863 30 0:11 sh
 6527 30 0:02 ps -a
 6245 32 0:12 sh
 6374 32 2:46 nroff -mm
$
```

This sums up what's happening at the seven active terminals. Note that each user has his own shell process. (There we are on terminal 30.)

Summary: ps—process status report

name	options	arguments
ps	[-a, -f]	

Description: **ps** prints information about processes currently in the system. The output consists of the process identification number (PID), the terminal (TT), CPU time used (TIME), and the command (COMMAND). The PID is a number uniquely assigned to the process. By default, **ps** reports on processes initiated at the user's terminal.

Options: **−a**
This option displays **ps** information for all terminals, not just the user's.
−f
This option prints a full list of information about each process, including status, priority, and size information.

Well, perhaps the shell is just another program, but it is a rather special and ingenious program. We've seen it can recognize and run commands and redirect input and output. Now let's see how it handles those UNIX programs known as shell scripts.

Shell Scripts

UNIX lets you use standard UNIX commands as building blocks to construct new commands of your own devising. The shell makes this possible. Normally, the shell takes its input from the terminal. (Its normal input consists of the commands you type.) But, like other UNIX programs, it also can take input from a file. A file containing such UNIX commands is called a shell script. For example, we can use an editor to create a file with the following command line:

```
ls -l
```

Suppose we name this file **ll** (for long list). Then we can have the shell run this command by typing

```
sh ll
```

and the command in the **ll** file is executed. The **sh** command invokes the shell, and the shell runs the instructions found in the **ll** file. (Actually, using **sh** creates a new shell which then takes over control. When it finishes running the shell script, the new shell "dies," returning control to your original shell. See the box on multiple shells.)

Multiple Shells

There is just one shell program in UNIX System V, but there are many instances of the shell. Each time you log in, the system starts up a shell process for you. (A process is a program being run.) Each other user has his or her own shell process. Of course, only one program runs at any moment, but UNIX switches from running your shell to running Laura's shell to running Pete's shell, and so on, attending to each of your needs in turn. Your shell process knows about your commands, but not Pete's, and vice versa. Thus, the separate shell processes keep your work from getting muddled up with the work of others.

More remarkable, perhaps, is the fact that you yourself can have more than one shell process going for you. For example, executing a shell script creates a new shell which runs the script and expires when it finishes. We can use **ps** to test this claim. First, create a file called, say, **do.ps,** and containing this command:

```
ps
```

Next, we will run this script, doing a **ps** before and after:

```
$ ps
  PID TT TIME COMMAND
 5004 30 0:04 sh
 5023 30 0:01 ps
$ sh do.ps
  PID TT TIME COMMAND
 5004 30 0:04 sh
 5089 30 0:00 sh do.ps
 5090 30 0:01 ps
$ ps
  PID TT STAT TIME COMMAND
 5004 30 0:04 sh
 5099 30 0:01 ps
$
```

The shell we were granted at login has a PID of 5004. The temporary shell that ran the shell script had a PID of 5089. Similarly, each invocation of **ps** has its own PID. If you make the script executable and type its name, that, too, creates a temporary shell. Try it and see.

You don't have to run a shell script to create a new shell. Just type **sh** and hit the <return> key. The screen may look the same, but you are using a new shell. Again, you can confirm this using **ps:**

```
$ sh
$ ps
  PID TT TIME COMMAND
```

```
5004 30 S      0:00 sh
5130 30 S      0:00 sh
5134 30 R      0:01 ps
$
```

> You can continue typing **sh**'s, creating a shell with a shell within a shell. . . . To reverse the process, type a <control-d>. Each <control-d> kills off the most recently created shell. Try it out. Of course, if you lose count and hit too many <control-d>'s, you will kill off the original shell and find yourself logged out!

Now suppose you just type

```
ll
```

Then you are informed

```
ll: cannot execute
```

But you need not accept this. Just type

```
chmod u+x ll
```

and try typing **ll** again. Now the command runs just by typing the filename! We'll discuss the **chmod** (change mode) command in Chapter 10, but what it does here is rather simple: it changes the mode of the **ll** file so that you **(u)** add **(+)** executable **(x)** status to the file. We now have a convenient abbreviation **(ll)** for a lengthier command **(ls -l).**

Let's summarize the main points before we move on to more interesting examples.

1. A shell script consists of a file containing UNIX commands.
2. A shell script can be run by typing **sh filename.**
3. If you use the **chmod** command (Chapter 10) to make the file executable, you can just type the filename to make it work:

```
filename
```

Shell scripts are quite versatile and flexible. First, you can include more than one command in script. Second, you can have your command use command line arguments, just like the built-in commands do. Third, you can create loops and other programming features in a script. We'll look at the first two features now, and in Chapter 12 we'll look at some more advanced uses of shell scripts.

Multiple Commands

You aren't limited to just one command per script. For example, when you've spent too many hours at the terminal, you might need a script like the following:

```
who am i
pwd
date
```

Just put one command per line, as if you were typing instructions from the terminal. Or you can put several commands on the same line by using the semicolon as a separator:

```
who am i; pwd; date
```

Put either version in a file called **huh,** and running **huh** will produce output such as

```
$ sh huh
fleezo   tty7    Apr 18  11:55
/usr/fleezo/stocks
Thu Apr 19 11:55:21 PST 1984
$
```

It would be nice if the script could print out descriptive messages. UNIX does not let us down here, for the **echo** command gives us the means. In its simplest form, which is all we need here, **echo** sends a copy of its arguments to the screen. For example,

```
$ echo 34
34
$ echo He spreads the burning sands with water.
He spreads the burning sands with water.
$
```

Summary: echo—echo arguments

name	options	arguments
echo		[any string of characters]

Description: **echo** writes its arguments on the standard output. Without arguments it produces an empty line.

Example: **$ echo say New York unique 10 times fast**
say New York unique 10 times fast
$

Now we can upgrade **huh** to the following:

```
echo You are
who am i
echo The directory you are in is
pwd
echo The date is
date
```

Running the new **huh** produces this sort of output:

```
$ sh huh
You are
fifi     tty14   Apr 19  12:08
The directory you are in is
/usr/fifi/cosmology/gravity
The date is
Thu Apr 19 12:08:23 PST 1984
$
```

(The output would be neater if we had a command that just gave the user's name without the other information. We'll show one possibility later in this chapter and a second version in Chapter 11.)

What if we want one of our scripts to use an argument? For instance, suppose you are in the directory **/usr/me** and you want a long listing of the **/usr/me/profits** directory. Can you type

```
ll profits
```

to get that listing? Well, you can type it, of course, but the shell will ignore the profits and just list your current directory. That is, your command is interpreted as

```
ls -l
```

and not as

```
ls -l profits
```

But there is a scheme that will not ignore your profits; that is our next topic.

Command Line Arguments for Shell Scripts

When you use the shell script, the shell does keep track of any arguments you type after the script name. Your script can use these arguments by referring to them by the following schemes: **$1** is the first argument, **$2** is the second argument, and so on. In addition, **$*** is short for all the arguments, and **$0** is short for the name of the shell script itself. The **$1** and its companions are called "positional parameters," for the number indicates the position of the original argument. Here is an example illustrating how the scheme works. First, here is the script itself, stored in the file **i.remember:**

```
echo This is the $0 command
echo My first argument is $1
echo My third argument is $3
echo Here are all my arguments: $*
```

Next, here is a sample invocation:

```
$ sh i.remember three cats each wearing three hats
This is the i.remember command
My first argument is three
My third argument is each
```

257

```
Here are all my arguments: three cats each wearing three hats
$
```

Thus **$1** is "three," and so on. Incidentally, the explicit numbering scheme only extends to **$9,** but the **$*** will encompass however many arguments you give.

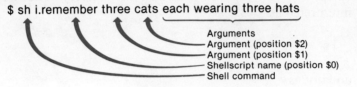

Scripts and arguments.

Now we can modify **ll** to make it more useful. One version would be

```
ls -l $1
```

Another possibility is

```
ls -l $*
```

How do they differ? The first version will list just one directory (the first one fed to it), while the second will list all the directories given to it.

Here is another example: Suppose we create a shell script containing the following command:

```
mv $1 $1.$0
```

Call the script **pig.** Then, assuming that you have a file called **porky,** what will the command

```
sh pig porky
```

do? Well, **$1** is the first argument **(porky),** and **$0** is the name of the script **(pig),** so this command is interpreted as

```
mv porky porky.pig
```

We now have a command that will add **.pig** to the name of any file! This could be quite useful to swinologists and to users of PIGTRAN (OGAY, OTAY . . .).

Another important feature of shell scripts is that they can use redirection and pipes. See if you can tell what the following shell script does (the **lp** command sends stuff to be printed on a line printer):

```
cat $* | lp
date >> prfile
echo $* >> prfile
echo >> prfile
```

The best way to check what this does is to run it on your system. But if you can't wait for that, here is what happens. The first line concatenates all the files you feed to the shell script as arguments. (Recall that **$*** stands for all the arguments to the shell script.) This combined file then is piped to the printer and printed. The next line adds the current time and date to the end of a file called **prfile.** (If no such file exists, it is created.) The next line adds the names of the files you printed to the end of **prfile.** The final line adds a blank line to **prfile.** Thus, the net effect of this shell script is to print some files and to keep a record of what files you printed and when. Note that the script uses a **prfile** in your current directory. If you wanted to use this command in various directories, you should be more specific about the name. For instance, Ben could establish an **Accounting** directory and use **/usr/ben/Accounting/prfile** as the storage file.

This should be enough to get you started with shell scripts. We will develop more examples in Chapter 11, and in Chapter 12 we will unveil further delights of this topic. Now let's look at another shell feature, shell variables.

Shell Variables

As the shell carries on its activities on your behalf, it has to keep track of a number of things, including the name of your home directory, what prompt you use, and where to look for commands. To do this, the shell uses "shell variables." We can think of variables as names that can have values assigned to them. The shell has "built-in" variables that keep track of your home directory, etc., but it also lets you define variables of your own. First we will look at some of the built-in variables, and then we will see how you can create and use your own variables.

Built-in Variables

To find out what variables your shell is using, just type the command **set:**

```
$ set
HOME=/usr/zeke
IFS=

MAIL=/usr/mail/zeke
PATH=.:/bin:/usr/bin
PS1=$
PS2=>
TERM=adm5
$
```

The shell prints out the variables it knows. The name to the left of each equals sign is the name of a variable, and the stuff to the right is the value of the variable. Thus, the variable **TERM** has the value **adm5.** It is a UNIX tradition (but not a requirement) that variable names are in uppercase. You may not have the exact same set of variables we have here, but this collection is typical. Let's describe what each one is. Then we can talk about how they are used and how they can be changed.

Standard Shell Variables

HOME: This is set to the pathname of your home directory.

IFS: (Internal Field Separator) This is set to a list of the characters that are used to separate words in a command line. Normally, this list consists of the space character, the tab character (produced by the tab key), and the newline character (produced by hitting the <return> key). They are "invisible" characters, so you don't see them. But you can see, for example, that the newline character produced a blank line.

MAIL: This variable's value is the name of the directory to which your mail is sent. The shell checks the contents of this directory every so often, and when something shows up, you are notified that mail has arrived for you.

PATH: This names the directories which the shell will search to find commands. A colon is used to separate the directory names; there are no spaces. The directories are searched in the order given. For example, if you give the command **cat,** the shell first searches your current directory (**.**) for an executable file by that name. If it doesn't find one there, then it looks in **/bin.** If it still hasn't found **cat,** it looks in **/usr/bin.** And if it still hasn't found a

cat program, the shell reports back that it can't find that command. Note that this particular sequence of directories in **PATH** means that if you have an executable file called **cat,** it is executed rather than the standard system **cat,** which would be in one of the subsequent directories. (Note: if the very first character in the string is a colon (:), the shell interprets that as **.:,** that is, as if the current directory is first on the list.

PS1: (Prompt String 1) This is the string used as your prompt. Normally (as in this example) it is set to **$,** but you can redefine it if you like.

PS2: (Prompt String 2) This prompt is used when UNIX thinks you have started a new line without finishing a command. You can continue a line, for example, by using a backslash (\ ) before hitting the < return > key:

```
$ echo 0 give me a ho\
> me where the buffalo roam
0 give me a home where the buffalo roam
$
```

See the section on metacharacters in this chapter for more information on \ and other special characters.

TERM: This identifies the kind of terminal you habitually use. Knowing this, the shell knows what to interpret as a backspace key, etc.

To use these variables we need a convenient way to specify the value of a particular variable, and we need a way to change that value. Let's look at these two points next.

Specifying the Value of a Variable

The shell uses the metacharacter **$** to specify the value of a variable. (What could be more American than denoting value with $?) Compare these two commands and responses:

```
$ echo TERM
TERM
$ echo $TERM
adm5
$
```

Using **TERM** prints the word literally, but using **$TERM** causes the *value* of **TERM** to be echoed. By using **echo** and **$** we can print out the value of any particular variable.

We also can use the **$** construction as part of other expressions. Suppose, for example, Zeke is working in a distant directory and wants to copy a file into his home directory. He could type

```
cp rainstats /usr/zeke
```

but he also could type

```
cp rainstats $HOME
```

The shell would see **$HOME** and know that Zeke wanted the value of the **HOME** variable, which is **/usr/zeke.** Then it would make that substitution.

That may not seem like much of a savings, but consider the possibilities for shell scripts. If Zeke wrote a shell script with the line

```
cp $1 /usr/zeke
```

only he could use it. But if he used

```
cp $1 $HOME
```

then anyone could use this script, and the copy would go to the home directory of the user. (Actually, we need to use the **export** command to make this use of the **HOME** variable work. We discuss **export** in a box later in this chapter.)

Here is another example. Remember that in discussing our **huh** script, we hankered for a command that yielded just the user's name. We can construct such a command very simply on those systems that carry a built-in variable set to the user's login name. If your system uses such a variable, it may have a name like **USER** or **LOGNAME.** Then you could create an executable file called **myname** containing the simple line

```
echo $LOGNAME
```

We will assume we have a **myname** function available from now on. If you don't have the proper shell variable, you can create one, using the information in the rest of this chapter. Or you can use the approach we give in Chapter 11. In the meantime, remember that the **myname** command outputs the user's login name.

Calling something a variable implies that you can change its value. And that we can do.

Setting Shell Variables

To create shell variables and to give them values, we give commands like these:

```
AGE=65
NAME=Scrooge
```

The form is

```
name=value
```

where "name" is the name of the variable and "value" is the value of the variable. Note that there must be no spaces between these items and the equals sign.

The shell variables we created are added to the list. We can check this by typing **set** to get the full list of shell variables:

```
$ set
AGE=65
HOME=/usr/zeke
IFS=

MAIL= /usr/mail/zeke
NAME=Scrooge
PATH=.:/bin:/usr/bin
PS1=$
PS2=>
TERM=adm5
$
```

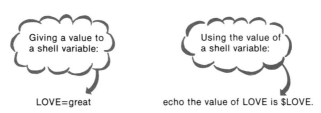

Giving a value to a shell variable:

LOVE=great

Using the value of a shell variable:

echo the value of LOVE is $LOVE.

Using shell variables.

Normally there should be no blanks or other **IFS** characters in the value-giving command:

```
$ set LUNCH=hot and sour soup
and: not found
$
```

This example just confused the shell. Use single quotes to get the whole expression:

```
$ LUNCH='hot and sour soup'
$ echo $LUNCH
hot and sour soup
$
```

As hinted earlier, we can redefine the built-in variables. Suppose you tire of the usual $ prompt. Then change it!

```
$ PS1=~~
~~myname
zeke
~~
```

(Recall that **myname** is a shell script that returns the user's login name.) If you want spaces in the prompt, use single quotes:

```
~~PS1='Your wish is my command: '
Your wish is my command: myname
zeke
Your wish is my command:
```

Of course, this new arrangement ends when you log out. In the next section we'll see how to make such arrangements more permanent.

Customizing Your Environment: Your *.profile* File

When you log in, a shell is created for you. Some shell variables (such as PS1 and PATH) are given to it at this time. Then the shell looks in your home directory for a file called **.profile** and follows the instructions it finds there. (The system treats **.profile** as a shell script.) Usually the system administrator provides you with a standard version of this file. (Remember, filenames beginning with a period are not listed by a simple **ls**. You need to use **ls -a** to see them.) The contents of this file will vary from system to system, but here is a typical example:

```
$ cat .profile
export MAIL PATH TERM
umask 22
MAIL=/usr/mail/bess
TERM=adm3
$
```

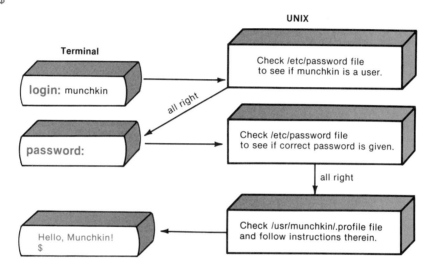

Condensed login procedure.

The **export** command makes the listed shell variables available to subshells; see the **export** box. The **umask** command affects who can read, write, and execute files you create. (The **chmod** command in the next chapter lets you change these permissions for individual files.) Next we have the two shell variables **MAIL** and **TERM** assigned values. Your file might have other entries. For example, it may have a shell variable called **EXINIT** which is used by the **vi** and **ex** editors to set up options.

Using *export*

Your login shell knows certain shell variables such as **HOME, MAIL,** and any variables you may have defined. When you start a new shell, however, (by running a shell script, say), that shell is ignorant of the old shell's variables. You can create a new variable in the new shell using one of the old names, but it will be a distinct variable, and old shell won't know it. The rule, you see, is that each shell's variables are private to itself. This exchange illustrates the point:

```
$ CAR=rolls <————————————————————— first CAR gets its value
$ echo $car
rolls
$ sh <————————————————————————————— create new shell
$ echo $CAR
  <————————————————————————————————— shell equivalent to "huh?"
$ CAR=vw
$ echo $CAR <——————————————————————— a second CAR gets its value
vw
$ <control-d> $echo $CAR <—————————— return to old shell
rolls <———————————————————— doesn't know about new shell's CAR
$
```

Sometimes we want the new shell to know the old shell's variables. Then we use the **export** command. Any shell variable used as an argument for this command will have copies of the variable and its value presented to all shells descending from it. Let's repeat the preceding exercise, but this time using **export.**

```
$ export CAR
$ CAR=rolls <————————————————————— first CAR gets its value
$ echo $car
rolls
$ sh <————————————————————————————— create new shell
$ echo $CAR
rolls <——————————————————— the new shell has a copy of the 1st CAR
$ CAR=vw <————————————————————————— the copy gets a new value
$ echo $CAR
vw
$ <control-d> $ echo $CAR <————————— return to old shell
rolls <———————————————————— original CAR has original value
$
```

As you can see, variables can be exported down to subshells, but they cannot be exported back up to parent shells.

To find out what variables are already exported, just type **export** without any arguments.

The neat thing about **.profile** is that you can use an editor to put in your own entries. If you want to have a different prompt, insert a line like this:

```
PS1='What next, Bess? '
```

If you don't have a variable set to your login name, you can create one:

```
LOGNAME=bess; export LOGNAME
```

Then you can use the **myname** script.

If you want to keep your own record of when you log in, insert a line like this:

```
date >> loginlog
```

Then each time you log in, the **date** command is run, and its output is diverted to the **loginlog** file, giving you a record of the date and time of your logins.

If you have a supply of shell scripts or other programs that you use often, here is a useful practice. First, establish a subdirectory to hold these executable files. Then add that subdirectory to your **PATH** search list. Then, no matter what directory you are in, you can run those programs just by typing the name. For example, Bess could establish a **bin** subdirectory and add this line to her **.profile:**

```
PATH=.:/bin:/usr/bin:/usr/bess/bin
```

A trickier way of doing the same thing is

```
PATH=$PATH:$HOME/bin
```

$HOME is converted to **/usr/bess**, then **:/usr/bess/bin** is added to the end of the original **PATH**. The advantage of this form is that it can be used in anyone's **.profile** without using the user's name explicitly.

Let's have one more example. If you like the personal touch in computers, you can add a line like

```
echo Welcome, Bess! I am glad you are back!
```

As you grow more familiar with the system, you will get your own ideas about what to put in your **.profile.** Feel free to use this opportunity; it's there for you.

In this chapter we have used several special characters, including **$** and **'**. At this point it may be useful to summarize the special characters we have encountered so far and to add a few more to the list.

Shell Metacharacters

The shell recognizes several characters ("metacharacters") as having special meaning, such as ***** and **/**. The shell also has ways to remove these special meanings. We'll summarize the more common metacharacters now and then show how to neutralize them.

Wildcard substitution: *** ? [ ]** (Chapter 7)
Redirection: **> >> < |** (This chapter)
Background process: **&** (This chapter)
Command separator: **;** (This chapter)
Continue command on next line: **** (This chapter)
Value of a variable: **$** (This chapter)

To this list add the backquote: **'**. Don't confuse this with the regular quote (**'**), which leans the opposite way. A pair of backquotes does for commands what the **$** does for shell variables. That is, a command name in backquotes is replaced by the output (or value, so to speak) of the command. Compare these two command-response pairs:

```
$ echo date
date
$ echo `date`
Mon May 21 11:22:05    PDT 1984
$
```

The backquotes are useful in shell scripts; see the Review Questions for examples.

Neutralizing Metacharacters

Now suppose you want to use some of these symbols literally, perhaps in a command like

```
echo Type a * if you are happy
```

Try it. You'll find that the * is replaced by a list of all your files! After all, that is what * means to the shell. To get around this difficulty, UNIX offers metacharacters that neutralize metacharacters. For this purpose it uses the backslash (\), single quotes ('), and double quotes (''). Let's see what each does.

The backslash negates the special qualities of whatever character immediately follows it. Unspecial characters are left that way. Here is an example:

```
$ echo \* \I \ \\ \[
* I \ [
$
```

Note that it even negates itself, so \ \ is rendered \. The single \ is read as \ *blank* and is printed as a blank, just as \I is printed as **I**.

Now suppose you wished to print the sequence ***?***. You could use

```
echo \*\?\*
```

or you could type

```
echo '*?*'
```

The single quotes turn off the special meaning of every character between them:

```
$ echo 'Send $100 to who?'
Send $100 to who?
$
```

The double quotes are slightly less restrictive. They turn off all the metacharacters *except* **$**, **`**, and \. Thus

```
$ echo `myname`
mariella
$ echo '`myname` is nice & sweet'
`myname` is nice & sweet
$ echo "`myname` is nice & sweet"
mariella is nice & sweet
$
```

The single quotes cause the backquotes and the **&** to be printed literally.

The double quotes also cause the **&** to be printed literally, but the **'myname'** is replaced by its output, **mariella.**

Once you use an opening single or double quote, the shell expects you to provide a closing quote, too. If you hit <return> before doing so, the shell shifts to its second prompt, telling you it expects more to the command:

```
$ echo 'The morning fog
> flowed into the
> low valleys.'
The morning fog
flowed into the
low valleys.
$
```

This gives you a means to print several lines with a single **echo.**

Another use for quotes is to combine several words into one argument. Suppose, for instance, that **additon** is a shell script. If we give the command

```
additon five fleet fools
```

then **$1** is **five, $2** is **fleet,** and so on, as usual. But if we say

```
additon 'five fleet fools'
```

then **$1** is the whole phrase **five fleet fools.**

There is another metacharacter useful in shell scripts. It is the # symbol, and it tells the shell to ignore what follows. You don't need a script to use it. For instance,

```
$ # this computer is not playing with a full stack
$
```

See? No reaction. The value of this metacharacter is that it lets you place explanatory comments in a shell script. For example, our **myname** script could look this way:

```
# myname:a command that returns the user's login name
echo $LOGNAME
```

Farewell, Dear Shell

This ends our discussion of the shell for a while. We've encountered many shell features in this chapter: command lines, redirection, job control, shell scripts, shell variables, the **.profile** file, and shell metacharacters. Using them can greatly enhance your UNIX powers and pleasures. We will use them in Chapters 11 and 12, and we suggest you play with these features until they become familiar. Using them will do much more for your understanding than just reading about them.

But now it is time to return to the nitty-gritty of learning some of the multitudinous commands known to the shell. We will resume that task in the next chapter.

Review Questions

1. Several commands are shown below. Some are correct, some have errors in them. Identify the incorrect commands, then fix them.

```
a. ls-l blackweb
b. ls rupart -s
c. ls -s-l
d. ps -a
e. cat duskhaven > lp
f. jolly > cat
g. PAL=ginny mae
h. NETWORTH = 45
```

2. The file **exc** contains the following line:
```
chmod u+x $1
```
What will these commands do?
```
sh exc fopman
sh exc exc
```

3. Our **huh** shell script had output like
```
you are
godzilla tty92 Feb 21 23:24
```
Modify the script so the output is
```
You are godzilla
```

4. Suppose you often **cd** to the **/usr/lisa/progs/pasc/proj** directory. What could you put into your **.profile** to make this easier to do?

5. Devise a shell script that will set a shell variable called **NAME** to the name of whatever user uses the script; assume the user is logged into her own account.

Answers

a. **ls -l blackweb;** should be a space before the -.

b. **ls -s rupart;** put the option in the right place.

c. **ls -s -l or ls -sl**

d. fine

e. **cat duskhaven | lp** or **lp duskhaven:** either sends the file **duskhaven** to the printer. The original command in this question would create a *file* called **lp** and place a copy of the contents of **duskhaven** there.

f. **cat jolly** or **cat < jolly;** the filename should be to the right of the redirection operator.

g. **PAL='ginnie mae';**

h. **NETWORTH=45;** remember, NO SPACES

2. The first command makes **fopman** into an executable file. The second makes **exc** into an executable file. Hereafter, the user can give commands like

```
exc nosecount
```

3. One way is to replace

```
echo You are
who am i
```

with

```
echo You are 'myname'
```

The backquotes cause 'myname' to be replaced by its value.

4. One possibility is to put in the line

```
PROJ=/usr/lisa/prog/pasc/proj
```

Then to reach that directory, just type

```
cd $PROJ
```

5. **NAME='myname'**

Exercises at the Terminal

1. Try out some pipes. To provide suitable tools, you can use the commands **wc,** which counts the words in its input, and **sort,** which sorts its input alphabetically. Create a file of text called **mystuff** and try these commands, then devise your own:

```
wc mystuff > savecount
cat mystuff | sort
sort mystuff | tee sorted | wc
```

2. Put a **ps** command in your **.profile** and find out the process number of the shell that reads that file. Is it the same shell that later interprets your commands?

3. Devise a shell script that cats a file and also copies it into your home directory. Make the copy have a name that adds **.cpy** to the original name.

4. Implement the personal command directory approach we outlined in the section on **.profile.**

10

File Management Commands and Others: *wc, sort, lp,* and *chmod*

In this chapter, you will find:

10 File Management Commands and Others: *wc, sort, lp,* and *chmod*

Introduction

Files are the heart of UNIX's storage system, so it is no surprise that UNIX has many commands for managing and manipulating files. In this chapter we will look at commands to count the number of words in a file, to give you a quick look at the beginning or end of a file, to sort a file, to compare files to each other, to print files, and to modify the permissions you and others have used your files. We also will mix in a few more commands to leaven the mixture. As you read through the descriptions, remember to sit down and try the commands out.

File Management Commands

Word counting: *wc*

The **wc** command tells you how many lines, words, and characters you have in a file. If you have a file called **gourd,** you find this information by typing:

```
wc gourd
```

and UNIX responds with, say,

```
79   378   2936 gourd
```

This response tells you that there are 79 lines, 378 words, and 2936 characters in the file **gourd.** You can have more than one file as an argument. For example, the command:

```
wc gourd mango
```

would produce a result like this:

```
 79   378   2936 gourd
132   310   2357 mango
211   688   5293 total
```

Not only does **wc** count the lines, words, and characters in each file, it also finds the totals for you!

The most commonly used options for **wc** are −**l,** −**w,** and −**c.** The first one counts lines only, the second counts words only, and the last option counts characters only. Of course, you can combine them as described in the preceding section. Hence:

```
wc -lw darkeyes
```

would count the number of lines and words in **darkeyes** but not the number of characters.

Summary: `wc`—word count

name	options	arguments
wc	[-lwc]	[filename(s)]

Description: **wc** is a counting program; by default, it works in the −**lwc** option, counting the lines, words, and characters in the named files. If more that one file is given, **wc** gives the counts for each file plus the combined totals for all files. If no file is given, **wc** uses the standard input—the terminal. In this case, you should terminate the input with a [control-d]. Multiple options should be strung together on the same hyphen.

Options: −**l** Counts lines
        −**w** Counts words
        −**c** Counts characters

Example: **wc** −**w** Essay
        This command would count the number of words in the file **Essay.**

File checking: *tail* and *sed*

These two commands give you a quick way to check the contents of a file. The **tail** command shows you the last 10 lines of a file. To see the last 10 lines of the file **feathers,** just type

```
tail feathers
```

The summary shows how to select more or fewer lines.

Our second aid, **sed,** actually is an editor that we will discuss in Chapter 11. But it does no harm to jump the gun a bit and tell you that this command prints the first 10 lines of the file **feathers:**

```
sed 10q feathers
```

You can replace the "10" with a different number if you wish to print a different number of lines.

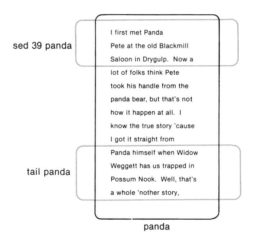

sed and **tail** look at a file.

Summary: `tail`—gives the last part of a file

name	options	arguments
`tail`	`[+/-number]lbc]`	filename(s)

Description:	**tail** shows the tail end of a file; by default, it delivers the last 10 lines. **tail** will only work with one file at a time.
Options:	**+ number** Start ''number'' from the beginning. **-number** Start ''number'' from the end. **lbc** Indicates whether ''number'' is to be counted in lines **(l)**, blocks **(b)**, or characters **(c)**. **l** is assumed if no letter is given.
Examples:	**tail −2Ø gate** Prints the last 20 lines of the file **gate.** **tail + 3Ø gate** Prints the file **gate** starting with the 30th character.
Note:	Constructions of the form **tail −15 −c gate** are not allowed; all the options have to be strung after one **+** or **−**.

Sorting: *sort*

One of UNIX's great labor-saving commands is the **sort,** which can sort files numerically or alphabetically. The sorting function can be used simply or with some fancy options. We will just take a basic look this time and will save the fancy stuff for Chapter 12. The **sort** function, when used without options, sorts files alphabetically by line. Actually, the idea of ''alphabetical'' order has to be extended since a file may contain nonalphabetic characters. The basic order used is called the ''machine-collating sequence,'' and it may be different on different machines. For UNIX, the following points are generally true:

1. Uppercase letters (capitals) are sorted separately from lowercase letters. Within each case, the standard alphabetical order is used.
2. Numbers are sorted by the first digit. The sorting order is 0,1,2,3,4,5,6,7,8,9.
3. The remaining symbols—ones like), %, +, and !—are not grouped together. Some may come between the numbers and the alphabet, and others before or after all numbers and letters.

Let's look at how a particular example might work. Suppose that the contents of **grabbag** are:

```
Here is a small
file with some
words in it
and also
some numbers like
1
23
and
102.

 The first line is blank; this one begins with a blank.
```

This is how the command

```
sort grabbag
```

would arrange them on one system:

```
 The first line is blank; this one begins with a blank.
1
102.
23
Here is a small
and
and also
file with some
some numbers like
words in it
```

Note that the line beginning "The first . . . " was not placed with the other alphabetical lines. The reason is that the first character of that line is a blank, not a "T," so the line was placed according to where blanks go. (The −**b** option will cause blanks to be ignored.) Also note that 102 is listed before 23! This is because **sort** treats numbers as words and sorts them by their first digit. (The −**n** option treats numbers as numbers and sorts them arithmetically; it would place the numbers in **file1** in the order 1, 23, 102.) Finally, notice that **sort** lists capital letters before lowercase letters.

If you feed more than one file to **sort,** it will sort them *and* merge the results. This is great for combining, say, inventory lists.

Normally, the **sort** function sends its output to the terminal. To save the results, you can use redirection. For example, to sort and merge the files **redsox** and **whitesox** and then store the results in a file called **pinksox,** type:

```
sort redsox whitesox > pinksox
```

Or, you can use the **-o** option described in the following summary.

Summary: sort—sorts and merges files

name	options	arguments
sort	[-b, -d, -f, -n, -o, -r]	filename(s)

Description: **sort** sorts and merges the lines from the named files and sends the result to the screen. In the default mode, lines are sorted by the machine-collating sequence, which is an extended alphabetical order encompassing letters, digits, and other symbols. Capital letters are sorted separately from small letters.

Options: **−b**
Ignore initial blanks when sorting.
−d
"Dictionary" order, using only letters, digits, and blanks to determine order.
−f
Ignore the distinction between capital and lowercase letters.
−n
Sort numbers by arithmetic value instead of by first digit.
−o filename
Place the output in a file called "filename" instead of on the screen. The name can be the same as one of the input names.
−r
Sort in reverse order.

Example: **sort −fr −o sortbag grabbag**
This command would sort the lines of the file **grabbag.** Capitalization will be ignored by the sorting process and the lines will be in reverse alphabetical order. The results will be stored in the file **sortbag.**

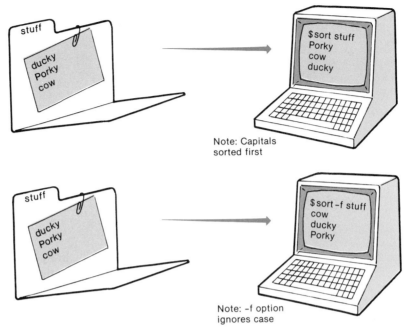

sort vs. *sort −f.*

File Comparison: *cmp, comm,* and *diff*

While cleaning up your filing system, you find two files with the same name but in different directories. Are they really the same? Or, let's say that you have two similarly named files. One is updated, but you don't remember which. Can you quickly compare the two? This is a small sample of the potential uses for some sort of system function that compares files. We will look at three UNIX possibilities.

The first is **cmp;** it is the simplest and tells you the least. It compares two files and finds the location (line and byte) of the first disagreement between the two. An interchange between you and UNIX might look like this:

```
% cmp rascal.p rascall.p
rascal.p rascall.p differ: char 48, line 21
```

The **comm** command tells you more, but it works successfully only with files sorted in the ASCII collating sequence. It prints out three columns. The first column lists lines found only in the first file; the second column lists lines found only in the second file, and the third column lists lines found in both files. Here is a typical user-UNIX dialogue:

```
% comm giftlist1 giftlist2
        Android, Arnold
                Falpha, Alpha
                Filename, Ronald
                Gossens, Waldo
                Goto, Dmitri
        Spumoni, Brunhilda
Spumoni, Hopalong
                Vlug, Merrimee
Yeti, Milo
                Zazzy, Quintus
```

The columns overlap, but you can see which lines are shared and which are not. In this case, only **giftlist1** contains ''Spumoni, Hopalong'' and ''Yeti, Milo.'' Only **giftlist2** contains ''Android, Arnold'' and ''Spumoni, Brunhilda.'' The rest of the names are in both lists. You can suppress the printing of any column you choose; the details for this are in the summary.

The **diff** command is the most powerful of the three. It finds the difference between two files and then tells you the most efficient way to make the first file identical to the second! It is a big help in updating files.

If we run **diff** on the same two files that we used **comm** on (i.e., we type **diff giftlist1 giftlist2**), we get this result:

```
0a1
> Android, Arnold
5c6
< Spumoni, Hopalong
- - -
> Spumoni, Brunhilda
7d7
< Yeti, Milo
```

This needs some interpretation. The **a, c,** and **d** stand for **append, change,** and **delete.** The numbers are line numbers, the ''< '' means a line from the first file, and the ''>'' means a line from the second file. We can paraphrase the output this way:

> Add to the beginning (line 0) of the first file, line 1 (''Android, Arnold'') of the second file.

Change line 5 of the first file ("Spumoni, Hopalong") to line 6 ("Spumoni, Brunhilda") of the second file.

Delete line 7 ("Yeti, Milo") of the first file.

Keep in mind that the goal of **diff** is to show how to make the first file identical to the second; thus, all the changes listed by **diff** apply to the first file only. Of course, if all you wanted to do was make the two files identical, you could just use the **cp** command to make a second copy.

Summary: `cmp`—compares two files, finding location of difference

name	options	arguments
cmp	−l	filename1 filename2

Description: **cmp** looks through the two input files and prints the byte and line number of the first difference between the two. You can use −for filename1 if you want one of the files to be the standard input.

Option: −l
The long option prints the byte number (decimal) and the differing bytes (octal) for each and every difference.

Example: **cmp −l remember**
This will print out the location of the first difference between what you type on the terminal (terminated by a <control-d> and what is in the file **remember.**

Summary: `comm`—find lines common to two sorted files

name	options	arguments
comm	[−1, −2, −3]	filename1 filename2

Description: **comm** reads the two named files (which should be in ASCII collating sequence) and produces three columns of output. The first column contains lines found only in the first file, the second column contains lines found only in the second file, and the third column contains lines found in both files.

Options: −**1** Don't print the first column.
               −**2** Don't print the second column.
               −**3** Don't print the third column.

Example: **comm −12 listA listB**
               This command will print only those lines found in both **listA** and **listB.**

Summary: `diff`—finds the difference between two files

name	options	arguments
diff	[-b, -e]	file1 file2

Description: **diff,** when the two arguments are text files, compares the files and produces output showing what changes to make in the first file in order to make it identical to the second file.

The output format uses "a" for *append,* "c" for *change,* and "d" for *delete.* The symbol " < " means a line from the first file, and " > " indicates a line from the second file. Numbers denote the lines affected. The following is an example:

```
8a1Ø,12
  >Barth, Garth
  >Cuddles, Misty
  >Dollar, Petro
```

This means to append line 1Ø to line 12 of file2 after line 8 of file1. Then, the three lines from file2 are shown.

Options: **−b**
Ignores trailing blanks in a line; other blank strings are considered equal regardless of length. Thus, this option would consider the following two lines to be the same:

    eye of a newt
    eye   of   a   newt

−e
Produces output in the form of **ex** editor commands.

Example: **diff −e giftlist1 giftlist2**
This command causes the output to be expressed as **ex** commands. If the files are the same as the example in the text, then the output would be:

```
7d
5c
Spumoni, Brunhilda
.
Øa
Android, Arnold
.
```

Notice that the commands include the period symbol that is needed to return to the command mode in **ex.**

Command	Operates on	Produces (if no options given)
cmp	Any two files (text or binary code).	Location of first difference, if any.
comm	Two sorted text files	Column 1: Lines only in first file. Column 2: Lines only in second file. Column 3: Lines in both files.
diff	Two text files.	Changes needed to make the first file just like the second file.

cmp, comm,* and *diff.

285

Redundancy Elimination: *uniq*

Suppose you have two mailing lists that you have sorted and merged together. You may have some addresses that are duplicated, and you might want to get rid of the repeated versions. You can do this with **uniq.** It will read a file, compare adjacent lines, reject repetitions, and print out the remaining lines on the terminal or into a file which you choose.

The file **weelist** has the following contents (we don't know why, it just does):

```
anchovies
apiaries
artichokes
artichokes
aviaries
```

The command:

```
uniq weelist
```

will produce the following output:

```
anchovies
apiaries
artichokes
aviaries
```

As you can see, **uniq** eliminated one copy of the word "artichokes" from the file. If you want to direct the output to a file, you need only to give the name of that file after the name of the file that is to be processed. Thus, the command:

```
uniq weelist newfile
```

would produce the same output, but would route it to the file **newfile** instead of to the screen.

Because **uniq** works by comparing adjacent lines, the duplicate lines must be next to the originals or else **uniq** won't spot them. Sorting the file first, using **sort,** will ensure that **uniq** works.

Summary: `uniq`—**remove duplicated lines from a file**

name	options	arguments
uniq	[-u, -d, -c]	inputfile [outputfile]

Description: **uniq** reads the input file, compares adjacent lines, and prints out the file minus the repeated lines. If a second filename is given, the output is placed in that file instead of on the screen.

Options: **−u**
Prints out only those lines that have no duplicates. That is, a line that appears two or more times consecutively, in the original file, is not printed at all.
−d
Prints out one copy of just the lines with duplicates, i.e., unique lines are not printed.
−c
Prints the usual output, but precedes each line with the number of times which it occurs in the original file.

Example: **uniq −d ioulist urgent**
This command would scan the files **ioulist** for lines that appear more than once consecutively. One copy of each such line would be placed in the file **urgent.**

Making a Printed Copy

Video terminals are fun, but for some purposes (conducting inventories, wrapping fish, etc.), you really need printed paper output. You can use the commands in this section to give you a printed output.

lp, lpstat, and cancel

The **lp** (for *l*ine *p*rinter) command sends one or more files to a line printer. Here is how to print the file **Fallreport:**

```
$ lp Fallreport
request id is pr2-46 (1 file)
$
```

(The line following the command provides a "request identification" for your printing job—more on that in a moment.)

Chaos would result, however, if this command sent your file directly to the printer, for other **lp** commands might arrive in the middle of your print job and interrupt it. Instead, this command sends a copy of your file to a printer "queue," where it waits its turn to be printed.

What if you sent the wrong file? Then use **cancel** to remove it from the queue or to halt the printing. Just use the request ID:

```
cancel pr2-46
```

Many installations have more than one printer. For example, a system might include a high-speed dot matrix printer and a slower, letter-quality printer. The **lp** command lets you specify which printer you want by using the **-d** option. For example, if a letter-quality printer were designated **pr1,** then you could send a letter to it with this command:

```
lp -d pr1 dearpres
```

If you don't specify the printer, the system will use a default value. For instance, our attempt to print **Fallreport** sent the text to **pr2,** as shown by the request ID assigned to it. If you like, you can establish your own default value by setting the shell variable **LPDEST** to the appropriate value.

To check up on the status of a printing request, just type

```
lpstat
```

and the system will report back to you. If you would like to know the status of the various printers, type

```
lpstat -p
```

To print several files, just list them all after the command:

```
lp Winterreport Springreport Summerreport Fallreport
```

Each file will be separated from its neighbors by a banner page proclaiming your identity and by a blank page. If you want the files printed as one unit, you can do something like this:

```
cat Winterreport Springreport Summerreport Fallreport | lp
```

Summary: `lp, cancel,` **and** `lpstat`

name	options	arguments
lp	[-d]	[filenames]
cancel		request ID.
lpstat	[-p,-t]	

Description: **lp** sends the named files to a line printer queue from whence they are printed in an orderly fashion. If you omit a filename, **lp** accepts input directly from your terminal; terminate the input with <control-d>. The **lp** command returns a request ID that can be used with **cancel. cancel** removes files from the queue and even halts the printer if necessary. Type **cancel** and follow it with the request ID. **lpstat** reports on the status of your requests when used without options.

Options: −**d** (for **lp**) Lets you select a printer.
−**p** (for **lpstat**) Reports on printer statuses
−**t** (for **lpstat**) Provides a total status report, covering printers and the printer queue

Example: **lp some stuff**
This prints the contents of the files **some** and **stuff**.

Permissions: *chmod*

The **chmod** (for "change mode") command gives you the final say on who can read and use your files and who can't. This command considers the UNIX users' world to be divided into three classes:

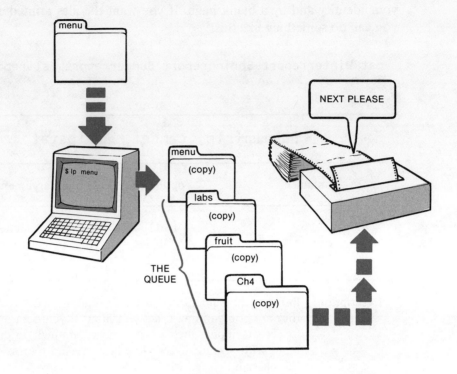

Using a line printer.

1. You, the user **(u).**
2. Your group **(g).**
3. Others **(o).**

What's this bit about a group? UNIX was developed at Bell Labs in order to be used in research there. So, originally, a "group" would correspond to a particular research group. What constitutes a "group" for you will depend on your system. Perhaps it might be students in the same class or workers in the same department, or it might be arbitrary. Whatever the system, users in the same group are assigned the same "group number," and this number is stored in the **/etc/passwd** file, which also contains your login name, your home directory assignment, and your encrypted password. So UNIX knows what group you are in and who else is in it (even if you don't).

In addition to three classes, there are three kinds of permissions that **chmod** considers.

1. Read permission (**r**)—this includes permission to **cat, more, lp,** and **cp** a file.
2. Write permission (**w**)—this is permission to change a file, which includes editing a file and appending to a file.
3. Execute permission (**x**)—this is permission to run an executable file; for example, a program.

You can check to see what permissions are in effect by using the **-l** option for **ls** on the pertinent files. For example, the command:

```
ls -l a.out expgrow.f
```

could produce this output:

```
-rwxr-xr-x 1 doeman        25957 Jan 27 15:44 a.out
-rw-r--r-- 1 doeman          671 Jan 27 15:17 expgrow.f
```

The symbols on the left (-rwxr-xr-x) contain the information about permissions. There are ten columns. The first, which contains a hyphen for these examples, contains a ''d'' for directories and other letters for special kinds of files. Don't worry about that column.

The next 9 columns are actually 3 groups of 3 columns each. The first group of three reports on user permissions, the second group of three on group permissions, and the final group of three on other permissions. We can spread out the 3 groupings for **a.out** like this:

rwx	r-x	r-x
user	group	other users

Within each grouping, the first column shows an ''r'' for read permission, the second column a ''w'' for write permission, and the third column an ''x'' for execute permission. A ''-'' means no permission.

Thus, for the **a.out** file shown above, the user has read, write, and execute permissions (rwx) for the file **a.out;** members of the same group have read and execute permissions (r-x), but no write permission. Other users also have read and execute permissions (r-x) but no write permission. Permissions for the **expgrow.f** account are similar, except no one has execution permission.

What does this all mean? It means that anyone on the system could read or copy these two files. Only the user, however, could alter these two files in this directory. (However, if you copied this file into your directory, you would then be able to write as well as read and execute.) Finally, anyone who wanted to could run the program **a.out** by typing the name of the file. (If the other user were in a different directory, he would have to use the full pathname of the file.) In most systems, these particular permissions are established by default; **chmod** lets you change them.

The **chmod** command is used a bit differently from most other UNIX commands. The simplest way to use it is to type **chmod** and then type in a space. Then comes an "instruction segment" with three parts and no spaces. The first part of the segment consists of one or more letters identifying the classes to be affected, the next part is a "+" or "−" sign for adding or subtracting permissions, and the final part is one or more letters identifying the permissions to be affected. After the instruction segment is another space and the name(s) of the file(s) to be affected by the changes. This may sound a little confusing, but it is simple once you see a few examples. So, here are some examples:

```
chmod g+w growexp.f
chmod go-rx a.out
```

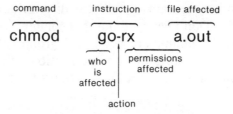

Parts of a *chmod* command.

The first example grants other members of your group **(g)** the right to write **(w)** in the file **growexp.f**. The second example takes away both read **(r)** and execute **(x)** privileges from members of your group **(g)** and from others **(o).** If we repeated the **ls -l** command now, the result would be:

```
-rwx------ 1 doeman          25957 Jan 27 15:44 a.out
-rw-rw-r-- 1 doeman            671 Jan 27 15:17 expgrow.f
```

You can include more than one permission instruction by separating them by commas. For instance:

```
chmod g+w,o-r project.big
```

would let other group members write in the **project.big** file and would deny other users permission to read that file. There should be no spaces within the instruction segment.

You can use **chmod** on your directories. Just use the directory name instead of the filename. Just what are the effects of these permissions on directories? Read permission for a directory lets one read (using **ls,** for example) the names of the files in the directory. Write permission lets one create new files in the directory and remove files from the directory. Finally, execute permission for a directory lets one **cd** to that directory.

Perhaps you wonder what the point is in changing permissions for yourself **(u).** First, you can create a shell script file of UNIX commands. If you give that file ''execute'' status, then typing that filename will cause the commands in the file to be executed. We talked about that in Chapter 9. Secondly, by removing write permission, you can protect yourself from accidentally changing a valuable file.

Summary: chmod—change modes or permissions on files

name	instruction components	argument
chmod	ugo,+−,rwx	filename(s) or directory name(s)

Description: **chmod** grants or removes read, write, and execute permissions for three classes of users: user (you), group (your group), and others. A **chmod** command has three parts: the command name (**chmod,** of course), the instruction string, and the name of the file to be affected. The instruction string also has three parts: letter(s) indicating who is affected, a + or − symbol indicating the action to be taken, and letter(s) indicating which permissions are affected. The code is as follows:
who:
   u the user
   g the user's group
   o others (everyone other than **u** or **g**)
action:
   + add permission
   − remove permission

> permission:
>   r read
>   w write
>   x execute

Example: Suppose you (login name booky) gave the command **ls −1** and found the following permissions for your **payroll** file:

```
−rwxrwxrwx 1 booky  1776 Jan 4 9:33 payroll
```

If you wanted to remove the write and execute permissions for your "group" and "other" users, type:

```
chmod  go−wx  payroll
```

The "g" refers to group, the "o" to others. The "−" means remove permissions "w" and "x".

Messages: *mesg*

Normally, accounts are set up so that if someone tries to write to you while you are on a terminal, you will get a message to that effect. This makes a UNIX system a friendly and neighborly environment. Sometimes, however, you may not want to be interrupted. For those times, UNIX gives you ways to turn off the messages; the **mesg** command controls attempts to **write** to you.

To prevent people from reaching you with **write,** type:

```
mesg n
```

When you feel more open to the world, you can reestablish your communication links with:

```
mesg y
```

If you forget your state, just type:

```
mesg
```

and UNIX will let you know your current state. The command will endure until you log out.

mesg y may be included in the standard **.profile** file. You can change that if you like, so that you can log in with **mesg n.**

Summary: `mesg`—permit or deny messages from `write`

name	options	arguments
`mesg`		`[-y, -n]`

Description: Typing **mesg y** allows other users to communicate with you using **write.**
Typing **mesg n** forbids other users from communicating with you using **write.**
Typing **mesg** will cause UNIX to reply with "is y" or "is n," as the case may be.

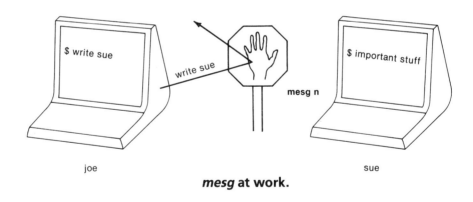

mesg **at work.**

Commands for Your Terminal: *tty* and *stty*

The **tty** command tells you the pathname of your terminal. For example, the command:

```
tty
```

might elicit the response

```
/dev/tty08
```

This means you are using terminal number 8 and the terminal is treated as a file in the /**dev** (for device) directory.

The **stty** command is used to set terminal options, such as the "baud rate" (transmission speed), parity, echo, and which key is the erase key. Much of **stty** concerns the interface between the terminal and the computer, but we will just look at some of the less technical aspects. Normally, the system takes care of these matters for you, but you might want to change some of the choices.

The first step is to determine the current situation. Type:

```
stty
```

and UNIX will report back the baud rate and option settings that are different from the default (standard) values. Here is a sample response to that command:

```
speed 9600 baud; —parity
erase =^h; kill = @;
brkint inpck icrnl onlcr tab3
echo —echoe echok
```

What does this all mean? First, the **speed 9600 baud** indicates the rate at which information is sent back and forth between the terminal and the computer.

Next, the single words, with or without a leading hyphen, refer to various communication conventions and modes. For instance, **echo** means that each character you type is echoed back to the terminal. Thus, when you type the letter Q, the letter Q appears on the screen. Preceding one of these words with a hyphen reverses its meaning. Hence **-echo** would tell the computer not to echo back the characters you type. (Some terminals handle echoing internally, so the **echo** mode would produce a double echo for them.) Chances are you needn't tamper with these modes.

Finally, there are entries of the form **erase = ^ h.** This particular entry means that the erase character has been set to <control-h>.

Suppose you want to change some of these values. You can use the **stty** command to do so. Here are some examples:

```
stty 2400 <――――――――――――――――――――――――――――― set the baud rate to 2400
stty -echo <――――――――――――――――――――――――――――― set the no echo mode
stty erase % <―――――――――――――――――――――――――――― set the erase character to %
```

To set erase or kill to a control character, you can type first an escaped carat (\^) then the corresponding letter. Thus, to set the erase character back to < control-h > , type

```
stty erase \^h
```

You should be cautious with such changes. For example, changing the baud rate just changes the computer end. You would also have to change the rate at the terminal end, perhaps by resetting switches.

To make such a change permanent, place the instruction in your **.profile** file, as described at the end of this chapter.

Using the UNIX clock: *time* and *calendar*

Never let it be said that UNIX won't even give you the time of the day; it gladly informs you whenever you give the **date** command. UNIX can support the **date** command because it keeps track of the time internally. This ability helps it to perform such diverse tasks as timing commands **(time)** and providing you with a reminder service **(calendar).**

time

The **time** command tells you how long a simple command takes. Its general form is:

```
time COMMAND
```

After you give this instruction, the COMMAND (which can be any UNIX command or program execution) is run, and when it is finished, you are given a breakdown of how much time was used. The output of **time** looks like this:

```
15.0 real
5.2 user
2.1 sys
```

These times are in seconds. The time labeled "real" is the elapsed time from when you first give the command until the command is completed. Because UNIX is a time-sharing system, it may have been doing some other tasks during that time period, so "real" time doesn't really represent how much time was devoted to your needs. The next two times relate just to the CPU time spent on your command. The "user" time is time spent executing the command, and "system" time is the additional time spent in the system as a result of the command.

These "time" commands are very important when you are renting CPU time which can cost $180 per hour or more.

calendar

The **calendar** command provides a built-in reminder service. (Don't confuse it with the **cal** command, which generates monthly and yearly calendars.) Actually, you don't even execute the **calendar** command. Your responsibility is to create a *file* named **calendar** in your login directory. In this file, you place dated reminders such as:

```
September 22       Dentist at 2:30
9/24          dinner at Antoine's, 8pm
PAY AUTO INSURANCE Sept 28
```

Early each morning, UNIX will look through all the login directories for files named **calendar.** Whenever it finds one, it will read the file and look for lines containing the date for today or tomorrow. The lines that it finds, it will mail to the directory's owner. Thus, you receive a reminder via **mail** the day before the date and, then, on the day itself.

The date can be anywhere on the line, and you can use abbreviations as above. However, **calendar** does not recognize dates where the day precedes the month. Thus, you won't be reminded of lines containing dates such as ''25 December'' or ''25/12.''

Summary: `time`—time a command

name	option	argument
`time`		command name

Description: **time,** when followed by a command name, runs the named command and gives you a breakdown of the time used. Three times are given.

    ''Real'' or elapsed time—This is the actual time that passes from the moment you initiate the command until the command is finished. If UNIX is switching back and forth between your demands and those of other users, all that time is included, too.

    ''User'' time—This is the CPU time used solely for the execution of your command.

    ''System'' time—This is additional CPU time spent in the system in the course of setting up and servicing the command.

Example: **time cc woo.c**

    This command will cause the command **cc woo.c** to run. When execution of the command is finished, UNIX will print out the time summary for **cc woo.c:**

```
1.1 user
0.9 sys
```

1.1 sec was used to execute the command; another 0.9 sec was spent in the system supporting the command execution, and 4.0 (i.e., 6.0 − 1.1 − 0.9) seconds were spent time-sharing.

Summary: `calendar`—a reminder service

Description: To use this service, create in your login directory a file called **calendar.** Put notes to yourself in this file. Every line in this file containing a recognizable date is mailed by UNIX to you twice: (1) on the day before the date listed and (2) on the date itself. The date can be anywhere on the line. It should include the month and the day *in that order,* and you can use reasonable abbreviations.

Examples: The **calendar** file can contain entries such as:

```
Buy goose March 19
call gus mar. 20 at 3 pm
3/23 Report due
```

Conclusion

We've looked over quite a few UNIX commands in this chapter, and that should give you an idea of the power and variety of the UNIX system. Once again we urge you to try them out and to experiment. You may even wish to look through the manual, for in many cases we have given only the more common options.

Review Questions

Explain what each of the following commands are used for.

1. chmod

2. mesg

3. time

4. calendar

5. sort

6. diff

7. lp

Several commands are shown below. Some are correct, some have errors in them. Identify the incorrect commands and then correct them. You may as well describe what the command does, too.

8. wc-w blackweb

9. tail blackweb

10. sort -f-b iou.list

11. tail blackweb -15

12. comm -3 stallion Stallion

13. cat Rupart > lp

14. blackweb > wc

Answers:

1. changes modes or permission on files.

2. Permits or denies messages from **write**.

3. Times a command.

4. A reminder service.

5. Sorts a file.

6. Finds differences between two files.

7. Sends material to a line printer.

8. **wc -w blackweb;** counts words in the file **blackweb.**

9. Correct; shows the last 10 lines of the file **blackweb.**

10. **sort -f -b iou.list or sort -fb iou.list;** sorts the contents of **iou.list** in machine-collating order, but ignores the difference between capital and small letters and ignores the initial blanks.

11. **tail -15 blackweb;** shows the last 15 lines of **blackweb.** (The incorrect version given in Question 4 would show the last 10 lines of **blackweb** and would then look for a file called **−15**; of course, if you had a file by that name, then the original instruction would be correct.)

12. Correct; shows in column 1 those lines that are only in the file **stallion** and shows in column 2 those lines that are only in the file **Stallion**; both files, however, need to be sorted for this to work correctly.

13. **cat Rupart | lp or lp Rupart;** sends the file **Rupart** to be printed on the line printer. The original command given in Question 6 would create a *file* called **lp** and would place a copy of the contents on **Rupart** there.

14. **wc < blackweb** or **wc blackweb**; counts the lines, words and characters in the file **blackweb**. The < and > operators require a command or executable file on the left, and a filename on the right.

Exercises at the Terminal

1. While in your home directory, do the following:

   A. List the contents of your home directory.
   B. Count the number of files you have using the command sequence shown earlier in the chapter (with pipes).
   C. Find your longest file.
   D. Read the beginning of three files using **sed** and pipe the results through **more.**

2. Create two new files using an editor as follows:

   A. file **AA** contains

   $$
   \begin{array}{l}
   3 \\
   4 \\
   1 \\
   a \\
   b \\
   c
   \end{array}
   $$

   file **BB** contains

   B. Now try the following commands:
   ```
   sed AA BB
   tail AA BB
   cmp AA BB
   comm AA BB
   diff AA BB
   cat AA > > BB
   head AA BB
   sort AA
   sort BB
   wc -l B*
   ```

3. Try a few commands like:
   ```
   who | sort | more
   who | sort | tee CC
   sed CC
   ```

11

MORE TEXT PROCESSING: *cut, paste, sed,* and *nroff*

In this chapter you will find:

11   More Text Processing: *cut, paste, sed,* and *nroff*

Introduction

Today, much computing effort goes into the creation and the alteration of text. Therefore, it is not surprising that UNIX has many facilities dealing with text processing. There are many aspects to this subject. First, there is the basic process of creating text files. We have seen how to use editors such as **ex** and **vi** to do this. Next, we may need to modify a file, perhaps to correct the spelling of a word we've persistently misspelled or to change a name in a form letter. Or we may wish to rearrange text. Another need is to format the file, that is, to set margins, to line up the right-hand side of the text, to control line spacing, and the like. These tasks, too, can be accomplished using the standard editors, but often they can be done more conveniently and efficiently using the UNIX commands **cut** and **paste** for rearranging, **spell** for proofreading, **sed** for editing, and **nroff** for formatting. All four of these tools are designed to work as "filters," so let's discuss this unifying feature before we move to the individual commands.

UNIX Filters

Many UNIX utilities, including **pr, wc, sort,** and those discussed in this chapter, are designed to be "filters." Typically, a filter takes input from the standard input (usually your terminal), processes it somehow, and sends the output to the standard output (usually your screen). By using UNIX redirection and pipes, a filter can just as easily take its input from a file or from another command instead of from the terminal. (Also, most filters can take input from files used as arguments.) Similarly, you can use UNIX redirection and pipes to route the output of a filter to a file or to another command. This agility makes for a flexible, powerful system. You don't need one command for keyboard input and a separate command to handle files. You don't need a carload of complex programs when you can achieve the same results by linking the right combination of filters together with pipes. Designing programs to act as filters is an important part of the UNIX philosophy.

Note that a filter adds nothing superfluous to its output; *sort* doesn't preface its output with a merry

```
All right, sweetheart, here's your output!
```

This may make UNIX utilities seem a little cold and impersonal, but you wouldn't want a message like that piped along to **wc** or **lp** along with the rest of the output.

(If you don't use pipes and do want the personal touch, you can make shell scripts like this:

```
echo There! It\'s all sorted.
sort $*
```

We used a backslash before the single quote metacharacter, for we want it to be a simple apostrophe.)

Now let's get on to particulars by looking at **cut** and **paste**.

Rearranging Text: *cut* and *paste*

The traditional cut-and-paste method consists of cutting up a manuscript and pasting the parts together in a new order. The UNIX commands accomplish a similar aim. They do, however, concentrate on vertical cuts and pastes.

Extracting Vertical Slices: *cut*

The *cut* command has two modes. One (the **-c** option) selects columns from a file, the second mode (the **-f** option) selects out fields. Let's take the first mode first. To use it, follow the **-c** (no intervening spaces) with the numbers of the columns to be passed on. Use a hyphen to indicate ranges and a comma to separate entries. Here are some examples:

```
cut −c2,4,6      Pass columns 2, 4, and 6
cut −c2−6        Pass columns 2 through 6
cut −c2−6,10−12  Pass columns 2 through 6 and 10 through 12
```

The numbers must be in increasing order.

This form of *cut* is useful for tables or files in which data is organized by columns, for example, data left over from the punched card era. Suppose the file *stuff* looks like this:

```
Owen        Danny       234 606 899833
Gershwin    Matthew     543 105 229381
Plaut       Julie       423 636 596215
```

Then we could have this exchange with the computer:

```
$ cut -c1-15,31-33 stuff
Owen           234
Gershwin       543
Plaut          423
$
```

We get back columns 1 through 15 and columns 31 through 33. Because **cut** is a filter, we could pipe the output to **sort** if we wanted the output sorted.

The **-f** option works similarly, but now the numbers refer to fields rather than columns. That is, the command

```
cut -f1-3,5
```

means to print fields 1 through 3 and 5. And what is a field? It is a string of characters marked off by a "delimiter." A delimiter is a character used to indicate the boundaries of a field. For *cut,* the delimiter is assumed to be the tab character (see box), but you can use the **-d** option to reset the delimiter. Let's give an example doing that, since a tab character is difficult to see. We'll use a colon for a delimiter. First, we create a file **morestuff** with colon-delimited fields:

```
Fennel:Douglas:Saint Bernard:55
Snapp:Ginger:Collie:43
```

Then feed the file to **cut,** specifying the delimiter and the desired fields:

```
$ cut -f2,4 -d: morestuff
Douglas:55
Ginger:43
$
```

Here we print out the second and fourth fields. Note that there are no spaces in the options. If you want a space or a shell metacharacter to be a delimiter, quote it:

```
cut -f1-4 -d" "
```

Remember our shell script **myname** in Chapter 9? We can use **cut** to construct another version:

```
who am i | cut -f1 -d" "
```

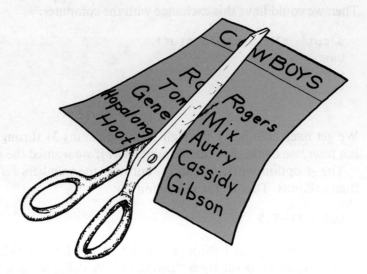

The *cut* command can select fields from a file.

This prints the first field of the *who am i* command, and that is just the user's login name.

The Tab and Space Characters

Many keyboards have a tab key. Sometimes it is labeled "tab," sometimes it features an arrow: −>. Hitting it causes the cursor to move to the right, typically 8 spaces at a time. A tab produces "absolute" moves, that is, it moves to predefined locations on the screen. Thus, whether the cursor is in column 1 or 6, a tab moves the cursor to column 9. (A "relative" move would move the cursor, say, 8 spaces from the current cursor position.)

A tab is part of the ASCII character set; it's character number 9. The space also is a character, character number 32. Each, for instance, takes up the same amount of storage space as "B" or as any other alphabetic character. One consequence of this is that text containing tabs may look like text containing spaces but nonetheless be different. Suppose, for example, that the tabs are spaced by 8 and that you type

```
sam[tab]adams
```

It would appear like this on the screen:

```
sam     adams
```

Typing

```
sam[space][space][space][space][space]adams
```

also produces that appearance:

```
sam        adams
```

But the first takes up just 9 memory slots (8 letters, 1 tab), while the second uses 13 memory slots (8 letters, 5 spaces).

The unexpected presence of tabs may produce surprises when you do editing. In **vi,** for instance, you may try to remove one space and find that 8 disappear, for you really were removing a tab.

The chief values of tabs are saving storage space and producing nicely aligned columns of data. This second point means that tabs often occur in the sort of text used with **cut,** and that is one reason why the tab is used as the default delimiter for **cut.**

Putting It Together: *paste*

The **paste** command is the reverse of **cut.** It takes two or more input files and pastes them together, side by side. If two files are pasted, then the first line of the first file is pasted to the first line of the second file, and so on. The default "glue" that holds the lines together is the tab character. (Aren't you glad we had a box on it!) For instance, suppose we have the following two files, as revealed by **cat:**

```
$ cat fname
gene
fred
elmo
brinleigh
$ cat lname
smith
flint
jardine
snerch
$
```

Then *paste* does the following:

```
$ paste fname lname
```

```
gene     smith
fred     flint
elmo     jardine
brinleigh        snerch
$
```

The tab between "gene" and "smith" causes "smith" to start in column 9 (one tab from the margin). But the last letter of "brinleigh" already is past the first tab stop, so the tab character pushes "snerch" to the next tab stop, column 17.

The **−d** option lets you change the pasting character. Here we change it to a space (we need to use quotes for a space character):

```
$ paste −d" " fname lname
gene smith
fred flint
elmo jardine
brinleigh snerch
$
```

The **paste** command also can accept input from the terminal or a pipe. For these cases, use a hyphen for one or more filenames. For instance, this would paste keyboard input between two other files:

```
paste fname − lname
```

You would type a < control-d > to indicate the end of the keyboard input.

A typical use for **cut** and **paste** in conjunction would be to extract some fields from a table of data and to paste them together in a different order.

Summary: cut—cut out selected fields of a file

name	options	arguments
cut	−c or −f, [−d]	[filename(s)]

Description: **cut** passes through the requested columns (−**c** option) or fields (−**f** option).

Columns are identified by number. Fields are recognized by a field delimiter (default is a tab) and identified by number. In either case, a hyphen is used to indicate a range of numbers and a comma is used to separate individual numbers or ranges. The list of identifying numbers follows the appropriate option without spaces.

Options:

−**c** *list*	pass on the columns in the list
−**f** *list*	pass on the fields in the list
−**d**	change the delimiter character to the one immediately following the **d**. A space or a shell metacharacter should be enclosed in double quotes.

Examples: **cut −c2−5,8 frip**

This command prints columns 2 through 5 and column 8 of the file **frip**

cut −f3,6 −d: fnip

This command prints fields 3 and 6 of the file **fnip**; the fields are separated by a colon.

Summary: `paste`—horizontally merge lines of files

name	options	arguments
paste	[−d]	filenames

Description: **paste** sticks together corresponding lines from the files given as arguments. All first lines are joined into one first line, and so on. Within the compound line, the original lines are separated by a tab character by default. A hyphen (−) can be used as a file name to indicate input from the standard input.

Option: −**d**   The character following the **d** is used to link together the input lines. If more than one character is given, they are used circularly; i.e., the first character is used, then the second, to the end of the list, and then that order is repeated.

> Example: `paste -d: fnip fnop`
> This command adds each line in **fnop** to the end of the corresponding line in **fnip**, separating the two with a colon.

Checking Your Spelling: *spell*

You have just completed an important letter, but you are worried about your spelling. You could sit down and check out each word with a dictionary, or you can let UNIX do that for you. Suppose your letter is in the file **sendcash**. You can give the command:

```
spell sendcash
```

and UNIX will then compare each word in your file with words in a spelling list it maintains. If one of your words is not on the list or is not derivable from some standard rules (adding an "s" or an "ing", etc.), that word is printed out on the terminal. (If you make gobs of spelling errors, you may need to use redirection to save all your errors in a file.)

Suppose **sendcash** looks like this:

```
Dear Ruggles,


    I'm at a real nice place. It's the sub-basement of Mildew
Hall at Forkney College; have you ever been their? If you
have, you will knoe that I need mony bad! Please, please
send some soon! The autochthons here are spooky. I'm
looking forward to recieving your next letter.
                                              Love,
                                              Buffy
```

The output of the **spell** command would look like this:

```
autochthons
Buffy
Forkney
knoe
mony
recieving
Ruggles
```

This example points out some of the pitfalls of **spell**. First, it may not recognize some proper names. Secondly, although it caught "knoe," "mony," and "recieving," it didn't catch the fact that "their" should have been spelled "there." **Spell** can check to see if a word is on its list, but it can't tell whether you used it correctly. Thirdly, **spell** doesn't tell you the correct spelling. Finally, you may know some words, such as "autoch-thons" and certain four-letter words, that are not on **spell**'s list. Nonetheless, **spell** is a big help, especially with long files.

Now let's see about editing files.

The *sed* Stream Editor

The **sed** command does wholesale editing work. It has many of the capabilities of **ed** or **ex,** but it is used differently. Instead of letting you interactively modify a file, it just takes a file as input, reads and modifies it one line at a time, and sends its output to the screen. You can think of the contents of the input file as streaming through the editor, modified as it flows through, hence the name *stream ed*itor. (The **sed** editor was developed from **ed**, not **ex,** which is why it is not the **sex** editor.) This design makes **sed** efficient for large files. Perhaps more importantly, it allows **sed** to be used with pipes and redirects; and this makes **sed** into a handy tool for many tasks. In particular, it often is used in shell scripts.

sed Basics

Give *sed* an input file and minimal instructions, and it will just print out the contents of the file line by line:

```
$ sed '' tale.start
    Once upon a time a delightful princess named Delita lived in
the Kingdom of Homania.  One day, as Princess Delita walked
amidst the fragrant flowers and artful bowers of the West Garden,
she spotted a glistening stone.  Picking it up, Delita discovered
that the stone looked wet but was dry to the touch.  Suddenly the
$
```

(**sed**'s first argument consists of its instructions, and it usually is enclosed in single quotes. Here we used single quotes containing nothing.) Used this way, **sed** reveals the contents of the file **tale.start** just as the **cat** command would. The difference, of course, is that **sed** will accept further instructions. For instance, look at this:

```
$sed 's/Delita/Melari/' tale.start
     Once upon a time a delightful princess named Melari lived in
the Kingdom of Homania.   One day, as Princess Melari walked
amidst the fragrant flowers and artful bowers of the West Garden,
she spotted a glistening stone.   Picking it up, Melari discovered
that the stone looked wet but was dry to the touch.   Suddenly the
$
```

Here we have added an *ed* substitution command to the command line. The command pattern here is

sed 'ed-command' filename

sed looks at each line in turn, applies the command if applicable, and prints out the result. In our example, the first, second, and fourth lines contained the word "Delita," so those lines were printed with the substitution of "Melari" for "Delita." The other lines were printed unchanged.

Note that the original file **tale.start** is left unchanged by **sed.** If you want to save your changes, you have to use redirection. For example, we could have typed

```
sed 's/Delita/Melari/' tale.start > tale.1
```

This command would have placed **sed**'s output in the file **tale.1** instead of on the screen.

Note, too, that **sed** is best used for wholesale changes to the whole file. It's great if you want to replace every Delita with Melari. If you want to change just one or two occurrences of a word and leave other occurrences of that word unaltered, you are better off using one of the regular editors.

We've just seen that **sed** can be used to make substitutions. What other abilities does it have at its disposal? Let's take a look.

sed Editing Instructions

A typical instruction has two parts: an address specification telling what lines are affected, and a command telling what to do to the affected lines. If there is no address given, then all lines are affected. The address can be specified numerically or by pattern matching, much as in **ed.** The commands, too, largely stem from **ed.** We've listed the most common commands in Table 11-1. They work much as they do in **ed,** and we'll bring out details in the examples to come. **sed**'s normal method, as we have said, is to

sed 's/trout/trout/g' brook

sed is a stream editor.

print out the modified line if a change has taken place and to print out the original line if no change was made. This norm is overridden by the **-n** option, which causes only those lines affected by a **p** command to be printed. We'll give an example soon, but first let's see how to specify an address.

Table 11–1 Common *sed* Commands

Command	Action
a\	appends following line(s) to affected lines
c\	changes affected lines to following line(s)
d	deletes affected lines
g	makes substitutions affect every matching pattern on a line instead of just first
i\	inserts following line(s) above affected lines
p	prints line, even under the **-n** option
q	quits when specified line is reached
r filename	reads filename, appends contents to output
s/old/new/	substitutes "new" for "old"
w filename	copies line to filename
=	prints line number
! command	applys command if line is not selected

315

Specifying Lines

sed uses two methods. The first is to specify an address with number. You can use a single number to indicate a particular line. For instance, to delete the third line of our sample file, try

```
$ sed '3d' tale.start
     Once upon a time a delightful princess named Delita lived in
the Kingdom of Homania.   One day, as Princess Delita walked
she spotted a glistening stone.   Picking it up, Delita discovered
that the stone looked wet but was dry to the touch.   Suddenly the
$
```

Or you can use two numbers separated by a comma to indicate a range of lines:

```
$ sed '2,4 s/e/#/' tale.start
     Once upon a time a delightful princess named Delita lived in
th# Kingdom of Homania.   One day, as Princess Delita walked
admidst th# fragrant flowers and artful bowers of the West Garden,
sh# spotted a glistening stone. Picking it up, Delita discovered
that the stone looked wet but was dry to the touch. Suddenly the
$
```

Here the substitution command affected just the second through fourth lines. (Recall that a simple substitution command affects just the first occurrence of a pattern on a line. Thus only the first "e" on each affected line is replaced by a "#".)

The second approach to identifying lines is to specify a pattern; the pattern is contained between slashes. The next example prints only those lines containing "Kingdom"; it uses the **-n** option, which suppresses printing of those lines not affected by a **p** command.

```
$ sed −n '/Kingdom/p' tale.start
the Kingdom of Homania. One day, as Princess Delita walked
$
```

What if we omitted the **-n**? Then the "Kingdom" line would be printed twice, and the rest once.

The patterns can be literal, as in the last example, or they can involve certain metacharacters. This next example, for instance, deletes lines containing "princess" or "Princess":

```
$ sed '/[Pp]rincess/d' tale.start
amidst the fragrant flowers and artful bowers of the West Garden,
she spotted a glistening stone.  Picking it up, Delita discovered
that the stone looked wet but was dry to the touch. Suddenly the
$
```

We'll take up **sed**'s pattern matching scheme after we finish with more basic matters.

One of the more basic matters is that these two modes (numerical, pattern) of specifying lines can be combined. For instance, to delete all lines from line 1 through the first line containing ''fragrant'', do this:

```
$ sed '1,/fragrant/d' tale.start
she spotted a glistening stone. Picking it up, Delita discovered
that the stone looked wet but was dry to the touch. Suddenly the
$
```

Now let's look a bit further at some of the commands.

sed Command Highlights

The last few examples show how to use the **d** and **p** commands. These work much as in **ed,** but **ed**'s **a, c,** and **i** commands have become **a \, c \,** and **i \.** We'll use the append command (**a **) to show the proper form for using these three commands:

```
$ sed 'a\
> Hey la la! Doo de dah!' tale.start
     Once upon a time a delightful princess named Delita lived in
Hey la la! Dooh de dah!
the Kingdom of Homania. One day, as Princess Delita walked
Hey la la! Dooh de dah!
amidst the fragrant flowers and artful bowers of the West Garden,
Hey la la! Dooh de dah!
she spotted a glistening stone. Picking it up, Delita discovered
Hey la la! Dooh de dah!
that the stone looked wet but was dry to the touch. Suddenly the
Hey la la! Dooh de dah!
$
```

Since we didn't give any sort of line identification, our addition was added after every line of the original. (Adding a blank line instead of our choice would have double-spaced the original.) Note, too, how the append command is used. First comes the **a**, then the backslash (\ ), which indicates that the shell should look at the next line. The > prompt shows that shell *is* looking at the next line. This next line contains the text to be added, and the closing quote mark indicates the end of the command. You could add more than one line by using more backslashes:

```
$ sed 'a\
> doobie doobie\
> do' dumbsong
```

The insert command (**i** \ ), works much the same, except it places the new line(s) before each of the original lines. The change line command (**c** \ ) has the same form, too:

```
$ sed 'c\
> Oh marvelous delight! Sing to me!' tale.start
Oh marvelous delight! Sing to me!
Oh marvelous delight! Sing to me!
Oh marvelous delight! Sing to me!
Oh marvelous delight! Sing to me!
Oh marvelous delight! Sing to me!
Oh marvelous delight! Sing to me!
$
```

Each of the original 6 lines was changed to the new text. Of course, you usually would attach some sort of address specifier to a change command so that it would affect just some lines.

The **q** command causes the editor to quit after it reaches the specified line:

```
$ sed '2q' tale.start
     Once upon a time a delightful princess named Delita lived in
the Kingdom of Homania. One day, as Princess Delita walked
$
```

As we mentioned in Chapter 10, this form is useful for looking at the beginnings of files.

The next command we wish to highlight is the substitution command. We've already seen that the form of this command is *s*/oldpattern/ newpattern/ where newpattern replaces oldpattern. In this form, the command affects only the first occurrence of oldpattern in a line. Adding the *g* command (for global) to the end of the instruction makes every occurrence in the line affected. Compare these two examples:

```
$ sed '1s/e/#/' tale.start
 Onc# upon a time a delightful princess named Delita lived in
$ sed '1s/e/#/g' tale.start
 Onc# upon a tim# a d#lightful princ#ss nam#d D#lita liv#d in
```

One very important feature of the *s* command is that it can use **sed**'s pattern-matching abilities for oldpattern. Let's see how that works.

Pattern-Matching in *sed*

sed uses patterns to specify lines in its substitution command. These patterns can be literal, or they can use metacharacters to specify more general patterns. The scheme is similar to the shell's filename expansion scheme (*, ?, and all that), but is not quite the same. Table 11-2 shows the metacharacters used by **sed**. (You can use these same metacharacters in **ex**, **ed**, and **vi**.) Look the table over, then look at our examples.

Table 11–2 Common *sed* Metacharacters for Pattern Matching

\	Turns off the special meaning of the following character
^	Matches the beginning of a line
$	Matches the end of a line
.	Matches any single character
[ ]	Matches any one of the enclosed characters; characters can be listed (**[aqg4]**) or be given as a range (**[c–h]**)
[^ . . .]	Matches any character not in the . . . list
pat*	Matches zero or more occurrences of pat, where **pat** is a single character or a . or a **[ ]** pattern
&	Used in the newpattern part of an s command to represent reproducing the oldpattern part

Quick Examples

Here we will run through some brief examples illustrating the use of the metacharacters of Table 11-2.

/**Second**/	Matches any line containing ''Second''
/^**Second**/	Matches any line *beginning* with ''Second''
/^$/	Matches an empty line, that is, one with nothing between

	the beginning and end of the line. Note that this does not match a line of blank spaces, since a space itself is a character.
/c.t/	Matches lines containing "cat", "cot", and so on. Note that this pattern can be part of a word. For instance, "apricot" and "acute" would be matched.
/./	Matches lines containing at least one character.
/\./	Matches lines containing a period. The backslash negates the special meaning of the period.
/s[oa]p/	Matches "sop" or "sap", but not "sip" or "sup" or "soap"; only one letter is permitted between the "s" and the "p"
/s[^oa]p/	Matches "sip" or "sup" but not "sop" or "sap"
s/cow/s&s/	Replace "cow" by "scows"
/co*t/	Matches "ct" or "cot" or "coot" or "cooot", etc. That is, it matches a "c" and a "t" separated by any number (including zero) of "o"s. Note that use of the * is different from the shell's use.

Now let's see how these can be used and combined in the context of **sed** commands.

Simple *sed* Solutions

Here we will go through some examples that are typical of the problems **sed** can solve.

Suppose we want to remove all the blank lines from a file called **rawtext**. We could do this:

```
sed '/^$/d' rawtext
```

However, as we pointed out previously, this only locates empty lines. The text might contain lines that are not empty but which only have blanks. The next command gets those lines, too:

```
sed '/^ *$/d' rawtext
```

Note that the * follows a blank, so the search pattern says to find lines that contain only zero or more blanks between the beginning and the end of the line.

Suppose we want to add a blank line to each line. One solution is one we suggested in passing earlier:

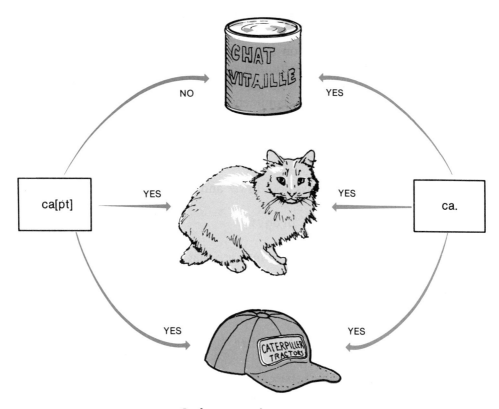

***Sed* can match patterns.**

```
$ sed 'a\
> ' rawtext
```

Here we have appended a line consisting of one blank space to each line. Another approach is

```
$ sed 's/$/\
> /'rawtext
```

This time we substituted a carriage return for the end of the line. The carriage return is an invisible character, and we made the substitution by typing a backslash and then <return>.

Next, suppose we want to print out all lines containing the word "hopefully":

```
sed -n '/[Hh]opefully/p' rawtext
```

We use the **−n** option to suppress the printing of other lines, and we use **[Hh]** to catch both capitalized and uncapitalized occurrences.

Now suppose we want to remove all the comments from a FORTRAN program. FORTRAN comments have a C in the first column, so this would work:

```
sed '/^C/d' prog.f
```

If your system allows both lower and uppercase, use

```
sed '/^[cC]/d' prog.f
```

Note that we use the ^ to indicate that the C (or c) must be at the beginning of a line.

We have a letter we wish to print, and we would like to shift the left margin 5 spaces to the right:

```
sed 's/^/     /' letter
```

We just substitute 5 spaces for the beginning of each line.

We have a file in which we want to change "Bob" to "Robert" and "Pat" to "Patricia." Oops! How do we make more than one command? Read on.

Multiple Commands

Sometimes you may need more than one editing command. Just add them in, one command to a line. (Be sure to enclose the entire command list in single quotes.)

```
$ sed 's/Bob/Robert/g
>       s/Pat/Patricia/g' actii
```

Each time a new input line is accepted, it is subjected to each command in the order given. For example,

```
$ sed 's/cat/dog/g
>       s/dog/pigs/g ' petreport
```

would first convert all **cats** to **dogs** and then all **dogs** (including former **cats**) to **pigs.**

There is one problem with our first example. A line like

```
Patience is needed, Pat.
```

will become

```
Patriciaience is needed, Patricia.
```

because **sed** searches don't distinguish between patterns that are complete words and those that are just part of a word. The pattern /**Pat** /(with a space) will pass up "Patience", but it also would miss "Pat" followed by a period. We have to anticipate ways in which "Pat" might not be followed by a space:

```
$ sed 's/Bob/Robert/g
>       s/Pat[ \.,;:\!?\'\'"\]]/Patricia/g' actii
```

Have we thought of all the possibilities? Perhaps not. And did we put backslashes in the right place? Maybe we should try another approach:

```
$ sed 's/Bob/Robert/g
>       s/Pat[^a-z]/Patricia/g' actii
```

Instead of thinking of all the possible ways "Pat" might be used, we simply eliminate the possibility we don't want, namely, that "Pat" is the beginning of a word. (Recall that **[^a-z]** means any character other than those from a through z.)

Tags

However, our pattern still has a fault. When something like **Pat!** is found, the whole string, including the !, is replaced by **Patricia**, and the ! is lost. We need a way to replace the **Pat** while keeping the !. We can do this with "tags." To "tag" part of a pattern, enclose it with a \ (to the left and a \ ) to the right. Then, in the **newpattern** part of the command, we can refer to the first such enclosed pattern a \ **1**, the second as \ **2**, and so on. Using this method gives us this command:

```
sed 's/\(Pat\)\([^a-z]\)/\1ricia\2/g' actii
```

Here the \1 stands for **Pat** and the \2 stands for **[∧a-z]**; we simply squeeze ricia in between these two patterns. Just as & gives us a means to refer to an entire expression, the \(. . . \) and \1 notation lets us refer to a part of an expression.

Shell Scripts and *sed*

If you find yourself using a particular **sed** concoction often, you may wish to put it into a shell script. For instance, our double-space example could be rendered

```
sed 'a\
' $*
```

and placed in the file **twospace.** Once that file was made executable, we can type

```
twospace jane.letter | pr | lp
```

to format the letter and print it. Or we could make the printing part of the script:

```
sed 'a\
' $* | pr | lp
```

This last example points out how **sed** lends itself to UNIX programming and to shell scripts. Since it produces an output instead of modifying the original file, it can be made part of a piping process linking various UNIX utilities. This convenience is, of course, one of the chief justifications of the "filter" approach to designing programs.

Here is one more example. Suppose you want a program that sorts one or more files alphabetically and prints out the first 10 lines. You can use the following script:

```
sort $* | sed 10q
```

Once you start making use of UNIX tools in this fashion, you are on the road to being a true UNIXer.

Well, enough said about **sed**—it is time to inspect **nroff**.

Text Formatting With *nroff* and *troff*

A text formatter handles such tasks as setting up margins, line-spacing, paragraph formats, and so on. The UNIX text formatters are **nroff** and **troff. nroff** (new runoff) formats material for a line printer, while **troff** formats material for a typesetter. **troff** is the more versatile of the two, for it can select different types styles and sizes and draw boxes. Aside from a few matters like that, the two accept the same instructions. We will use **nroff** as an example, but what we say applies equally well to **troff**.

You have three levels of simplicity and power on which to use **nroff**. The simplest and least powerful level is to use **nroff** unadorned upon an ordinary file. The next level, which brings a great leap in power, is to use an **nroff** "macro." This involves placing a few **nroff** commands into a file of text. The most powerful level, which brings a great increase in complexity, involves putting many **nroff** commands into a file. We'll start with the first level, then look a bit at the second level, and touch upon the third.

Level 1: nroff:

First, get a file with some text. Here are the contents of the **speachify** file:

```
Eighty-seven years before the present time,
a group of men
who could be termed,
with some degree of appropriateness, the ancestors of us here
today and of this distinguished nation, assembled
themselves with the intention, a great intention, we might
add, and one that proved successful,
of modifying for the purpose of improvement our already noble and
notable nation.
```

Now feed this file to **nroff**:

```
nroff speachify
```

Oops! The output runs off the screen! Like **pr, nroff** formats the text to a printed page of 66 lines, so enough blank lines are added to our input to bring the total of 66. We can use **sed** to look at the beginning:

```
$ nroff speachify | sed 10q
Eighty-seven years before the present time, a group of men who
could be termed, with some degree of appropriateness, the
ancestors of us here today and of this distinguished nation,
assembled themselves with the intention, a great intention, we
might add, and one that proved successful, of modifying for the
purpose of improvement our already noble and notable nation.
```

Now we can see what **nroff** hath wrought. First, it has "filled" each line. That means it tries to use enough words in each line to make it as close as possible to the maximum line length without exceeding it. For **nroff** this maximum length is 65 characters by default, including spaces. Secondly, it has "right-justified" or "adjusted" the text. This means spacing out the text so that the right margin is even. That's about all this simple usage does, so let's move on to the next level.

Level 1.5: Messing Around

We didn't mention this level in our introduction because it is not really a level of using **nroff**. Rather, it is a level of experimenting with **nroff**, seeing how **nroff** commands (or "requests") are made, and what they do.

First, what does a typical **nroff** command look like? Here are a few:

```
.ce
.sp 3
.ti 8
```

That's the typical appearance: a period followed by two lowercase letters followed (possibly) by an argument.

Next, how are they used? They are placed in the text file. Each command is placed on a line of its own and at the far left of the line. When **nroff** reads the file, it assumes that any line beginning with a period is a **nroff** request. If it doesn't recognize what follows, it ignores it. Otherwise, it implements the request when it outputs the following text. For example, let's add **.ce** to our text and see what happens. First, here is the new text:

```
.ce
```

```
Eighty-seven years before the present time,
a group of men
who could be termed,
with some degree of appropriateness, the ancestors of us here
today and of this distinguished nation, assembled
themselves with the intention, a great intention, we might
add, and one that proved successful,
of modifying for the purpose of improvement our already noble and
notable nation.
```

Submit it to **nroff:**

```
nroff speachify | sed 10 q
```

and get this output:

```
        Eighty-seven years before the present time,
a   group  of  men  who  could  be  termed,  with  some  degree  of
appropriateness,  the  ancestors  of  us  here  today  and of this
distinguished nation,  assembled themselves with the intention, a
great  intention,  we  might  add, and one that proved successful,
of modifying for the purpose of improvement our already  noble and
notable nation.
```

The result is that the line following the request was centered. Perhaps that is why **.ce** is labeled the centering request.

Positioning an *nroff* request.

Of course, you can read in the manual what these "embedded" commands do, but actually using them makes it clearer. To save you the time of constantly reediting a file to put in new requests, here is a shell script that lets you test out one request at a time:

```
# nrtest -- a shell script for testing nroff
sed 'i\
'$2 $1 | nroff | sed 20q
```

This script inserts its second argument at the beginning of the file named by the first argument. The output is filtered through **sed** so that we get just the first 20 lines, about a screenful.

Let's put the script in a file called **nrtest** and use it to see the effect of adding an argument to the **.ce** request.

```
$ nrtest speachify .ce4
                  Eighty-seven years before the present time,
                            a group of men
                          who could be termed,
         with some degree of appropriateness,  the  ancestors  of us here
         today and of this distinguished nation, assembled themselves with
         the  intention,  a  great  intention,  we  might  add,  and  one that
         proved successful,  of modifying for the  purpose  of  improvement
         our already noble and notable nation.
$
```

Now 4 lines are centered! (**nroff** will accept either **.ce4** or **.ce 4**; we use the first form so that our shell script will take the whole request as **$2**.)

Here is another example:

```
$ nrtest speachify .1130
   Eighty-seven years before the
       present time, a group of men
    who could be termed, with some
   degree of appropriateness, the
     ancestors of us here today and
     of this distinguished nation,
     assembled themselves with the
     intention, a great intention,
         we might add, and one that
           proved successful, of
       modifying for the purpose
```

```
of  improvement  our  already
noble  and  notable  nation.
```

This time we used a **.11** (line length) request to produce a line 30 characters long.

Not all **nroff** requests produce discernible results when inserted at the front of a file, but Table 11-3 consists of some that do. We've included a brief description, but it's fun to try them out yourself. Try, for instance, a **.tra#e$o%** request.

Table 11–3. Some *nroff* Requests

`.ce N`	center next N lines
`.in N`	indent text N spaces
`.hy N`	turn on auto-hyphenation for N >= 1, off for N = 0.
`.ll N`	set line length to N characters
`.ls N`	set line spacing to N (2 = double-spaced, etc.)
`.na`	don't justify right margin ("no adjust")
`.nf`	don't fill text
`.sp N`	put in N blank lines
`.ti N`	temporarily (next line) indent N spaces
`.tr abcd..`	replace "a" with "b", "c" with "d", etc.

The space between request and argument can be omitted.

Let's move on to the topic of macros now.

Level 2: *mm* Macros

The term "macro" signifies a command or instruction that is constructed from several more basic units. **nroff** lets you construct you own macros from the basic instructions. The chief tool here is the **.de** request that lets you define a single symbolism to represent several requests. For example,

```
.de PP
.sp
.ti5
..
```

defines **.PP** to mean space one line and temporarily indent 5 spaces. The **..** marks the definition's end.

You could study **nroff** assiduously and create your own set of macros, but most users use a "macro package." This is just a set of predefined macros designed to handle common situations, such as creating paragraphs, making footnotes, and the like. System V features the **mm** (for "memorandum macros") package.

Macros are used the same way ordinary requests are. Here, for example, we will insert the **mm** macros for a title (**.TL**) and for an indented paragraph (**.P 1**):

```
.TL
A Stirring Speech
.P 1
Eighty-seven years before the present time,
a group of men
who could be termed,
with some degree of appropriateness, the ancestors of us here
today and of this distinguished nation, assembled
themselves with the intention, a great intention, we might
add, and one that proved successful,
of modifying for the purpose of improvement our already noble and
notable nation.
```

Now that we have the instructions in place, how do we get them noticed? We have a choice. We can invoke **mm** as an option in two ways:

```
nroff -mm speachify
```

or

```
nroff -cm speachify
```

The second version uses a precompacted version of the macros that runs faster and is the one that usually should be used. In fact, this second option is used often enough that System V allows us simply to type

```
mm speachify
```

to produce the same effect.

(These are the corresponding **troff** commands:

```
troff -mm speachify
troff -cm speachify
mmt speachify )
```

With either evocation of **nroff**, we get this output:

A Stirring Speech

Eighty-seven years before the present time, a group of men
who could be termed, with some degree of appropriateness, the
ancestors of us here today and of this distinguished
nation, assembled themselves with the intention, a great
intention, we might add, and one that proved successful, of
modifying for the purpose of improvement our already noble and
notable nation.

(Here we've suppressed the large number of blank lines following the text.)

As you can see, the **.TL** macro centered the title and surrounded it with blank lines. The **.P 1** macro produced a paragraph with the first line indented five spaces. Notice that the right margin is not justified. This is the default choice for **nroff -mm; troff -mm** uses justified margins as a default.

There you have the essence of **mm**: embed appropriate macros in the text. The next step would be to learn **mm**'s 87 macros. That's a bit more than we care to cover here. Instead, we will concentrate on some of the more common examples. If you need to learn more, Volume III of the System V documentation devotes nearly 200 pages to **nroff** and **troff**, with 80 of these pages specifically about **mm**. Meanwhile, you can find some typical **mm** macros in Table 11-4. We will give examples using most of them.

Table 11–4 Some *mm* Macros

Macro	Meaning and Typical Usage
.AF	Define company name for memos; place company name in double quotes on same line. ("Bell Laboratories" is the default.)
.AL	Start an automatically numbered list; used with **.LI** and **.LE**
.AU	Author's name; place on same line and enclose in quotes
.DL	Start a list marked with dashes; used with **.LI** and **.LE**
.FC	Formal close; ends a letter with "Yours very truly,"
.FE	Marks the end of a footnote.
.FS c	Marks the start of a footnote, with c being the footnote marker.
.I	Italics (underlined in **nroff)**
.LE	List end; marks the end of a list. (See **.AL, .DL.**)
.LI	List item; text starting next line is the next item in a list. (See **.AL, .DL.**)
.MT N	Specifies memo type. N=0 gives memo form. N values of 1, 2, and 3 add

various labels. N=4 yields a released-paper form, and N=5 results in a letter style.

.ND   New date: Place desired date on same line in quotes.

.P N   Start paragraph. N=0 is a block paragraph, N=1 is an indented paragraph (5 spaces by default)

.R   Roman font

.SG   Adds a signature line, using the name from **.AU**

.TL   Uses the next line for a title

Making a Letter

Let's use some macros to put together a simple letter. Here is the original text:

```
.AU "Bart Bargletoot"
.MT 5
.P 0
Dear Flossie,
.sp
.P 1
Well here I am in the Big City!
Cousin Bert tells me they have upward of 40,000 folks here at
Great Forks, and that's not counting those outside the city
limits!
The hustle and bustle is quite amazing, but I'm adjusting to it.
Though it does seem strange to walk by people without either
giving a ''howdy.''
.P 1
I'm missing you, of course. You would have loved the eating
place Bert and Bette (that's Bert's fiancee) tolk me to last
night.
It was all-you-can eat ribs'n'chicken with three hotnesses
of barbeque sauce to choose from.
I was the only one there with enough sense to use one of their
big trays for piling up the vittles.
The others put food on little dishes, then put the dishes on the
tray —seems kinda dainty to me.
.P 1
Well, give my love to Geezer, Flopnose, and TS.
I'll see you
soon.
.FC
.SG
```

We show the output in Fig. 11-1. As you look at the input and output versions, please note these points. First, unlike most **nroff** commands, the **.AU** command has its associated text on the same line. One reason for this is that the author's name doesn't necessarily appear in the output text in the same position it does in the input text. In this case, for example, the name doesn't appear until the end of the letter, as requested by the **.SG** signature macro there. Second, the letter wound up dated. That is one effect of the **.MT 5** macro. Since UNIX systems keep track of the date, we don't have to supply that information. Third, note that we can mix in regular **nroff** requests like **.sp** with the **mm** macros. Mixing requests with macros can create disaster, but some requests (including all are examples aside from **.in, .hy,** and **.na**) are safe to use. Again, Volume II of the System V documentation gives the details. Fourth, note how we started each sentence on a new line. It is not necessary to do this, but it makes it simpler to add or remove sentences later, particularly if you use a line editor such as **ed** or **ex**.

```
                                                           May 17, 1984

Dear Flossie,

    Well here I am in the Big City! Cousin Bert tells me they
have upward of 40,000 folks here at Great Forks, and that's not
counting those outside the city limits! The hustle and bustle is
quite amazing, but I'm adjusting to it. Though it does seem
strange to walk by people without either giving a "howdy."

    I'm missing you, of course. You would have loved the
eating place Bert and Bette (that's Bert's fiancee) took me to
last night. It was all-you-can eat ribs'n'chicken with three
hotnesses of barbeque sauce to choose from. I was the only one
there with enough sense to use one of their big trays for piling
up the vittles. The others put food on little dishes, then put
the dishes on the tray—seems kinda dainty to me.

    Well, give my love to Geezer, Flopnose, and TS. I'll see you
soon.

                          Yours very truly,

                          Bart Bargletoot
```

Fig. 11-1

It's not too difficult to produce a letter if you are happy with the form these **mm** macros produce. We should point out that we have just used default values for many things. These can be overridden. If, for example, you want to use a different date, a different closing, a different indentation, a different line spacing, you can. But that takes us deeper into **mm** than we care to go. Instead, let's look at another common task, creating a memo.

A Simple Memo

There are several macros specifically designed to go at the beginning of a memo. The ones we will use are **.TL**, **.AF**, **.AU**, and **.MT**. An important point is that, if present, these macros must be used in this order. (Thus, in our letter, we put **.AU** before **.MT**). We will use **.FS** and **.FE** to create a footnote. Also we will use **.DL**, **.LI**, and **.LE** to create a dashed list. First, we create the input text.

```
.ND "May 19, 2832"
.TL
Calashian Hats
.AF "Galactic Express Travel"
.AU "Gauis Cho McLeod"
.MT 0
.P 0
Tourists are choosing to visit the planet Calash*
.FS *
System 2301.234.08 of the Canopus Sector
.FE
in rapidly increasing numbers, drawn, no doubt, by the colorful
and exotic civilization that the Calashian settlers have created.
Some visitors, unfortunately, have experienced difficulties
because of their ignorance of local customs.
Please advise our clients
.I
not to wear hats
.R
while visiting Calash.
This may seem odd in view of the fact that Calash is renown for
the variety of hats worn by the inhabitants.
Bear in mind, however, that the Calashians have evolved an
elaborate hat code; to wear a hat is to make a statement about
oneself.
Here are some examples:
```

```
.DL
.LI
An orange billed cap with a yellow plume indicates the wearer to
be in a snappish mood and seeking like company.
.LI
A dark blue conical hat with mauve braiding indicates a wearer
willing to debate philosophical matters with anyone who will
provide him wine.
.LI
A purple sombrero with green trim indicates a wearer of vast
wealth looking for an evening of amiable frivolity.
.LE
.P 0
The point here is that by wearing a hat, a tourist unknowingly
creates unforeseeable attitudes towards himself.
One recent visitor, for instance, was soundly slapped with a
yellow fish by several young ladies before getting rid of his
hat.
.P 0
Please impress upon all our Calash-bound clients the importance
of this matter.
.SG
```

The **.MT** 0 request causes our text to be arranged in memo format; see Fig. 11-2 for the result.

Note how the memo layout is set up for you. Note, too, how the list procedure works. First we declare the type of list (**.DL**). Then we precede each list item with **.LI**. And we mark the end of the list with **.LE**. If we were to change the **.DL** to **.AL**, then the items would be labelled with the numbers 1, 2, and 3 instead of dashes. Several other list varieties and variations are available.

In creating a footnote, we use **.FS** and **.FE** to mark the bounds of the footnote. We follow the **.FS** with the footnote symbol used in the main text, and this symbol is then used to mark the beginning of the footnote.

The company name comes out in boldface, and the italicized portion (after the **.I**) comes out underlined. This assumes your printer is equipped to do so.

Once you have tried your hand at a few examples like ours, you may wish to burrow into the manual yourself and find what else you can do. Other

Galactic Express Travel

subject: Calashian Hats   date: May 19, 2832

                                           from: Gaius Cho McLeod

Tourists are choosing to visit the planet Calash in rapidly
increasing numbers, drawn, no doubt, by the colorful and exotic
civilization that the Calashian settlers have created. Some
visitors, unfortunately, have experienced difficulties because of
their ignorance of local customs. Please advise our clients not
to wear hats while visiting Calash. This may seem odd in view of
the fact that Calash is renown for the variety of hats worn by
the inhabitants. Bear in mind, however, that the Calashians have
evolved an elaborate hat code; to wear a hat is to make a
statement about oneself. Here are some examples:

—An orange billed cap with a yellow plume indicates the
    wearer to be in a snappish mode and seeking like
    company.

—A dark blue conical hat with mauve braiding indicates a
    wearer willing to debate philosophical matters with
    anyone who will provide him wine.

—A purple sombrero with green trim indicates a wearer of
    vast wealth looking for an evening of amiable
    frivolity.

The point here is that by wearing a hat, a tourist unknowingly
creates unforeseeable attitudes towards himself. One recent
visitor, for instance, was soundly slapped with a yellow fish by
several young ladies before getting rid of his hat.

Please impress upon all our Calash-bound clients the importance
of this matter.

                                           Gaius Cho McLeod

---

 * System 2301.234.08 of the Canopus Sector

Fig. 11-2

features include macros for numbered and unnumbered topic headings and subheadings and macros for abstracts.

Level 3: Naked *nroff*

On this level you are free to use the basic **nroff** requests as you desire. Probably the most profitable way would be to create your own set of macro definitions. However, please note that the **mm** macro package is able to deal with most situations. Most typically, the basic **nroff** requests are used to supplement the macro commands.

We haven't reached the end of the text formatter story yet. UNIX has two more utilities designed to work with **nroff** and **troff**. We will take a brief look at them now.

Formatting Helpmates: *tbl* and *eqn*

Document preparation often involves putting together tables of data, and technical documents often make use of equations. The **tbl** and **eqn** programs use their own instruction set to convert descriptions of tables and equations into **nroff** and **troff** requests. We'll outline how to use them without going into details. Suppose, for example, you are creating a table. You would include the material for the table between the **.TS** (table start) and **.TE** (table end) macros. The enclosed material would include the **tbl** instructions and the data to be used. Before and after this material would be the normal text of the document. Since **tbl** should act on the table before **nroff** reaches it, you could use a command like this, assuming the document is in the file **Report:**

```
tbl Report | nroff -mm
```

Or you can use the −**t** option of **mm:**

```
mm -t Report
```

The **eqn** program is used similarly.

Conclusion

This chapter has taken us further into the world of text processing and of filters. We have seen how **cut, paste, sed,** and **nroff** each stake out its own territory in the business of modifying and shaping text. Because these programs can be linked to each other and to other programs using pipes, they become tools that can be combined in a multitude of ways to accomplish a multitude of tasks. Suppose, for instance, you want to paste together two files of names and that you want the names to be separated by three spaces. **paste** won't do that, for it only places one character between joined lines. But you can pipe **cut**'s output to **sed** and have **sed** replace that one tab with three spaces, and the job is done.

So when you have a job to do, first ask yourself if there is a UNIX command that will do it. If the answer is no, then ask if there is a combination of UNIX commands that will do the task. The more you learn about UNIX, the more likely it is that your answer will be yes.

Review Questions

1. Devise commands to do the following in the file **firdata:**
   a. Print columns 4 and 22.

      b. Print columns 4 through 22.

      c. Set the field delimiter to an asterisk and print fields 2 through 4 and 6 through 8.

  2. Devise a **sed** command to do each of the following tasks to the file **essay:**

      a. Replace every instance of Edgar with Elgar.

      b. Print lines 10 through 15 of the file.

      c. Put every occurrence of San Francisco Treat in double quotes.

      d. Delete lines containing the sequences ude or aked.

Answers

  1. a. `cut -c4,22 firdata`

     b. `cut -c4-22 firdata`

     c. `cut -d"*" -f2-4,6-8 firdata`

  2. a. `sed 's/Edgar/Elgar/g' essay`

     b. `sed -n '10,15p' essay`

     c. `sed 's/San Francisco Treat/"&"/g' essay`

     d. `sed '/ude/d`
```
        /aked/d ' essay
```

Exercise at the Terminal

Copy our memo text (or make up your own) and find the effect of changing **.MT 0** to **.MT 1**, **.MT 2**, and so on.

12

Information Processing: *grep, find,* and *Shell Scripts*

In this chapter, you will find:

- Graphics Utilities
  - Using *graph* and *plot*
- Where Do We Go From Here?
- Review Questions
- Exercises at the Terminal

12   INFORMATION PROCESSING: *grep, find,* and *Shell Scripts*

In the cool confines of the Programming Division of Dray Conglomerate, Delia Delphond took off her softball cap and shook her auburn curls loose. She had just finished updating the statistical files for her softball team, the Byte Boomers. Now she copied the files for the other teams in the company league; it was her turn to put together the league stats. First, she used **sort** to put together a league masterfile of batting statistics arranged alphabetically by player. Then, using the field-specification option of **sort,** she created a file listing the players in descending order of batting averages. Next, again using the field-specification **sort** option and piping it through **sed 10q,** she created files giving the top ten players for each of several categories: home runs, RBIs, hits, runs, triples, doubles, walks, stolen bases, and strike-outs. Curious about how her team was doing, she used **grep** to find Byte Boomers on the top ten lists. Good, they were making a fine showing. The name D. Delphond, in particular, appeared in several lists. Smiling, she turned her attention to the team statistics. Using **awk,** she had UNIX sum up the "at bats," the hits, etc., for each team and calculate the team averages. Then, she went on to handle the pitching stats.

Delia enjoyed going through the statistics, but she didn't care much for her next task, preparing a press summary for the company paper, *Draybits.* She'd much rather bat than write. However, with the help of a UNIX editor, she put together a blurb of rather irregular line length. She ran the file through **spell** and corrected the errors that had shown up—words such as "avarage" and "notewordy." Next she invoked a shell script of hers that first sent the file through **nroff** to tidy it up and, then, forwarded the result through **mail** to the *Draybit's* newspaper editor.

She leaned back in her chair and relaxed for a few moments. Not for too long, however, for she had her regular work to do, too. Besides being a nifty shortstop, Delia was a prolific Pascal programmer (a ppp, for short). She had scattered her program files through several subdirectories, and now, she decided to gather them together in one place. She created a directory for that purpose and then set up a **find** command that would locate all her files whose names ended in **.p** and move them to the new directory.

Delia checked the time (using **date,** of course). It was time for her next project, the long-awaited salary raise! She put her cap back on at a jaunty angle, picked up the analysis she had prepared using the UNIX system, and set off for the President's office; Dray wouldn't have a chance.

* * * *

Introduction

There is more to be said of UNIX than can be squeezed into a book this size. So far, we have concentrated on the more basic operations. Now we will turn to a few UNIX commands and utilities that take you beyond the basics. Many of them are really useful only when you deal with large numbers of files and directories. (Both "commands" and "utilities" are programs run by UNIX; we are using the word "utility" to indicate a program more elaborate than a "command.") We will describe some of the simpler examples, such as **grep,** in fair detail. Others, such as the powerful **awk,** are rather extensive in scope and rules, and we will give them just a brief introduction.

Finding Stuff: *grep* and *find*

These commands are useful when you have to look through several files or directories to find a particular file entry or file. The **grep** command lets you find which files contain a particular word, name, phrase, etc. The **find** command lets you find files that satisfy some criterion of yours (having a certain name, not used for two months, having a certain suffix, etc.) and, then, have something done to those files (print the names, move them to another directory, remove them, etc.). We introduced **grep** in Chapter 7; now let's take a more complete look.

File Searching: *grep*

Sometimes, through necessity or curiosity, you may want to search through one or more files for some form of information. For example, you may want to know which of several letter files contain references to the Wapoo Fruit Company. Or you may have a set of files constituting a large C program and you want to know which ones use a certain function. Let's look at a simpler example using just one file. On most systems, there is a file called **/etc/passwd** that contains information about the system users. (See the following box.) Suppose you want to find out more about someone using the login name of "physh" and your system does not have the **finger** command. Then, you can have the **/etc/passwd** file searched for the word "physh" and the line(s) containing that word will be printed out. To do this, give the command:

```
grep physh /etc/passwd
```

The response might look like this:

```
physh:xMTyUrR:Ø1:1Ø:Jon Foreman:/usr/physh:/bin/sh
```

This line from the **/etc/passwd** file is interpreted in the following box; the important point is that the pattern of the command was:

```
grep pattern filename
```

Thus, the basic manner of using **grep** is pretty simple. On the other hand, the following explanation will be a little lengthy. That's because we will describe some additional features of **grep** that you may want to use.

The */etc/passwd* File

The UNIX system has to keep track of who is allowed to use the system, of login names, group memberships, passwords, and user identification numbers. UNIX may want to know your phone number and, on multiple shell systems, which shell you use. All this information is kept in the */etc/passwd* file. Let's look at the sample line we used in the section on **grep** and see how such a file can be set up.

```
physh:xMTyUrR:2Ø1:1Ø:Jon Foreman:/usr/physh:/bin/sh
```

The line is broken up into seven "fields," with each separated from the adjoining fields by a colon (:). (We will discuss fields again when we revisit **sort.**)

1. The first field contains the user's login name; (physh).
2. The second field contains the user's password; (xMTyUrR).
   Don't panic—the password is encrypted into a secret code.
3. The third field contains the user identification number; (2Ø1).
4. Next comes the user's group number; (1Ø).
5. Then, the personal information; (Jon Foreman).
6. The sixth field contains the user's home directory; (/usr/physh).
7. The final field gives the user's login shell; (sh).

> If a user has not set up a password, the field will be empty, but the colons will be left as place keepers; thus the line would look like this:
>
> ```
> luscious::1313:24:Lucy, ext. 777:/usr/luscious:/bin/csh
> ```

More generally, **grep** is used this way:

```
grep option(s) pattern filename(s)
```

Let's look at each part of this form, starting with "filename(s)" and working backwards.

Filenames

You can give one filename or several for **grep** to search. When you use more than one filename, **grep** will tag each line that it finds with the name of the file that the line was in. For example, if we type:

```
grep dentistry boyd carson douglass ernst
```

the response might look like this:

```
boyd:without which the undoubted charms of dentistry would be
boyd:unless, of course, you are speaking of dentistry.
boyd: I would rather suffer the agonies of amateur dentistry
douglass:in dentistry. Aside from that, he was in no way
```

Here, three lines containing "dentistry" were found in the **boyd** file, while one was found in the **douglass** file, and none were found in the remaining files.

You can use "wild-card" substitution for filenames when using **grep.** Consider the commands:

```
grep reverse *.c
```

and

```
grep Renaldo /usr/phoebe/*
```

The first would search for "reverse" in all files ending in **.c** (i.e., C-language files) in your current working directory. The second would search all the files in the **/usr/phoebe** directory for "Renaldo."

Patterns

So far, we have used single words for the pattern. In general, the pattern can be a "string" or, else, a limited form of "regular expression." A "string" is just a sequence of ordinary characters. All the examples that we have used so far for **grep** patterns are strings. A "regular expression," on the other hand, may include characters with special meanings. For example, we will see that **grep** recognizes the pattern "b.g" as representing any three-character string beginning in "b" and ending in "g." The pattern "b.g" is a regular expression, and the "." in it is a special character playing much the same role that a "?" does when used in a shell command. Like the shell, **grep** recognizes certain regular expressions for patterns, but the rules it uses, as we shall see later, are not the ones used by the shell.

Strings merit a closer look since most of the time that you use **grep,** you probably will use strings. If the string is just a single word, you can use it just as in the previous examples. But, what if you want to find something like "Los Angeles"? The command:

```
grep Los Angeles cityfile
```

will not work, for **grep** will think that the pattern sought was "Los" and that "Angeles" was the name of the first file to be searched. To avoid this confusion, you can place the pattern in single quotes; that is, use:

```
grep 'Los Angeles' cityfile
```

and all will be well.

When **grep** looks for a string, it doesn't care whether it finds the string by itself or embedded in a larger string. For example, the command:

```
grep man moon
```

will not only find the word "man" in the **moon** file, it will also find such words as "woman," "mantra," and "command," for they all contain the string "man" within them. Some implementations of **grep** have a **-w** option (whole words only) that picks up only lines that contain the pattern as an isolated word. If your system lacks that option, you might try putting spaces in the pattern, as in ' man ', but that will fail to pick up lines in which "man" is the first or last word and, also, those constructions such as "man." or "man," because these all lack one of the specified spaces. (Remember, a space is a character, too.)

You may run into problems if the pattern *string* you use contains some of the special characters used by UNIX (e.g., * or ?) or by **grep** regular expressions (e.g., . or [).

Sometimes, it is sufficient to enclose the pattern in single quotes. For instance, the command:

```
grep * froggy
```

will confuse UNIX, but the command:

```
grep '*' froggy
```

will cause the system to search the **froggy** file for lines containing the symbol "*".

You also can use the backslash (\) to turn off the special meaning of a character, as we described in Chapter 9:

```
grep \? dinnerreview
```

Forms of Regular Expression

Now we can take a look at the forms of regular expressions recognized by **grep.** Basically, these forms (with some omissions) are the same as those used by **ed** and **ex.** Here's a rundown of the most important rules:

1. A period (.) in a pattern stands for any one character; it plays the same role in **grep** patterns as the ? does in UNIX shell wild-card substitution. Thus, the command:

```
grep 'c.n' horply
```

will find such strings as "can" and "con," but not "coin," since "coin" has two characters, not one, between the "c" and the "n."

2. A string in brackets (i.e., enclosed in []) matches any one character in the string. (This is the same as the UNIX shell's use of brackets.) Thus, the pattern:

```
[wW]easel
```

will match "weasel," or "Weasel," but not "wWeasel." You can use a hyphen to indicate a range of characters. For example,

```
[m-t]ap
```

would match the strings "map," "nap," etc., up to "tap."

3. Preceding a string in brackets with a caret (^) causes **grep** to make matches using the characters *not* in the list. For instance,

```
[^m-t]ap
```

would match strings like "cap" and "zap" but not strings like "map" and "tap."

4. A regular expression preceded by a ^ will match only those lines that begin with the expression. Thus, the command:

```
grep '^James' slist
```

would find the first of the following lines and would skip the second:

James Watt
Henry James

5. Similarly, a regular expression followed by a $ will match only those lines with the expression at the end. Therefore,

```
grep 'James$' slist
```

would find "Henry James" but not "James Watt" in the preceding example.

You can use both the ^ and the $ if you want to find only lines that match the pattern in their entirety. For example, the command:

```
grep '^The King of Red Gulch$' oddfile
```

would find the line

"The King of Red Gulch"

and skip over the line:

"The King of Red Gulch sauntered over to Doc Buzzard's table."

6. A backslash (∖) followed by any character other than a digit or parentheses matches that character, turning off any special meaning that character might have. For instance, suppose you wanted to search a file for mentions of FORTRAN files, which have names ending in ".f". You can type:

```
grep '\.f' forttext
```

If you omitted the ∖, **grep** would interpret the period as described in rule 1.

Options

Grep options are indicated in the usual way, using flags. Here are some that you may find useful:

1. The **-n** option precedes each found line with its line number in the file. Here is a sample command and the response:

```
grep -n FORTRAN Johnletter

237: wanted to search a file for mentions of FORTRAN files,
```

2. The −**v** option causes **grep** to print those lines that *don't* match.
3. The −**c** option prints a count of the number of lines that match, but doesn't print the lines themselves. If you are searching several files, it prints the name of each file followed by the number of matching lines in that file.

Summary: grep—search a file for a pattern		
name	**options**	**arguments**
grep	[-n, -c, -v]	pattern [filename(s)]

Description: **grep** searches the named files for lines containing the given pattern and then prints out the matching lines. If more than one file is searched, the name of the file containing each line is printed, too. If no filename is given, **grep** looks to the standard input; thus, **grep** can be used with pipes. The pattern can be a single string, or it can be a limited form of regular expression as described in the text. A pattern containing spaces or special characters such as "*" should be set off by single quotes. Normally, **grep** will match any string containing the pattern; for example, "hose" matches "whose."

Options: −n   Precedes each matching line with its line number.
             −c   Prints only a count of matching lines.
             −v   All lines but those matching are printed.

Example: **grep −n hop peter bugs**
             This command searches the files **peter** and **bugs** for occurrences of the string "hop." It prints the matching lines along with line numbers.

Finding Files: *find*

The **find** command searches for files that meet some criterion. You can search for files that have a certain name or are a certain size or files not accessed for a certain number of days or having a certain number of links; and this is just a partial list. Once the files are found, you can have the pathnames printed out, you can have the files themselves printed or removed or otherwise acted upon. The search will begin at the directory you specify and will then descend down all its subdirectories and all their subdirectories, etc., leaving no nook or cranny unexplored (except, of course, for forbidden nooks and crannies like those in some English muffins). A branching search such as this is termed "recursive."

It would be difficult to fit the capabilities of the **find** command into the usual format for commands, so **find** has its own unique structure. The basic sequence goes like this:

find directory pathname   search criterion   action

The "directory pathname" is the pathname of the directory that will be recursively searched (all subdirectories, etc.) for the desired files. The "search criterion" identifies the files that are sought. The "action" tells what to do with the files once they are found. The criterion and the action

351

are identified with special flags, which we will discuss soon. Here is an example of a **find** command:

```
find /usr -name calendar -print
```

The directory pathname is **/usr,** so the search starts here and proceeds recursively through all directories branching off this directory. The search criterion is **-name calendar;** this means UNIX will search for files bearing the name **calendar.** Finally, the action is **-print,** meaning that each time a file is found that meets the search criterion, its pathname is displayed. The output might look like this:

```
/usr/flossie/calendar
/usr/nerkie/calendar
/usr/sluggo/calendar
```

This would tell us which users were using UNIX's **calendar** feature.

Naming the directory is straightforward, but the search criterion and action sections need further discussion.

Search Criteria

Find recognizes several search criteria. They take the form of an identifying flag word (a hyphen joined to a word, e.g., −**name**) followed by a space and a word or number. Here are the more common ones.

A. Finding a file by name:

Use the −**name** flag followed by the desired name. The name can be a simple word as in the preceding example, or it can use the shell wild-card substitutions: **[ ], ?,** and ***.** If you use these special symbols, place the name in single quotes. Here are some examples of acceptable uses.

Criterion	Files sought
-name nail	Files named "nail."
-name '*.c'	All files whose names end in ".c".
-name '*.?'	All files for which the next to last character is a period.

B. Finding a file by last access:

Use the −**atime** flag followed by the number of days since the file was last accessed. Plus and minus signs may be used to indicate greater than or less than.

Criterion	Files sought
`-atime 7`	Files last accessed exactly 7 days ago.
`-atime -14`	Files accessed more recently than 14 days ago.

    C. Finding a file by last modification:

Use the −**mtime** flag followed by the number of days since the file was last modified. Plus and minus signs may be used to indicate greater than or less than.

Criterion	Files sought
`-mtime 20`	Files last modified 20 days ago.
`-mtime +45`	Files modified more than 45 days ago.

    D. Finding files modified more recently than a given file.

Use the −**newer** flag followed by the name of a file.

Criterion	Files sought
`-newer slopware`	Files modified more recently than **slopware** was.

Actions

You have three flag options to choose from for the action section of the command: −**print,** −**exec,** and −**ok.**

    A. The −**print** option.

This option prints the pathname for every file found that matches the criterion.

    B. The −**exec** option.

This option lets you give a command to be applied to the found files. The command should follow the flag and should be terminated with a space, a backslash, and then a semicolon. A set of braces, i.e., { }, can be used to represent the name of the files found. For example,

```
find . -atime + 100 -exec rm {} \;
```

This command would find and remove all files in your current directory (and its offshoots) that haven't been used in over 100 days.

    C. The **ok** option.

This option is just like the −**exec** option except that it asks for your "ok" for each file found before it executes the command. For instance, if you gave the command:

```
find . -atime +100 -ok rm {} \;
```

and the system found a file called **first.prog** that satisfied the criterion, the system would then query you:

```
<rm . . . ./first.prog> ?
```

If you reply with the letter **y**, the command is executed; otherwise it is not. A command along the lines of this example is a handy aid in cleaning up your file systems.

For Advanced Users: More Complex Forms of *find*

You can expand each of the basic sections of the **find** command to pinpoint more exactly what you want done.

The Directory Pathname

You actually can give a list of directories to be searched. For instance,

```
find /usr/lester /usr/festus . -name '*.p' -print
```

would search lester's home directory, festus's home directory, and your current directory for files whose names end in ".p" and would then print the pathnames of those files.

The Search Criterion

The search criteria we have given are called "primaries." You can combine them or act upon them in the following three basic ways.
   1. The ! operator negates a primary. It should precede the primary and would be isolated by spaces on either side.

Criterion	*Meaning*
`-newer fops`	Files revised more recently than **fops.**
`! -newer fops`	Files not revised more recently than **fops.**
`! -name '*.f'`	Files whose names do not end in ".f".

2. Listing two or more criteria in a row causes **find** to seek those files that simultaneously satisfy all criteria.

Criteria	*Meaning*
`-name calendar -size +2`	Files named **calendar** having a size greater than 2 blocks.
`-size +2 -size -6`	Files whose size is greater than 2 blocks and less than 6 blocks.

3. Separating two criteria with a **-o** flag (a space on either side) causes **find** to search for files that satisfy one or the other criterion.

Criteria	*Meaning*
`-name turk -o -name terk`	Files named **turk** or **terk.**
`-atime +7 -o -mtime +14`	Files that haven't been accessed within 7 days or modified within 14 days.

Summary: `find`—find designated files and act upon them

name	arguments
`find`	directory pathname(s) search criteria action(s)

Description: **find** searches the named directories recursively for files matching the specified criteria. It then performs the specified actions on the files.

Search Criteria: In the following, "n" represents a decimal integer. It can be given with or without a sign. With no sign, it means n exactly; + n means greater than n; −n means less than n.

−name filename	Files named "filename."
−size n	Files of size n blocks (one block is 512 bytes).
−links n	Files with n links.
−atime n	Files accessed n days ago.
−mtime n	Files modified n days ago.
−newer filename	Files modified more recently than the file "filename."

Actions:	**−print**
	Print the pathnames of the found files.
	−exec command \ ;
	Executes the given command upon finding a file; the symbolism { } represents the found file.
	−ok command \ ;
	Same as **−exec,** except your approval is requested before each execution; reply with a **y** to have the command executed.
Note:	There is a procedure for combining criteria. A ! (isolated by spaces) before a criterion negates it. Giving two or more criteria means that all must be satisfied by the file. Separating two criteria by an **−o** (isolated by spaces) means one *or* the other. Escaped parentheses, i.e., \ (and \ ), can be used to clarify groupings.
Examples:	**find . −name boobtube −print**
	This command searches through the current directory and all its offshoots for a file named **boobtube.**
	find . −atime +30 −atime −60 −exec mv { } ./old \ ;
	This command finds all files in the current working directory (and its offshoots, and their offshoots, etc.) that have been used within 60 days but not within 30 days. These files then are moved to the directory **./old.**

Revisiting Sort: Using Fields

When we discussed **sort** in Chapter 9, we saw that it sorted files on the basis of the beginning of each line. This is useful, for example, if you have a mailing list in which people are listed last name first. But you might want to sort that same list on the basis of city or state. You *can* do that, too, providing you have set up your file accordingly. The key is to break up each line into "fields." As will be shown, you can instruct **sort** to look only at certain fields when sorting. Thus, you can set up the file so that last names are in the first field and states in, way, the sixth field. Having the **file** sorted by the sixth field would then sort the file by state.

Fields and Field Separators

What makes up a field? That is a matter of definition. If you don't specify differently, fields are nonempty, nonblank strings separated by blanks. For example, in the line:

line	McHaggis,	Jamie	33883	Sea	Drive,	Tuna	Gap,	California	94889
Field number	1	2	3	4	5	6	7	8	9

Fields in a line.

the first field is "McHaggis," the fifth field is "Drive," and the last field is "94888." For some types of files, the blank is a fine field separator, but not for a mailing list. The reason is that a metropolis such as "Hogback" uses one field but a town like "San Luis Obispo" uses three fields, and this would throw off the numbering of the field containing the state.

line	Blugston,	Eve	13	Jowl	Drive,	Hogback,	AR	72777		
Field Number	1	2	3	4	5	6	7	8		
Field Number	1	2	3	4	5	6	7	8	9	10
line	Blugstone,	Frappo	896	Jewel	Road,	San	Luis	Obispo,	CA	93401

A problem with using a blank as a field separator.

To get around this sort of problem, you can choose your own field separator. A common choice is the colon. You could make a file entry look like this:

```
McHaggis:Jamie::33883 Sea Drive:Tuna Gap:California:94888
```

In this case, the first field is the last name, the second field is the first name, the third field (empty, in this case) is the middle name or initial, the fourth field is the street address, the fifth field is the city, etc. Note that a field now can have spaces within it, as the fourth field does, or it can be completely empty, as is the third field. The value of the empty field is that it is a

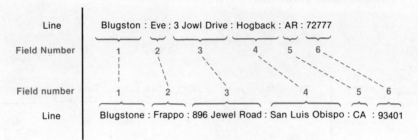

Using a colon as a field separator.

place keeper; even though a middle name is missing in this case, the address is still in the fourth field. Also notice that we haven't left any spaces at the beginning or ends of the fields. This, as you may remember, is because a space itself is a character. Therefore ": Wickley :" is a field containing 9 characters (the first and last being the space character), and it would be sorted differently from the 7-character field ":Wickley:". The **-b** option of **sort** would ignore leading blanks but not the trailing blanks in a field, so it is simpler to just leave out extra blanks in the first place. Of course, you also could carefully use the exact same number of blanks for each entry.

Using Fields With *sort*

But, how does **sort** know to use a colon instead of a blank as a field separator? You have to use the **-t** option to tell it so. When you use this option, you follow the **-t** with the symbol that is to be the field separator; the symbol follows the "t" directly with no spaces. Thus, to use the colon as a separator, you would use **-t:** as the flag.

Next, how do you tell **sort** which fields to use? You include a flag consisting of a plus sign followed by a number. This tells **sort** how many fields to *skip*. For example, the command:

```
sort -t: +4 maillist
```

tells **sort** to recognize colons as a field separator and to skip 4 fields before comparing lines in the **maillist** file. This means the comparison will start with the fifth field, which, in the preceding address example, corresponds to the city, and will proceed to the end of the line.

Suppose that when you run the previous command, two lines are identical from the fifth field on to the end of the line. How does **sort** decide to arrange these two lines? It looks at the complete line and sorts them on that basis. A definite example will help clarify this and later points, so let's suppose that **maillist** contains these entries:

```
Morgan:Joe::315 Second Street:Riesenstadt:Ca:94707
Vegetable:Joe:Fritz:1002 Market Pl.:Riesenstadt:CA:94707
Morgan:Joe::315 Second Street:Redville:OH:40817
Morgan:Joe::315 Second Street:Hot'n'wet:TX:72727
Antibody:Aristotle:Asis:26 Furtz Way:Redville:OH:40822
Zircon:Bilbo:Nagy:1313 Ratgut Blvd.:Hot'n'wet:TX:72702
```

Then, the result of **sort −t + 4 maillist** is:

```
Zircon:Bilbo:Nagy:1313 Ratgut Blvd.:Hot'n'wet:TX:72702
Morgan:Joe::315 Second Street:Hot'n'wet:TX:72727
Morgan:Joe::315 Second Street:Redville:OH:40817
Antibody:Aristotle:Asis:26 Furtz Way:Redville:OH:40822
Morgan:Joe::315 Second Street:Riesenstadt:CA:94707
Vegetable:Joe:Fritz:1002 Market Pl.:Riesenstadt:CA:94707
```

The last two lines in the sorted list have the same city, state, and zip code, so the tie was decided by looking at the rest of the line and, alphabetically, "Morgan" precedes "Vegetable."

You also can tell **sort** where to stop the comparison by using a flag consisting of a minus sign followed by a number. This tells **sort** to stop at the end of the numbered field. Thus,

```
sort -t: +4 -6 maillist
```

would mean to sort the file on the basis of the fifth and sixth fields. If two or more lines have identical fifth and sixth fields, they are then sorted further on the basis of the whole line as before.

Multiple Fields

With **sort,** you can create your own sorting scheme by using multiple fields. **Sort** will first sort the file using the first field pattern you give it. Then, within a block of lines that are identical for those fields, it will sort further using the next field pattern you give. For example, consider the command:

```
sort -t: +0 -1 +5 maillist
```

The first field pattern is "**+0 −1**", which is simply the first field; in this case, the last name. So, first, the file is sorted by last name. The second field pattern is "**+5**", which means field 6 to the end of the line. (Whenever a "plus" field option is given without a "minus" field option, the pattern comparison goes to the end of the line.) In this case, the second pattern corresponds to state and zip code. Thus, all those address lines containing the same last name are further sorted on the basis of state and zip code. This command would yield:

```
Antibody:Aristotle:Asis:26 Furtz Way:Redville:OH:40822
Morgan:Joe::315 Second Street:Riesenstadt:CA:94707
Morgan:Joe::315 Second Street:Redville:OH:40817
Morgan:Joe::315 Second Street:Hot'n'wet:TX:72727
Vegetable:Joe:Fritz:1002 Market Pl.:Riesenstadt:CA:94707
Zircon:Bilbo:Nagy:1313 Ratgut Blvd.:Hot'n'wet:TX:72702
```

Note how the various Morgans are arranged in order of state, not city.

On the other hand, the command:

```
sort −t: +5 −6 +1 maillist
```

would sort the file first by state. Then, those with the same state would be sorted by field 2 (first name) to the end.

To repeat the main point of this section, when you give a series of field ranges by which to sort, the sorting is done first by the first range and, then, ties are resolved by the next range, and so on. Any remaining ties are resolved by looking at the whole line; **sort** always has a reason for putting lines where it does.

Subdividing a Field

You can refine the sorting process even further. Within each field, you can have **sort** skip over a certain number of characters. This is done by adding a decimal point to the field number and following it with the number of characters to be skipped. For instance,

```
sort +2.3 inventory
```

would skip the first two fields and three characters when sorting the file **inventory;** that is, it would start at the fourth character of the third field.

Flag Options and Fields

Several of the **sort** options we discussed in Chapter 7 can be applied globally or just for certain fields. The choice is controlled by the placement of the option letter. Consider the following two commands:

```
sort -r +4 -5 somefile
sort +4r -5 somefile
```

In the first command, the **r** (reverse) option is invoked universally. Lines will be in reverse order on the basis of field 5, and ties will be resolved by applying reverse order to the whole line. In the second command, the **r** option applies only to the initial ordering using field 5; ties are resolved by applying normal order to the whole line. If a field locator option has any additional options appended, then all global options are overriden for that field. That is, if the instruction is:

```
sort -n +4 -5 +6r somefile
```

then, the −**n** option will apply to field 5 but not to field 7. (Remember, the +6 means skip 6 fields, so the −**r** option will begin with field 7.)

Summary: sort—sorts files

name	options	arguments
sort	[-tc, +n.m, −n.m]	[filename(s)]

Description: **sort** options allow you to sort files on the basis of chosen fields within a line.

Options: −tc
This option sets the field separator to be the character "c".
(A blank is the default.)
+ n.m
sort skips n fields and, then, m characters before beginning comparisons. A "+n" is the same as "+n.0".
−n.m

sort stops comparison after skipping n fields from the beginning plus m characters. A "−n" is the same as "−n.m".

Notes:

The b, d, f, n, and r options can be appended to the field locator flags; this causes the option to apply to just that field. Options appearing before the field locators apply globally except that all global flags are turned off for fields with a local flag.

If multiple fields are specified, sorting is first done by the first field given. Lines having that field identical are then sorted by the second specified field, etc. Remaining ties are resolved by looking at the whole line.

Example: **sort −t: −r +2 −3 +5n sauerbrot**

The field separator is declared to be a colon. The file **sauerbrot** is sorted in reverse order by field 3. Lines having the same field 3 are further sorted numerically by the sixth field to the end of the line; the numerical sorting is not in reverse order. Lines identical to this point are then sorted on the basis of the whole line, again using reverse order.

Of the **sort** options we discussed in Chapter 7, the following can also be used but limited to a field: **b, d, f, n,** and **r.** The method is (as in the preceding discussion) to append the letter to the field number.

Sort is so flexible and has so many options that you should be able to tackle about any sorting problem that comes up except, perhaps, multiple-line records (where the information for each entry is spread over more than one line) and your laundry.

A Quick Peek at *awk*

Suppose you have a file in which the first column is the name of an item, the second column is its price, and the third column is the number sold. You want to add a fourth column giving the money value of the sales, but you don't want to make the calculation yourself. (Why get a computer if you have to do the work yourself?) Can you get UNIX to help? You have a file of names, debts, and last payment dates. You want to create a file containing information about everyone who owes more than $50.00 and hasn't paid in two months. Can UNIX help you? The answer to both questions (surprise!) is yes, providing you know how to use **awk.**

Awk is one of the most interesting of the UNIX utilities, and although we don't have space here to explain it completely, we wanted to give you an idea of what it can do and how it works. In UNIX-speak, **awk** is a "pattern scanning and processing language." By pattern scanning, we mean that **awk** can look through a file for certain patterns. In this, it is like **grep** except that **awk** is both more general (the patterns can be rather sophisticated) and more specific (the patterns can be limited to particular fields within a line). Processing means that once **awk** finds an appropriate line, it can do something with it, e.g., print it, change it, or sum numbers in it.

One important type of use of **awk** is as a file processor. Given a file consisting of three columns of numbers, for example, **awk** can produce a new file consisting of the original three columns plus a fourth that is the arithmetic product of, say, the first two columns. Indeed, **awk** can do many of the same things that the popular Visicalc program can. **Awk** works with text as well as numbers. For example, a simple **awk** program can scan an address list and print out those people who live on a certain street. (**Grep** could do something similar, but **grep** would be fooled by entries containing people with the same name as the desired street.)

Awk was created by Alfred Aho, Brian Kernighan, and Peter Weinberger of Bell Labs. Some suspect a connection between the name of the utility and the names of the authors, but this is at best an awkward conjecture.

There are two methods of using **awk.** One method is to type something in the form:

```
awk program filename
```

where "program" consists of the instructions and "filename" is the name of the file **awk** is to act upon. The second method is to type:

```
awk -f file filename
```

where "file" is the name of the file containing the program instructions. This second method is, perhaps, a bit more difficult, but is much less likely to produce syntax error messages when you use symbols in the program that also have special meaning to the shell. We will confine our examples to the second method.

A program consists of one or more program lines. A program line consists in general of two parts, a pattern and an action; the action is enclosed in braces. Here's one possible line:

```
/rotate/ { print }
```

The pattern is "rotate" (simple string patterns are enclosed in slashes) and the action is "print." Using this, the **awk** program finds lines containing the string "rotate" and prints them; it is equivalent to using **grep rotate** filename.

Learning to use **awk** consists of learning the many possibilities for defining patterns and learning the possible actions. (Actually, the "print" action is not needed here, for a line that matches a pattern is printed automatically if you omit giving any action. Also, if you give an action without a pattern, that action is performed on all lines.)

We won't go into the many pattern-defining options, but we will let you in on the secret of using fields. Fields are defined as they are for **sort;** that is, fields are strings separated by blanks. Again, as in **sort,** you can choose some other character to be a field separator, but the method of doing so is different. (One way is to use the **-F** option followed immediately—no spaces—by the chosen character.) **Awk** has a labeling system for fields; $1 is the first field, $2 is the second field, and so forth. $Ø has a special meaning; it stands for the entire line. These field labels can be used in patterns and actions both. Here are some examples.

Pattern	Meaning
/fish/	Any line containing the string "fish."
$1 ~ /fish/	Any line whose first field contains the string "fish."
$3 ~ /fish/	Any line whose third field contains the string "fish."
$1 !~ /fish/	Any line whose first field does not contain the string "fish."

Action	Meaning
{print $2}	Print only the second field.
{print $4, $2}	Print the contents of the fourth field, then of the second field.
{print $2, $2+$4}	Print the second field, then the sum of the second and fourth fields.
{s=$2+$4;print s}	Add the second and fourth fields, and print the sum.

Note the use of " ~ " and "!" in the patterns. The tilde (~) means the pattern to the right is contained in the field to the left. The ! ~ combination means the pattern to the right is not contained in the field to the left. Also note that the **print** instruction can be used with individual fields and with combinations of fields.

You can do arithmetic in the action parts: + is addition, − is subtraction, * is multiplication, and / is division. You can include more than one action by separating them by a semicolon, as in the preceding example.

Let's take a look at a simple example using some of these ideas. Let's take a file called **sales** that contains six columns of information. The first column is the name of an item, the second column is the selling price of the item, and the next four columns are quarterly sales figures for the item. (This is such a simple example that the prices remain constant for a year.) The file looks like this:

```
carts     29.99  45  13  55   22
corks      0.02  30  20  25   93
doors     49.99  40  15  20   25
geese     15.00   2   8   1  128
nighties  50.00  11  23  15   82
```

We would like to add two more columns: total items sold, and total cash sales. We create a file called, say, **addup** that looks like this:

```
{total=$3+$4+$5+$6, print $0, total, total*$2}
```

This action contains two parts separated by a semicolon. The first part sums the sales and cleverly calls the total "total." The second part prints the original line ($0), followed by the total, and, then, the total*$2, which means "total" times the second column.

The command:

```
awk -f addup sales
```

produces this output:

```
carts     29.99  45  13  55   22  135  4048.65
corks      0.02  30  20  25   93  168  3.36
doors     49.99  40  15  20   25  100  4999
geese     15.00   2   8   1  128  139  2085
nighties  50.00  11  23  15   82  131  6550
```

You could save the output in a file called **sumsales** by using redirection:

```
awk -f addup sales > sumsales
```

This introduction just scratches the surface of **awk.** The on-line manual has a concise summary of **awk,** but the Bell Labs publication, *Awk—a pattern scanning and processing language* (also published in the *Support Tools Guide*), by A. V. Aho, B. W. Kernighan, and P. J. Weinberger, is easier to read and is much more informative. It also is much longer.

More on Shell Scripts

Shell scripts can do much more than what we've shown so far. Indeed, a full description is quite beyond the scope of this book. But we would like to add three more shell script skills to your repertoire. The first skill is making a shell script interactive, letting it and the user indulge in a dialogue. The second skill is creating a loop, letting the same script cycle through several times so that it can process several items. The third skill is creating a script that chooses between different alternatives. You may wish to review the sections in Chapter 9 on shell scripts and shell variables before reading on.

Interactive Shell Scripts: *read*

An interactive program allows two-way communication between the program and the user. We already have a way to have a script speak to the user: just use the **echo** command. The **read** command gives the user the means to talk back. For example, let's put the following shell script in the file **hello:**

```
echo Hello! What\'s your name\?
read NAME
echo Golly, $NAME, it\'s a privilege to meet you.
```

(We used the backslash to turn off the special meanings of the shell metacharacters in the messages.) When the user types a response to the first **echo,** the **read** command assigns that response to the shell variable **NAME.** Then the next **echo** prints out that value again.

```
$ sh hello
What's your name?
Rembrandt da Vinci
Golly, Rembrandt da Vinci, it's a privilege to meet you.
$
```

The **read** statement takes in one line of input. You can use more than one variable after a **read.** In that case, the first variable gets the first word, the second variable the second word, and so on. Any leftover words get assigned to the last variable. Any leftover variables get assigned nothing. In our example, there was just one variable, so all the words were assigned to it. Here is a revised **hello** using more than one variable.

```
echo Hello! What\'s your name\?
read NAME1 NAME2
echo Golly, $NAME1, it\'s a privilege to meet you.
echo Are you any relation to Vicky $NAME2?
```

And here is a sample run:

```
$ sh hello
Hello! What's your name?
Alexander the Great
Golly, Alexander, it's a privilege to meet you
Are you any relation to Vicky the Great?
$
```

As advertised, the first word was assigned to **NAME1** and the rest of the input line was assigned to **NAME2.**

Now that we know how to make an interactive script, let's move on to one way of making loops.

The *for* Loop

The simplest way to set up repetition in a shell script is to use what is known as a **for** loop. Here is a simple example. (For heuristic reasons, we have shortened the noble epic song contained therein.)

```
for i in horse duck cow chicken
do
   echo Old Macdonald had a $i
   echo Eeii eeii ooo
done
```

Before explaining this script, let's see what it does. (Assume it is in the file **McFarm.**)

```
$ sh McFarm
Old Macdonald had a horse
Eeii eeii ooo
Old Macdonald
had a duck
Eeii eeii ooo
Old Macdonald had a cow
Eeii eeii ooo
Old Macdonald had a chicken
Eeii eeii ooo
$
```

Now the intent should be clear. The **i** is a shell variable. The list of animals are values the variable assumes in succession. The instructions between **do** and **done** are executed with **i** set to the first value **(horse)** from the list. Then **i** is set to the next value **(duck),** and the instructions between **do** and **done** are executed again. This continues until all the variables have been used.

You can use any name you like for the variable. We could replace **i** with **beast** and **$i** with **$beast,** and the program would work the same. However, **i** is the name most often used. The general form is

for variable-name **in** value1 value2 . . .

do
    commands
done

The indentation is not necessary, but it makes it easier to see where loops start and stop.

A **for** loop also can get variable values from outside the shell. Here is a modified **McFarm:**

```
for i in $*
do
  echo Old Macdonald had a $i
  echo Eeii eeii ooo
done
```

Recall that **$*** stands for all the arguments of a script. Thus our new version works like this:

```
$ sh McFarm snake moose muskrat
Old Macdonald had a snake
Eeii eeii ooo
Old Macdonald had a moose
Eeii eeii ooo
Old Macdonald had a muskrat
Eeii eeii ooo
$
```

Now the variable **i** took on each of the three arguments in turn for a value.
    The combination

```
for i in $*
```

occurs so frequently that UNIX accepts the abbreviation

```
for i
```

as having the same meaning. This means we could rewrite the last version of **McFarm** as

```
for i
do
  echo Old Macdonald had a $i
  echo Eeii eeii ooo
done
```

This version would work the same, cycling through each argument given to the script.

There are many ways to get values to a **for** loop variable. Here are some of them:

1. List the values explicitly, as in

   ```
   for name in kathleen kate tana georgiana anita
   ```

2. Take the values from shell script arguments, as in

   ```
   for i in $*
   ```

   or the equivalent

   ```
   for i
   ```

3. Take filenames from a directory as values. The shell expands combinations (other than $*) involving * and ? into filenames. Thus

   ```
   for file in *
   do
     cat $file
   done
   ```

   would cat in succession each file in the current working directory, and

   ```
   for file in FORT/*.f
   do
      mv $file old$file
   done
   ```

   adds the prefix *old* to all the FORTRAN files in the *FORT* directory.

4. Take values from a shell variable. Here is yet another revision of **hello:**

   ```
   echo Hello! What\'s your name\?
   read NAME
   for N in $NAME
   do
       echo $N
   done
   echo is quite a name.
   ```

   Running it, we get

   ```
   $ sh hello
   Hello! What's your name?
   Willie Joe Frogflapper
   Willie
   Joe
   Frogflapper
   is quite a name.
   $
   ```

The **read** command gave the value "Willie Joe Frogflapper" to **NAME.** Then **N** was assigned each name from this list, one at a time. Thus each cycle through the loop printed just one name.

Notice that a **for** loop can have other commands before and after it.

5. Take values from the output of a command. Recall that the backquotes allow us to obtain the output of a command. Using this, we can rework **McFarm** to take names from a file called animals:

```
for i in `cat animals`
do
   echo Old Macdonald had a $i
   echo Eeii eeii ooo
done
```

Then the words in the file **animals** are used as successive values for **i.**

The **for** loop is invaluable when you want to process several files in some manner. Many commands, of course, already can handle several files. For example, to do a word count on several files, you can just type

```
wc phys chem biol astr
```

The **wc** command already has a loop mechanism built in, so you don't have to make a loop to use it. But some commands don't work that way. For instance, we used a loop earlier with the **mv** command in order to change the names of several files. Or if you wanted to sort a bunch of files, returning each sorted output to the corresponding original file, you could use a loop:

```
for file in $*
do
   sort -o $file $file
done
```

Similarly, you often need a loop to apply two or more processes in turn on a set of files:

```
for file in $*
do
   spell $file > sp.$file
done
```

Here each file in turn is checked for spelling, with the misspelled words redirected to an appropriately named new file.

Now that we've seen the basics of looping, let's try choice-making.

Choosing Actions: the *case* Statement

Many software packages are "menu-driven"; that is, they offer you a "menu" of choices and ask what you want. The **case** statement makes it easy to set up shell script menus. Here is a simple example showing how a **case** statement works:

```
echo Please enter the number of the program you wish to run:
echo '1 date              2 who'
echo 3 ls
read choice
case $choice in
1) date ;;
2) who ;;
3) ls ;;
*) echo That wasn\'t one of the choices! Bye. ;;
esac
```

We used quotes in the first **echo** to preserve the spacing; otherwise **echo** ignores what it conceives of as surplus spaces. Now let's see what the script does. Assume the script is in the file **askme**. Here are two sample runs:

```
$ sh askme
Please enter the number of the program you wish to run:
1 date              2 who
3 ls
1
Mon May 21 14:23:52 PDT 1984
$ sh askme
Please enter the number of the program you wish to run:
1 date              2 who
3 ls
why
That wasn't one of the choices! Bye.
$
```

When we entered a "1," then the case statement caused the command with the **1)** label to be run. The command labeled ***)** was executed when something other than 1, 2, or 3 was entered. The double semicolon (;;) is used to end each choice, and the **esac** (**case** spelled backwards) marks the end of the **case** statement.

There is nothing magical about using numbers to label the cases. We could just as easily have used letters. Just remember to follow each choice with a) when using it as a label:

```
echo Please enter the letter of the program you wish to run:
echo 'a date              b  who'
echo  c  ls
read choice
case $choice in
a) date ;;
b) who ;;
c) ls ;;
*) echo That wasn\'t one of the choices! Bye. ;;
esac
```

The general form of the **case** statement is

case value **in**
choice1)   commands ;;
choice 2   commands ;;

. . .

esac

The list of choices is scanned to find the first one that matches the value. The choice labeled ***)** matches any value, so it often is used as the last choice to act as a catch-all. (Making it the first choice would cause the first choice to match any value, and the **case** would not be searched any further. So don't do that.) If no choices match and if there is no ***)** choice, then nothing is done, and the program moves on to whatever comes after the **case** statement.

Let's look at a few more examples.

```
echo Which of these words means a short, obese lump of a person?
echo dotterel drotchel fadge fustilugs
read answer
case $answer in
fadge) echo Correct you are! ;;
dotterel | drotchel | fustilugs) echo Nope, $answer is wrong. ;;
*) echo Very wrong: $answer is not even a choice! ;;
esac
```

Aha! Something new! The | here is *not* a pipe. Rather, it serves as an "or." It lets us attach more than one label to the same response. Let's put this in a file **quiz** and see if it works.

```
$ sh quiz
Which of these words means a short, obese lump of a person?
dotterel drotchel fadge fustilugs
drotchel
Nope, drotchel is wrong.
$
```

So far our examples have used a shell variable for the value-part of a **case** statement. As the next example shows, we also can use shell script arguments:

```
case $1 in
dog) echo Man\'s best friend ;;
[aeiouAEIOU]*) Echo word beginning with a vowel ;;
??) echo a two-letter word ;;
*) echo I don\'t know ;;
esac
```

Notice, too, that we can use the shell's pattern-matching skills in formulating the choices. Put the script in the file **whatisa** and run it a few times:

```
$ sh whatisa owl
word beginning with a vowel
$ sh whatisa dog
Man's best friend
$ sh whatisa cat
I don't know
$ sh whatisa oo
word beginning with a vowel
$
```

The last example (**oo**) illustrates our earlier claim that a **case** stops after the first match. That is, **oo** matches the **??** pattern, but since it also matches the preceding pattern for vowels, the **case** doesn't check any further than the first match.

The **case** value portion can be a shell variable or a shell script argument or anything else that produces a value. For example,

```
case `pwd` in
```

would be a valid beginning of a **case** statement. The backquotes cause the output of **pwd,** namely, the current working directory, to be the value against which the choices are compared.

What if you want more than one command to be executed for a given choice? Then just use the standard conventions of the command line. That is, you can separate commands on one line by a semicolon, and you can use a backslash to extend a command to the next line. See Chapter 9 for more details.

In summary, the **case** statement is a powerful and flexible tool. The value portion of the statement can come from shell variables, shell-script arguments, or command outputs. The patterns that are matched to this value can use shell metacharacters such as ***, ?,** and **[ ].** The patterns can also use the metacharacter | to mean "or", so that more than one pattern can correspond to a given command. The commands themselves can use pipes and redirection, and more than one command can be attached to a given choice. Beyond all that, you can use **case** statements in **for** loops and vice versa. And still we have left much unsaid!

What Else?

If you wish to learn more on shell scripts, you can find a substantial discussion in Volume II of the System V Documentation. The discussion includes more commands often used in shell scripts, such as **test, eval,** and **shift.** It also covers more control structures, such as an **if** statement and a **while** loop.

Graphics Utilities

A picture is worth 10,000 words! And, until recently, a computer picture would cost about $10,000. However, the price of computer graphics is dropping significantly as more people value its use. *If* you have a graphics terminal connected to UNIX, there are several graphics utilities that might be available to you.

These utilities can be arbitrarily divided into three categories depending on the type of service provided. The first type of graphics utility is the simplest.

1. Take a file of numbers (data) and plot it.

   graph and **tplot** are the standard System V commands.

   plot2d and **qdp** are versions available on some systems.

2. Take a file of numbers (data) and manipulate it in order to create bar charts, pie charts, histograms, etc.

graphics consists of a series of System V utilities that offers this capability. See also **stat,** a package of commands under **graphics.**

S is a much larger AT&T package available on some systems.

3. Take a file of drawing instructions, like "arc", "line" and "circle" and use them to build pictures.

graphics and **ged** provide this capability for most System V computers.

plot10 from Tektronix is a sophisticated commercial version.

The **graphics** set of utilities available for System V is too complex to discuss in this book. Interested users can refer to Volume 1 of the manual for a summary of commands and to Volume 2 (or 3 depending on the system) of the manual for more information.

The simpler commands **graph** and **tplot** can be illustrated with a short example.

Using *graph* and *plot*

Suppose that you have a file called **data4** that contains the following numbers:

```
1  100
2  200
3  300
4  400
```

If you give the command

```
graph < data4 | plot
```

you would see a graph like the one shown in the following drawing.

There are several options available in **graph** that allow you to change the graph size, label axis and points, and so on. The on-line manual gives the details.

Where Do We Go From Here?

If you have read through this book diligently and have mastered UNIX so far, then you have finished the book! Congratulations on your accom-

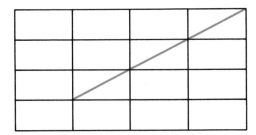

Graph using *graph* and *plot* commands.

plishments and a hearty "thank you" from the authors for your intelligence and understanding.

However, you have not finished learning UNIX. In this book, we have discussed about 40% of UNIX's commands and, maybe, 20% of UNIX's utilities. We have chosen those commands and utilities that should change the least over the next few years. (The major utilities that we have *not* mentioned are those written for the programmer.) In addition, new software is constantly being developed. However, as we mentioned in Chapter 1, UNIX software is designed to work well and to lead a long and useful life. New programs generally will not replace old ones, but will add to them to give you more computing power, without making your past skills obsolete. And, in a similar manner, revisions to this book will be primarily to correct the author's errors (if there are any!) and to add new material, rather than to change the UNIX commands.

If you have any suggestions to make concerning this book, please write to us in care of the publisher.

Review Questions

A. For each *grep* pattern on the left, indicate which pattern(s) following it would be matched.

1. 'to'	**a.** hot	**b.** to	**c.** toad	**d.** stool	**e.** To
2. 't.n'	**a.** tin	**b.** stun	**c.** nation	**d.** stony	**e.** tnuch
3. 'a[o-t].'	**a.** art	**b.** act	**c.** task	**d.** tort	**e.** at

B. Describe what each of the following *find* commands would do.

1. find $HOME −name '*.c' −exec mv { } $HOME/cdirect \ ;

2. find . −name '*.c' −size +3 −ok rm { } \ ;
3. find /usr \ (−size + 10 −atime + 20 \) −o −size + 30 −print

C. The questions in this section refer to a file named *maillist* whose contents are as follows:

```
Morgan:Joe::315 Second Street:Riesenstadt:CA:94707
Vegetable:Joe:Fritz:1002 Market Pl.:Riesenstadt:CA:94707
Morgan:Joe::315 Second Street:Redville:OH:40817
Morgan:Joe::315 Second Street: Hot'n'wet:TX:72727
Antibody:Aristotle:Asis:26 Furtz Way:Redville:OH:40822
Zircon:Bilbo:Nagy:1313 Ratgut Blvd.:Hot'n'wet:TX:72702
```

1. What order would each of the following commands produce?
   a. sort −t: +3n −4 +6n maillist
   b. sort −t: +3n −4 +6nr maillist
   c. sort −t: +6.3n maillist
2. Create an instruction that would sort **maillist** by state, and then by city within state, and then by name within city.

D. create a shell script that searches */etc/passwd* for those names given as arguments to the script.

Answers:

A. 1. b,c,d; **2.** a,b,d; **3.** a,c.

B. 1. Search your home directory recursively for files whose names end in ".c" and move them to the directory ~ /**cdirect.**

2. Search your current working directory recursively for files whose names end in ".c" and have a size in excess of 3 blocks. Then for each found file, ask user if it should be removed.

3. Search the /**usr** directory recursively for all files that either are bigger than ten blocks and haven't been used in over 20 days or else are bigger than 30 blocks. Print the pathnames of these files.

C. 1.a.

```
Antibody:Aristotle:Asis:26 Furtz Way:Redville:OH:40822
Morgan:Joe::315 Second Street:Redville:OH:40817
Morgan:Joe::315 Second Street:Hot'n'wet:TX:72727
Morgan:Joe::315 Second Street:Riesenstadt:CA:94707
Vegetable:Joe:Fritz:1002 Market Pl.:Riesenstadt:CA:94707
Zircon:Bilbo:Nagy:1313 Ratgut Blvd.:Hot'n'wet:TX:72702
```

C. 1.b.

```
Antibody:Aristotle:Asis:26 Furtz Way:Redville:OH:40822
```

```
Morgan:Joe::315 Second Street:Riesenstadt:CA:94707
Morgan:Joe::315 Second Street:Hot'n'wet:TX:72727
Morgan:Joe::315 Second Street:Redville:OH:40817
Vegetable:Joe:Fritz:1002 Market Pl.:Riesenstadt:CA:94707
Zircon:Bilbo:Nagy:1313 Ratgut Blvd.:Hot'n'wet:TX:72702
```

C. 1.c.

```
Zircon:Bilbo:Nagy:1313 Ratgut Blvd.:Hot'n'wet:TX:72702
Morgan:Joe::315 Second Street:Riesenstadt:CA:94707
Vegetable:Joe:Fritz:1002 Market Pl.:Riesenstadt:CA:94707
Morgan:Joe::315 Second Street:Redville:OH:40817
Antibody:Aristotle:Asis:26 Furtz Way:Redville:OH:40822
Morgan:Joe::315 Second Street:Hot'n'wet:TX:72727
```

C. 2. sort −t; +5 −6 +4 −5 +0 maillist

D.
```
for name in $*
    do
        grep $name /etc/passwd
    done
```

Exercises at the Terminal

1. Duplicate as many features as you can of those described in the introductory story.

2. Devise an interactive version of the **cp** command. Have it query the user for the name of the file to be copied and for the name to be given the copy.

3. Devise an interactive program that will copy, link, or change the name of a file, as the user selects. If you like, you can have this shell procedure call upon the shell procedure of Exercise 2.

Appendices

List of Appendices

In this section, you will find:

- A Quick Index to Commands
- Bibliography
  - The Bell System Technical Journal
  - UNIX Manuals
  - Other Documentation
- CP/M and UNIX
- ASCII Table
  - Numerical Conversion
  - ASCII Definitions
- Glossary
- A Summary of UNIX Abbreviations
  - Shell Abbreviations for Files and Directories
  - Abbreviations Used by *grep, ed, edit*, and *ex*
  - Abbreviations Used by the C-Shell History Function
- UNIX Command Reference
  - Starting Up
  - Manipulating Files and Directories
  - Communication
  - Housekeeping Utilities
  - On-Line Help
  - Text Processing and Formatting
  - Information Handling
  - Running Jobs and Programs
  - Adjusting Your Environment
  - Graphics
- *ex/vi* Command Reference
  - The *ex* Line Editor—A Quick Summary
  - The *vi* Screen Editor—A Quick Summary
- Entering and Exiting the UNIX Shell

A   A Quick Index to Commands

B Bibliography

This bibliography is divided into two parts that cover the following items:
1. Selected list of articles from the Bell System Journal
2. The UNIX Programmer's Manual.

The Bell System Technical Journal

One issue of the Bell Journal (Vol. 57, No. 6, Part 2) has become a UNIX classic. Published in July-August 1978, it contains several articles by the principal founders of UNIX. All of the articles are written at a technical level.

Here is a partial selection from the Contents page.
1. The UNIX Time-Sharing System by D. M. Ritchie and K. Thompson.
2. UNIX Implementation by K. Thompson.
3. A Retrospective by D. M. Ritchie.
4. The UNIX Shell by S. R. Bourne.
5. The C Programming Language by D. M. Ritchie, S. C. Johnson, M. E. Lesk, and B. W. Kernighan.
6. Document Preparation by B. W. Kernighan, M. E. Lesk, and J. F. Ossanna, Jr.
7. The Programmer's Workbench by T. A. Dolotta, R. C. Haight, and J. R. Mashey.
8. The UNIX Operating System as a Base for Applications by G. W. R. Luderer, J. F. Maranzano, and B. A. Tague.

UNIX Manuals

As with UNIX systems, the UNIX manuals may vary from system to system. The manuals are organized in two or three parts, with Volume 1 being of most interest to the new user. Volume 1 of the manual contains a complete, terse description of all UNIX commands. It is the same document as the on-line manual described in Chapter 3. Volumes 2 and 3 of the manual may vary and we describe one common version here.

Volume 1

Volume 1 of the UNIX System V User's Manual contains a list of all available UNIX commands. Volume 1 is divided into six sections as follows:

1. Common commands: ~ 200 commands.
2. System calls: ~ 50 commands.
3. Subroutines: ~ 60 commands.
4. File Formats
5. Miscellaneous Facilities: ~ 15 commands.
6. Games: ~ 14 commands.

About 60 of these commands from section 1 are presented in this book.

Volume 2 (and 3)

Whereas Volume 1 of the manual provides a complete description of each UNIX command, Volume 2 (or 3) provide supplemental information about commands and procedures. This information includes the following:

1. An Administrator's Manual with commands, device files, and procedures.
2. An Error Message Manual.
3. An Administrator's Guide to implementing and running UNIX.
4. A User's Guide with selected articles on
   a. Starting UNIX.
   b. Text editing.
   c. An introduction to the shell.
5. An Operator's Guide with system requirements, console operations, boot procedures, and other instructions.
6. A Document Processing Guide providing detailed descriptions of the **nroff** and **troff** utilities (including **tbl, eqn** and **mm**).
7. A Graphics Guide with administrative and user information.
8. A Shell programming guide describing the shell programming language and shell scripts.
9. A Support Tools Guide with information about tools such as **awk, yacc, lex,** and **make.**
10. An Assembler User's Guide.
11. A Common Link Editor Reference Manual.

Generally, this section of the manual offers a good source of information for users of this book.

ASCII Tables

Numerical Conversion

DECIMAL-HEXADECIMAL-OCTAL-BINARY-ASCII
NUMERICAL CONVERSION

DEX X_{10}	HEX X_{16}	OCT X_8	Binary $P\ X_2$	ASCII	Key
0	00	00	0 000 0000	NUL	CTRL/1
1	01	01	1 000 0001	SOH	CTRL/A
2	02	02	1 000 0010	STX	CTRL/B
3	03	03	0 000 0011	ETX	CTRL/C
4	04	04	1 000 0100	EOT	CTRL/D
5	05	05	0 000 0101	ENQ	CTRL/E
6	06	06	0 000 0110	ACK	CTRL/F
7	07	07	1 000 0111	BEL	CTRL/G
8	08	10	1 000 1000	BS	CTRL/H, BACKSPACE
9	09	11	0 000 1001	HT	CTRL/I, TAB
10	0A	12	0 000 1010	LF	CTRL/J, LINE FEED
11	0B	13	1 000 1011	VT	CTRL/K
12	0C	14	0 000 1100	FF	CTRL/L
13	0D	15	1 000 1101	CR	CTRL/M, RETURN
14	0E	16	1 000 1110	SO	CTRL/N
15	0F	17	0 000 1111	SI	CTRL/O
16	10	20	1 001 0000	DLE	CTRL/P
17	11	21	0 001 0001	DC1	CTRL/Q
18	12	22	0 001 0010	DC2	CTRL/R
19	13	23	1 001 0011	DC3	CTRL/S
20	14	24	0 001 0100	DC4	CTRL/T
21	15	25	1 001 0101	NAK	CTRL/U
22	16	26	1 001 0110	SYN	CTRL/V
23	17	27	0 001 0111	ETB	CTRL/W
24	18	30	0 001 1000	CAN	CTRL/X
25	19	31	1 001 1001	EM	CTRL/Y
26	1A	32	1 001 1010	SUB	CTRL/Z
27	1B	33	0 001 1011	ESC	ESC, ESCAPE
28	1C	34	1 001 1100	FS	CTRL<
29	1D	35	0 001 1101	GS	CTRL/
30	1E	36	0 001 1110	RS	CTRL/=

31	1F	37	1 001 1111	US	CTRL/-
32	20	40	1 010 0000	SP	SPACEBAR
33	21	41	0 010 0001	!	!
34	22	42	0 010 0010	,,	,,
35	23	43	1 010 0011	#	#
36	24	44	0 010 0100	$	$
37	25	45	1 010 0101	½	½
38	26	46	1 010 0110	&	&
39	27	47	0 010 0111	'	'
40	28	50	0 010 1000	(	(
41	29	51	1 010 1001	)	)
42	2A	52	1 010 1010	*	*
43	2B	53	0 010 1011	+	+
44	2C	54	1 010 1100	,	,
45	2D	55	0 010 1101	-	-
46	2E	56	0 010 1110	.	.
47	2F	57	1 010 1111	/	/
48	30	60	0 011 0000	0	0
49	31	61	1 011 0001	1	1
50	32	62	1 011 0010	2	2
51	33	63	0 011 0011	3	3
52	34	64	1 011 0100	4	4
53	35	65	0 011 0101	5	5
54	36	66	0 011 0110	6	6
55	37	67	1 011 0111	7	7
56	38	70	1 011 1000	8	8
57	39	71	0 011 1001	9	9
58	3A	72	0 011 1010	:	:
59	3B	73	1 011 1011	;	;
60	3C	74	0 011 1100	<	<
61	3D	75	1 011 1101	=	=
62	3E	76	1 011 1110	>	>
63	3F	77	0 011 1111	?	?
64	40	100	1 100 0000	@	@
65	41	101	0 100 0001	A	A
66	42	102	0 100 0010	B	B
67	43	103	1 100 0011	C	C
68	44	104	0 100 0100	D	D
69	45	105	1 100 0101	E	E
70	46	106	1 100 0110	F	F
71	47	107	0 100 0111	G	G
72	48	110	0 100 1000	H	H
73	49	111	1 100 1001	I	I

74	4A	112	1 100 1010	J	J
75	4B	113	0 100 1011	K	K
76	4C	114	1 100 1100	L	L
77	4D	115	0 100 1101	M	M
78	4E	116	0 100 1110	N	N
79	4F	117	1 100 1111	O	O
80	50	120	0 101 0000	P	P
81	51	121	1 101 0001	Q	Q
82	52	122	1 101 0010	R	R
83	53	123	0 101 0011	S	S
84	54	124	1 101 0100	T	T
85	55	125	0 101 0101	U	U
86	56	126	0 101 0110	V	V
87	57	127	1 101 0111	W	W
88	58	130	1 101 1000	X	X
89	59	131	0 101 1001	Y	Y
90	5A	132	0 101 1010	Z	Z
91	5B	133	1 101 1011	[	[
92	5C	134	0 101 1100	\	\
93	5D	135	1 101 1101	]	]
94	5E	136	1 101 1110	∧	∧
95	5F	137	0 101 1111	—	—
96	60	140	0 110 0000	`	`
97	61	141	1 110 0001	a	a
98	62	142	1 110 0010	b	b
99	63	143	0 110 0011	c	c
100	64	144	1 110 0100	d	d
101	65	145	0 110 0101	e	e
102	66	146	0 110 0110	f	f
103	67	147	1 110 0111	g	g
104	68	150	1 110 1000	h	h
105	69	151	0 110 1001	i	i
106	6A	152	0 110 1010	j	j
107	6B	153	1 110 1011	k	k
108	6C	154	0 110 1100	l	l
109	6D	155	1 110 1101	m	m
110	6E	156	1 110 1110	n	n
111	6F	157	0 110 1111	o	o
112	70	160	1 111 0000	p	p
113	71	161	0 111 0001	q	q
114	72	162	0 111 0010	r	r
115	73	163	1 111 0011	s	s
116	74	164	0 111 0100	t	t

117	75	165	1 111 0101	u	u
118	76	166	1 111 0110	v	v
119	77	167	0 111 0111	w	w
120	78	170	0 111 1000	x	x
121	79	171	1 111 1001	y	y
122	7A	172	1 111 1010	z	z
123	7B	173	0 111 1011	R	R
124	7C	174	1 111 1100	/	/
125	7D	175	0 111 1101	T	T
126	7E	176	0 111 1110	~	~
127	7F	177	1 111 1111	DEL	DEL, RUBOUT

P=Parity bit; "1" for odd number of 1s, "0" for even number of 1s.

D   Glossary

argument—An item of information following a command. It may, for example, modify the command or identify a file to be affected.

assembly language—A mnemonic code representing the basic instructions understood by a particular computer.

background—Running of system so that the terminal is left free for other uses.

backup—A file copy set aside as insurance in case something happens to the original.

baud rate—The rate at which information is transmitted between devices; for example, between a terminal and the computer. One baud is one unit of information (a bit) per second. A hundred baud is about 9 characters a second or 110 words a minute.

Berkeley Software Distribution—UNIX versions developed at the University of California, Berkeley. They bear names such as BSD 2.7 and BSD 4.2.

bit—The smallest unit of information or memory for a computer. A bit can have the value "0" or the value "1," and it forms the basis of the binary coding used internally by computers.

block—A standard chunk of memory used as a unit by the computer; a block typically consists of 512 bytes.

Bourne Shell—The UNIX shell used by the standard Bell Labs UNIX.

buffer—A temporary work area or storage area set up within the system memory. Buffers are often used by programs, such as editors, that access and alter text or data frequently.

bug—A design error in the hardware or software of a computer system.

byte—A unit of information or memory consisting of eight bits. A byte of memory will hold one character.

call—To summon a program into action.

change mode—To alter a set of parameters that describe a file, telling who can use it and how it can be used. The **chmod** command is used to do this.

character—A letter, numeral, punctuation mark, control character, blank, or other such symbol.

character string—A series of characters; for example, "gofats" and "hot&#$23".

chip—A small chunk of silicon bearing the equivalent of a large number of electrical components; an integrated circuit.

clobber—To wipe out a file.

command—An instruction to the computer. A command typically is a character string that is typed in at a keyboard and is interpreted by the computer as a demand for a particular action.

command interpreter—A program that accepts commands from the keyboard and causes the commands to be executed. The shell is the UNIX command interpreter.

command line—A line consisting of one or more commands, each followed by its arguments, if any.

compiler—A master program that converts a high-level computer language (such as FORTRAN) into machine language.

concatenate—To string together two or more sequences, such as files, into one longer sequence. The **cat** command, for example, concatenates files.

control characters—Characters that are typed by pressing a key down while the <control> key is depressed. For instance, a <control-h> is typed by pressing the <h> key while the <control> key is depressed.

CPU—Abbreviation for Central Processing Unit. This is the part of the computer in which calculations and manipulations take place.

C Shell—The standard shell provided with Berkeley Standard versions of UNIX.

cursor—A marker on the screen, which is usually a rectangle of light or an underline mark.

directory—A file containing a list of associated files and subdirectories.

directory pathname—The complete name by which the directory is known; the pathname gives the sequence of directories by which the directory is linked to the root directory.

echo—To repeat a stream of characters. For example, the commands you type to the computer are echoed on the screen.

editor—A program to assist you in writing material to be stored in files. Editors allow you to modify existing files and create new ones.

EOF—Abbreviation for End of File. Files are terminated with a particular "end of file" character, usually a <control-d>, that tells the system it has reached the end of the file.

escape—To divest a special character of its special meaning by preceding it with a backslash character. For example, the UNIX shell interprets a **?** to represent any single character, but a \? (an "escaped" question mark) is interpreted to be just a question-mark character.

event—A previous line of input from the terminal; usually either a command line or an attempted command line. The **history** function maintains a numbered list of the last several events that you have entered.

event identifier—A shorthand code used by you to identify earlier events on the history list.

execute—To run a command or program. (Not to be confused with "kill.")

field—A subsection of a line. Programs such as **sort** and **awk** can look at individual fields within a line.

field separator—The character used to separate one field from the next; a string of one or more spaces is the usual field separator.

file—A sequence of bytes constituting a unit of text, data, or program. A file can be stored in the system memory or on an external medium such as tape or disk.

filename expansion—The process by which UNIX matches filenames with metacharacters to actual filenames; for example, matching **?oo?** to **foot** and **loop.**

filling—Adjusting the line lengths in text so that all lines have about the same length.

flag—An argument to a command indicating a particular option or modification. UNIX flags usually are indicated by a leading hyphen.

foreground—Running under direct control of the terminal; the terminal cannot be used for anything else until a foreground job finishes or is halted.

formatting—Arranging text or data into a suitable visual form.

global—Having extended or general scope. For example, a global substitution of one word for another in a file affects all occurrences of the word.

hardware—The mechanical and electrical components of a computer system.

home directory—The directory assigned to you by the system manager; usually the same as your login directory. Additional directories that you create would stem from your home directory.

housekeeping—Keeping track of what files are where, of who is doing what, and the like.

input—Information fed to a command, a program, a terminal, a person, etc.

interactive—Allowing the computer and the user to carry on a dialogue.

interpreter—A master program that translates a high-level computer language (such as BASIC) into machine language, a line at a time. Interactive languages use interpreters instead of compilers.

interrupt—To break off a command or other process and, thus, terminating it; a signal that accomplishes this.

kill—To terminate a process before it reaches its natural conclusion.

learn—A computer-aided instruction program provided with some versions of UNIX.

line editor—An editor that works on a line as the basic unit. In general, the user identifies the line she wants changed and, then, indicates the change desired.

link—An entry in a directory file that links a user-assigned name for a file to the system's identification number for that file; a name you give to a file.

loading—Putting the machine-language instructions of a program into memory.

local—Having limited scope; the opposite of global.

login—The process of gaining access to the computer system to begin a session.

login directory—The directory you are placed in when you login; usually your home directory.

login name—The name by which the computer system knows you.

logout—The process of signing off the system.

machine-collating sequence—An extended alphabetical sequence that encompasses uppercase letters, lowercase letters, numerals, punctuation marks, and the various other characters recognized by the system.

machine language—The basic set of instructions understood by a given computer. These instructions are represented internally by means of a binary code.

macro—A compound instruction put together from simpler instructions.

mail—A computer system facility that allows the sending and holding of messages via the computer.

map—To assign a new interpretation of a terminal key. For example, in **vi,** one can map, say, the [@] key to represent the sequence [o] [esc] [j].

metacharacter—A character having a special meaning to UNIX. For example, the UNIX shell interprets the **?** character to stand for any single character.

microprocessor—The essential electronics of a computer miniaturized to a single chip.

modem—Short for MOdulator-DEModulator; a device for connecting a terminal or printer to a computer via a telephone line.

multitasking—Allowing more than one user to access the same program at the same time.

multiuser—Permitting more than one user to use the system at the same time.

network—The linking up of several computers.

null character—An invisible character whose internal code is Ø and which occupies no space if printed; not to be confused with a blank, which is invisible but occupies a space.

object file—A file containing machine-language code.

on-line—Connected to the system and in operation.

operating system—A master program that handles the varied tasks involved in running a computer system, including the user-computer interface.

option—A variation on or modification to a command, usually requested by use of a flag.

optional argument—An argument accepted but not required by a command.

output—Information produced by a command, program, etc., and sent elsewhere; for example, to the terminal, to a file, or to a line printer.

overwrite—To write on an existing file, eliminating what previously was there.

owner—The person who created a file.

page—To advance text on the screen by one screenful (or page) at a time.

password—A secret word, chosen by you, with which you can reassure the computer system that you are who you claim to be.

pathname—A name for a file or directory specifying the location of the file or directory in the directory system.

peripheral input-output—Input and output devices attached to a computer; e.g., terminals, printers, and tape drives.

permission—The yes-or-no specification of what can be done to a file. A file has read permission, write permission, and execute permission.

pipe—To make the output of one command or program into the input of another. Also, the UNIX operator (|) that accomplishes this.

pipeline—The program linkage established by performing one or more pipes.

process—A particular computer activity or job.

process ID—A unique, system-wide, identification number assigned to a process.

process status—The current state of the process: running, stopped, waiting, etc.

program—A sequence of instructions telling a computer how to perform a task. A program can be in machine language or it can be in a higher-level language that is then translated into machine language.

prompt—A character or character string sent from the computer system to a terminal to indicate to the user that the system is ready to accept input. Typical prompts are $ and %.

protection—Safeguarding a file from accidental erasure or from unwanted inspection of others. Protection can be accomplished, for example, by using **chmod** to deny others the right to read a file.

recursive—In reference to a directory system, the application to a directory, to all its offshoots, to all their offshoots, etc. In reference to a computer program, the describing of a program that calls itself.

redirection—The channeling of output to a file or device instead of to the standard output; the channeling of input from a file or device instead of from the standard input.

regular expression—A pattern representing a class of character strings. **grep,** for example, recognizes the regular expression **h.t** to mean any three-character string beginning with **h** and ending with **t.**

root directory—The base directory from which all other directories stem, directly or indirectly.

scope—The range over which an action or definition applies.

scroll—To shift text up or down one or more lines on the screen.

search and replace—In editing, an operation that finds one or more occurrences of a word or pattern and replaces it with another.

shell—A UNIX program that handles the interaction between user and system.

shell script—A file containing a sequence of shell commands. It can be used as input to the shell or be declared an executable file.

smart terminal—A terminal possessing some computer power of its own.

software—The programs used on a computing system.

special character—A character with special meaning beyond its literal one; a metacharacter.

standard input—Short for standard input device. The device from which a program or system normally takes its input; usually a terminal.

standard output—Short for standard output device. The device to which a program or system normally sends its output; usually a terminal.

stopped job—A job that has been halted temporarily by the user and which can be resumed at his command.

string—A sequence of characters.

subdirectory—A directory branching off from another directory.

time sharing—The allocation of computer resources among several users.

tools—Compact, well-designed programs designed to do a specific task well. Several tools can be linked together to perform more complex tasks.

user—A person using the computer system.

visual editor—An editor that shows a screenful of text at a time and allows the user to move a cursor to any part of the screen and effect changes there.

wild-card—A metacharacter used to represent a range of ordinary characters. Examples include the shell's use of * and **?.**

word processing—The use of editors and other computer programs to prepare, alter, check, and format text.

working directory—The directory in which your commands take place, given that no other directory is specified.

write—1. To place text in a file. 2. To use the **write** command to communicate with other users.

E   A Summary of UNIX Abbreviations

Shell Abbreviations for Files and Directories

The following three abbreviations can be used in representing the names of files and directories.

?   Represents (or "matches") any single character.

*   Matches any number of characters (including none)

[ ] Matches any *one* character from the list included between the brackets; a hyphen (-) can be used to indicate a range.

Examples:

Abbreviation	Some matches	No match
l?t	lit lot lst	lt lout
l*t	lot lout latent lt	lots allot
l[aou]t	lat lot	lout
l[3-6]	l3 l5	l2 l33
l[3-5] [7-9]?	l38q l472	l27n l38

The following two symbols can be used in identifying directories.

.   Your current working directory.

.. Parent directory to your current working directory.

Examples:

Abbreviation	Meaning
cp ../recipe .	Copy the file **recipe** from your parent directory into your current directory.
cd ..	Change directories to the parent directory of your current working directory.

Abbreviations Used by *grep, edit,* and *ex*

These abbreviations are used in search patterns.

. Matches any single character. (Works the same as the shell abbreviation **?**.)

[ ] Matches any *one* character found in the list between the brackets; a hyphen (-) can be used to indicate a range of characters.

∧ Matches beginning of line; i.e., the following pattern must begin the line.

$ Matches end of line; the preceding pattern must end the line.

Examples:

Abbreviation	Matching line	Nonmatching line
car.o	a carton of milk	carts of fish eyes
car[gt]	a cargo of gold	a tub of carp
∧car[gt]	cartoon of frog	a fine cartoon
car.o$	a fresh cargo	fresh cargos

Shell-Script Abbreviations

These are abbreviations used by the shell.

$Ø The name of the shell script.
$n The nth argument of the shell script.
$* The complete argument list of the shell script.

Suppose the following command has been given, where **freem** is a shell script:

freem click clack clock

Then, within the script,

$Ø represents **freem.**
$2 represents **clack.**
$* represents **click clack clock.**

AWK Abbreviations

Here are some more abbreviations.

$n	The nth field of a record (by default, a record is a line).
$0	The entire record.
NF	The number of fields in the current record.
NR	The ordinal number of the current record.
FILENAME	The name of the current input file.

Examples:

{print $3}	Print the third field.
{print $3/NR > > FILENAME}	Divide the contents of the third field by current line number and write the result at end of the current file.

F   UNIX Command Reference

How To Use This Summary:

1. This summary is best used as a quick reference for commands you have already used.
2. Type **boldface** text as shown.
3. Substitute your filenames for file, file2, etc.
4. Repeatable arguments are followed by ellipses (. . .).
5. Arguments in brackets [ ] are optional. Do not type in the brackets.
6. The number in parentheses ( ) following the entry refers to the page number of the command summary in the text.

Starting Up

LOGIN—sign on. (42)
PASSWD—change login password. (43)

Manipulating Files and Directories

CAT—concatenate and print. (88)
　　cat
Example:
　　cat file2 displays **file2** on terminal.

CD—change directory. (183)
　　cd
　　cd directoryname
Example:
　　cd /user/reggie/foods/carbo places you in the **usr/reggie/foods/carbo** directory.

CHMOD—change modes or permissions on files. (289)
　　chmod ugo, + −, rwx file . . . or directory . . .
Who:
　　u　Login owner (user).
　　g　Group.
　　o　Other users.

Op-codes:
+   Add permission.
−   Remove permission.
Permissions:
r   Read.
w   Write.
x   Execute.
Example:

> **chmod o-rwx private** removes read, write, and execute permissions for others from the file called **private.**

CP—make copy of files. (187)
cp file1 file2
cp file . . . (file, file . . . , directory)
Example:

> **cp flim flam** makes a copy of the file **flim** and calls it **flam.**

LN—makes file links. (193)
ln file . . . file . . . or file . . . directoryname
Example:

> **ln hist /usr/francie** links the file **hist** to the **/usr/francie** directory.

LP, CANCEL, and LPSTAT—Use the Line Printer
lp [-d] file . . .
cancel ID number
lpstat [-p] file . . .

Options:
-d Selects printer.
-p Reports printer status.

Example:

> **lp some stuff**
> Sends the files **some** and **stuff** to the printer

LS—list contents of directory. (83)
ls [-a,c,l,r , s + others] directory . . .
Options
         -a   List all entries.

-c	List by time of file creation.
-l	List in long format.
-p	Marks directories with a /.
-r	Reverses the order of the listing.
-s	Gives the size in blocks.

Example:

ls -c will list contents of current directory in order of time of creation.

MKDIR—makes a new directory. (181)

mkdir directoryname

Example:

mkdir Chapter4 creates a new subdirectory called **chapter4** in the present directory.

MV—move or rename files. (190)

mv filename1 filename2 or filename1 directoryname

Example:

mv gappy happy changes the name of the file **gappy** to **happy.**

RM—removes files. (186)

rm [-i, -r] file . . .

Options:

-i	Protects existing files.
-r	Deletes a directory and every file or directory in it. (Be careful!)

Example:

rm Rodgers removes the file **Rodgers.**

RMDIR—removes directories. (185)

rmdir directory . . .

Example:

rmdir budget65 removes directory **budget65** if it does not contain any files.

REDIRECTION OPERATORS—<, >, >> (238)

Example:

cat listA listB >> listC appends the files **listA** and **listB** to the file **listC.**

PIPES— | (243)

Example:

cat listA listB | lp joins two files and "pipes" the result to the line printer.

Communication

MAIL—receiving mail.

mail

Commands:

<return>	Reads next message, exits **mail** after last message
-	Goes back to previous message.
p	Prints message again.
s filename	Appends message to filename (default is **mbox**).
d	Deletes message, go on to next message.
q	Quits mail.
*	Provides a summary of **mail** commands.
<control-d>	Same as **q**.

Plus other commands. Differences may exist from system to system.

MAIL—sending mail. (62)

mail loginname(s)

Examples:

mail dick bob

(text of message here)

<control-d>

MESG—permit or deny messages from write. (294)

mesg [-y, -n]

Example:

mesg n prevents people from using **write** to interrupt you.

WRITE—write to another user. (69)

write loginname

(text of messages)

<control-d> when finished

Housekeeping Utilities

CAL—provides a calendar. (53)
 cal [month] year
Example:
 cal 05 1942 is the calendar for May 1942.

CALENDAR—a reminder service. (297)
 You create a file in your home directory called **calendar.** UNIX sends you reminders by mail.
Example:
 Your **calendar** file might look like:
 Buy goose March 19
 call gus mar. 20 at 3 pm
 3/23 Report due

DATE—gives date and time. (51)

PWD—prints working directory. (184)

WHO—Who is on the system. (55)
 who [am I]
Example:
 who Tells who is on the system.

On-Line Help

HELP—ask for help.

MAN—find manual information by keywords. (72)
 man section
Example:
 man cat displays the on-line manual explanation of **cat.**

Text Processing and Formatting

CUT—cut out selected fields of a file
 cut [-c, -d, -f] file . . .

Options:

    -c list   Pass on the columns in the list.

    -f list   Pass on the fields in the list.

    -dk   Change delimiter character to k.

Example:

    cut -f3, 6 -d: **address** Prints fields 3 and 6 of the file
                       address. Fields are separated by a colon.

EX—line-oriented text editor. (104)

    ex file

EQN—Formats mathematical text for **nroff** commands

    eqn (options) file . . .

    See the manual for details.

MN—Simplified package of **nroff** commands

    mm (options) file . . .

    See the manual for details.

NROFF—advanced text formatting.

    See Chapter 12 for details.

PASTE—Horizontally merge lines of a file

    paste (-d) file1 file2

Options:

    -dk Uses the character k to link together lines.

Example:

    paste -d: address date Adds each line of the date file to the corresponding line of the address file.

PR—Prints partially formatted file. (90)

    pr [-d, -l, -p, -t, -w] file . . .

Options:

    -d   Doublespace lines.

    -l k   Set page length to k lines.

    -p   Pause until a < return >.

    -t   Suppresses heading on each page.

    -wk   Set line width to k positions.

Example:
> **pr -p120 myths**
> Prints file **myths** on the terminal
> 20 lines at a time.

SED—Stream editor
> **sed [options]** file . . .

TBL—Format tables for **nroff** commands
> **tbl [options]** file . . .
> See the manual for details.

VI—the screen-oriented text editor. (134)
> **vi** file

Information Handling

AWK—pattern scanning and processing language. (362)
> See Chapter 12 and the AWK manual.

CMP—compares two files. (281)
> **cmp** filename1 filename2
> Example:
> **cmp Janice Susan** finds and prints by byte and line number the first difference between the two files.

COMM—finds lines common to two sorted files. (281)
> **comm [-1,-2,-3]** file1 file2
> Options:
> > **-1**   Don't print the first column.
> > **-2**   Don't print the second column.
> > **-3**   Don't print the third column.
> Example:
> **comm listA listB** prints three columns. First, lines only in **listA,** secondly, lines only in file **listB,** and thirdly, lines in both files.

DIFF—finds the difference between two files or directories. (281)
> **diff [-b,-e,-r]** file1 file2 or directory1 directory2

409

Options:
>   **-b**   Ignores trailing blanks.
>
>   **-e**   Output in the form of **ed** commands.

Example:
>   **diff giftlist1 giftlist2** shows how to make **giftlist1** like **giftlist2**.

ECHO—Echoes argument
>   **echo** [any string of characters]

Example:
>   **echo** You have just won $1,000,000.!!
>   You have just won $1,000,000.!!

FIND—finds designated files and acts upon them. (351)
>   **find** pathname searchcriteria action(s)

Search Criteria:

-name filename	Files named "filename"
-size n	Files of size n blocks.
-links n	Files with n links
-atime n	Files accessed n days ago.
-ntime n	Files modified n days ago.
-newer filename	Files modified more recently than the file "filename."

>   **+ others**

(Note "n" without a sign means exactly n, "+n" means greater than n, "-n" means less than n.)

Actions:

-print	Prints the pathname of the found files.
-exec command \ ;	Executes the given command upon finding a file; { } represent the found file.
-ok command \ ;	Same as **-exec**, except your approval is requested before each execution; replay with a **y**.

>   **+ others**

Example:
>   **find /usr/bob -ntime -10 -print** finds all files in **usr/bob** directory that have been modified within 10 days and prints pathnames.

GREP—search a file for a pattern. (344)

    grep [-n,-c,-v] pattern file . . .

Options:

        -n   Precedes each matching line with its line number.

        -c   Prints only a count of matching lines.

        -v   Prints all lines that do not match.

Example:

    grep hop bugs searches the file **bugs** for the word ''hop''.

SORT sorts and merges files (278, 356)

    sort [b,-d,-f,-n ,-o,-r] file . . .

Options:

        -b   Ignore initial blanks.

        -d   Dictionary order.

        -f   Ignore upper and lowercase letters.

        -n   Sort numbers by value.

        -o filename Outputs to file called filename.

        -r   Sort in reverse order.

Example:

    sort -fr -o sortbag grabbag sorts the file **grabbag** in reverse order, ignoring upper and lowercase letters. Results stored in **sortbag.**

SPELL—find spelling errors. (312)

    spell file . . .

TAIL—gives the last part of a file. (276)

    tail [-n] file

Options:

        -n   Start ''n'' lines from the end.

Example:

    tail -20 gate prints the last 20 lines of the file **gate.**

UNIQ—remove duplicated lines from file. (286)

    uniq [-u,-d,-c] inputfile [outputfile]

Options:

        -u   Prints only lines with no duplicates.

        -d   Prints one copy of lines with duplicates.

        -c   Prints number of times line is repeated.

Example:

uniq -d ioulist urgent scans the file **ioulist** for lines that appear more than once. One copy of each line placed in the file **urgent**.

WC—word count. (275)

wc [-l,-w,-c,] file . . .

Options:

-l	Counts lines.
-w	Counts words.
-c	Counts characters.

Example:

wc -w Essay counts the number of words in file **Essay.**

Running Jobs and Programs

CC (218)

cc [-c,-o] file . . .

Options:

-c	Creates object file suppressing loading.
-o filename	Uses filename for file **a.out.**

Example:

cc payroll.c compiles **payroll.c** file, with the executable program placed in **a.out** file

F77—compile FORTRAN programs. (223)

f77 [-c,-o] file . . .

Options:

-c	Creates object code file suppressing loading.
-o filename	Uses filename for **a.out.**

Example:

f77 payroll.f compiles **payroll.f** file, with the executable code placed in **a.out** file

KILL will terminate jobs. (248)

kill [-9] process ID

Option:

09	This is a sure kill.

NOHUP—Run a Command Immune to Hangups
> **nohup** command

Example:
> **nohup spell ch2 > spellch2 &**

PS—the Process Status Report. (250)
> **ps [-a]**

Options:
> **a** Displays **ps** information for all terminals.
> **+** many others

TEE—split output. (245)
> **tee [-i,-a]** file

Options:
> **-i** Ignores interrupts.
> **-a** Sends output to the end of named file.

Example:
> **ls -l /usr | tee -a clutter** produces the long listing of the **/usr** directory on the terminal and also appends it to the end of the file **clutter.**

TIME—will time a command. (297)
> **time** commandname

Example:
> **time cc woo.c** runs the command **cc woo.c** and prints execution time when finished.

Adjusting Your Environment

You can customize your UNIX environment by changing your .profile (be careful) and by creating executable shell scripts.

Graphics

GRAPH will draw a graph. (376)
> **graph** filename | **plot**

See Chapter 12 or the on-line manual for more details.

GRAPHICS—A Sophisticated Package of Graphics Commands.
graphics [options]
See the special Graphics Manual for details.

G *ex/vi* Command Reference

The *ex* Line Editor—a Quick Summary

The command for editing the file "filename" is

ex filename

If no such file exists yet, it will be created when this command is given.

Modes

Command Mode: Lets you use any commands described below.

To Enter: You are placed in the Command Mode when you invoke **ex.** To enter the Command Mode from the Text Mode, begin a new line with a period (.) and hit the <return> key. Command mode prompt is a colon (:).

Text Mode: Lets you use the keyboard to enter text.

To Enter: Use an **a, i,** or **c** command.

Open/Visual Mode:

To Enter: type **o** or **vc**

           to get back to **ex,** type **Q.**

Commands

In general, commands consist of an address and an instruction. The address identifies the lines to be affected.

Addresses

n	The nth line.
n,k	Lines n through k.
.	The current line.
$	The last (i.e., final) line.
+n	n lines after the current line.
-n	n lines before the current line.
$-n,$	The last n + l lines.
/**pat**	search forward for pat.

Instructions

For clarity, we will include simple forms of addresses with the instructions. Instructions shown with an address range will also accept a single address. Instructions operate on the current line if no other address is given.

n,k**p**	Print lines n through k.
n**a**	Append (text is added after line n).
n**i**	Insert (text is inserted before line n).
n,k**d**	Delete lines n through k.
n,k**c**	Change lines n through k to new text.
n,k**m**j	Move lines n through k to after line j.
n,k**co**j	Place a copy of lines n-k after line j.
s/pat1/pat2/	Replaces the first occurrence of "pat2" with "pat1" on the current line.
n**r** filename	Read and insert filename at line n.

Searches

/pattern   Causes **ex** to search for the next line containing a pattern.

A search pattern can be used in place of an address in a command. For example:

/slop/**d**	Delete the next line that contains "slop."
/dog/**s**/dog/hog/	Find the next line containing "dog" and replace the first occurrence of "dog" on that line with "hog."
/dog/**s**//hog/	Short form of the preceding command.

The Global Parameter *g*

The **g** parameter, when following an **s** command, makes the substitution affect all occurrences of "pat1" in a line. When preceding an **s** command, it makes the command affect all lines. Both uses can be made in the same command:

g/house/**s**//home/**g**	Substitutes "home" for "house" everywhere in the file.

The Undo Command u

A friendly command that lets you undo the last change made to the buffer.

Saving Text and Quitting the Editor

Editing work is done in a temporary buffer and must be ''written'' into a file to save it.

w	Writes the current text into a permanent file.
q	Quits the editor, if no changes since previous **w**.
wq	Write and quit.
q!	Emphatic form of quit. No changes recorded.
n,k**w** file2	Writes lines n through k into another file.
n,k**w** > >file3	Appends lines n through k to file 3.

The *vi* Screen Editor—A Quick Summary

The command for editing the file ''filename'' is

vi filename

If no such file exists yet, it will be created when this command is given.

Modes

Command Mode:	Lets you use the commands described below.
To Enter:	You are placed in a Command Mode when you invoke **vi**. To enter the Command Mode from the Text Mode, hit the <esc> key.

Text Mode:	Lets you use the keyboard to enter text.
To Enter:	Any of the following commands will put you in the Text Mode: **a, i, o, O, R,** and **c.**

Using *ex* Commands

While in the Command Mode, type a colon and follow it with the desired **ex** command; for example:

:g/dog/s//mango/g

or

:14,42w newfile

You are returned to the regular Command Mode after the **ex** command is executed.

Cursor Movement Commands

vi commands take place at the cursor location. These commands help you to place the cursor where you want it to be in the text. The cursor will not move beyond the bounds of the existing text.

j	Move the cursor down one line.
k	Move the cursor up one line.
h	Move the cursor left one space.
l	Move the cursor right one space.
<control-d>	Move the screen down a half page.
<control-u>	Move the screen up a half page.
<control-w>	Moves the screen up a full page.
<control-f>	Moves the screen forward a full page.
nG	Moves the cursor to the nth line of file.

Text Entering Commands

a	Appends text after cursor position.
i	Inserts text before cursor position.
o	Opens a new line below cursor position.
O	Opens a new line above cursor position.

Text Deletion Commands

x	Deletes character under cursor.
dw	Deletes from cursor to beginning of next word.
dd	Deletes line containing cursor.
d)	Deletes rest of sentence.
d}	Deletes rest of paragraph.

These commands can be preceded by an integer to indicate the number of characters, words, etc., to be affected.

Text Alteration Commands

The **R, cw, c)** commands need to be terminated with an < esc >.

r	Replace character under cursor with next character typed.
R	Write over old text, beginning at cursor position.
cw	Change word (beginning at cursor) to new text.
c)	Change sentence (starting at cursor) to new text.
J	Join next line down to line with cursor.
u	Undo last command.
U	Undo all changes to line with cursor.

Search Commands

/pattern	Search for next occurrence of ''pattern''.
?pattern	Search for preceding occurrence of ''pattern''.
n	Repeat the last search command given.

Text Moving Commands (also see Text Deletion Commands)

yy	Yank a copy of a line, place it in a buffer.
p	Put after the cursor the last item yanked or deleted.
P	Put before the cursor the last item yanked or deleted.
''c**Y**	Yank a copy of a line, place it in buffer c, where c is any letter from a to z.
''c**P**	Put after the cursor the contents of buffer c.

Saving Text and Quitting the Editor

Editing work takes place in a temporary work area and must be saved by ''writing'' it into a permanent file.

< esc >:**w**	Write the current text into the permanent file.
< esc >:**q**	Quit, if no changes since last **w**.
< esc >:**q!**	Emphatic form of quit, no changes written.
< esc >:**wq**	Write and quit.
< esc >**ZZ**	Write and quit.
< esc >:**n,kw** file2	Write lines n-k into another file.
< esc >:**n,kw** >> file2	Append lines n-k to another file.

Screen Enhancement Options

<esc>:**set nu**	Show line numbers
<esc>:**set wm=k**	Provides wrap margin at **k** characters from right.
<esc>:**set redraw**	Keeps screen display current.
+ others	

H   Entering and Exiting the UNIX Shell

One of the major problems facing beginning UNIX users is how to go from the shell to various utilities and how to get back to the shell again. Here are some examples:

	IN	OUT
ex filename	EX EDITOR	wq or q
mail	MAIL—RECEIVE	\<return\>
mail username	MAIL—SEND	.(lone period)
man Command	ON-LINE MANUAL	interrupt key
\<control-z\>	TO SUSPEND A JOB	fg
\<control-s\>	SCREEN OUTPUT	any key
login	UNIX SHELL	EOF
vi filename	VI EDITOR	\<esc\> wq or ZZ or :q!

Use the following keys for:

Interrupt: The "interrupt" signal stops most processes. On most systems, the signal is sent by typing \<control-c\>. Other common choices are the \<del\> or \<rub\> keys.

EOF: The "End-Of-File" character is usually transmitted by typing \<control-d\>.

In order to check which characters are used to control your terminal input and output, type in the UNIX command:

    stty

You should be given a list of characters presently used to:

1. Erase character.
2. Erase line.
3. End of file.
4. Control terminal output.
5. Other things.

These control characters can be changed as described in Chapter 10.

INDEX

Example:
diff giftlist1 giftlist2 shows how to make **giftlist1** like **giftlist2.**

ECHO—Echoes argument
    echo [any string of characters]
    Example:
        echo You have just won $1,000,000.!!
        You have just won $1,000,000.!!

FIND—finds designated files and acts upon them (351)
    find pathname searchcriteria action(s)
    Search Criteria:

-name filename	Files named "filename"
-size n	Files of size n blocks.
-links n	Files with n links
-atime n	Files accessed n days ago.
-ntime n	Files modified n days ago.
-newer filename	Files modified more recently than the file "filename."
+ others	

(Notes "n" without a sign means exactly n, "+n" means greater than n, "-n" means less than n.)

Actions:

-print	Prints the pathname of the found files.
-exec command \ ;	Executes the given command upon finding a file; { } represents the found file.
-ok command \ ;	Same as **-exec**, except your approval is requested before each execution; replay with a **y.**
+ others	

Example:
    find /usr/bob **-ntime** -10 **-print** finds all files in usr/ bob directory that have been modified within 10 days and prints pathnames.

GREP—search a file for a pattern. (344)
    grep [-n,-c,-v] pattern file . . .
    Options:

-n	Precedes each matching line with its line number.
-c	Prints only a count of matching lines.
-v	Prints all lines that do not match.

Example:
    grep hop bugs searches the file **bugs** for the word "hop."

SORT sorts and merges files. (278, 356)
    sort [b,-d,-f,-n ,-o,-r] file . . .
    Options:

-b	Ignore initial blanks.
-d	"Dictionary" order.
-f	Ignore upper and lowercase letters.
-n	Sort numbers by value.
-o filename	Outputs to file called filename.
-r	Sort in reverse order.

Example:
    sort -fr -o sortbag grabbag sorts the file **grabbag** in reverse order, ignoring upper and lowercase letters. Results stored in **sortbag.**

SPELL—find spelling errors. (312)
    spell file . . .

TAIL—gives the last part of a file. (276)
    tail [-n] file
    Options:

-n	Start "n" lines from the end.

Example:
    tail -20 gate prints the last 20 lines of the file **gate.**

UNIQ—remove duplicated lines from file. (286)
    uniq [-u,-d,-c] inputfile [outputfile]

Options:

-u	Prints only lines with no duplicates.
-d	Prints one copy of lines with duplicates.
-c	Prints number of times line is repeated.

Example:
    uniq -d ioulist urgent scans the file **ioulist** for lines that appear more than once. One copy of each line placed in the file **urgent.**

WC—word count. (275)
    wc [-l,-w,-c,] file . . .
    Options:

-l	Counts lines.
-w	Counts words.
-c	Counts characters.

Example:
    wc -w Essay counts the number of words in file **Essay.**

Running Jobs and Programs

CC (215)
    cc [-c,-o] file . . .
    Options:

-c	Creates object file suppressing loading.
-o filename	Uses filename for file **a.out.**

Example:
    cc payroll.c compiles **payroll.c** file, with the executable program placed in **a.out** file

F77—compile FORTRAN programs. (223)
    f77 [-c,-o] file . . .
    Options:

-c	Creates object code file suppressing loading.
-o filename	Uses filename for **a.out.**

Example:
    f77 payroll.f compiles **payroll.f** file, with the executable code placed in **a.out** file

KILL will terminate jobs. (248)
    kill [-9] process ID
    Option:
        09   This is a sure kill.

NOHUP—Run a Command Immune to Hangups
    nohup command
    Example:
        nohup spell ch2 > spellch2 &

PS—the Process Status Report. (250)
    ps [-a]
    Options:
        a   Displays **ps** information for all terminals.
       + many others

TEE—split output. (245)
    tee [-i,-a] file
    Options:
        -i   Ignores interrupts.
        -a   Sends output to the end of named file.
    Example:
        ls -l /usr | **tee -a clutter** produces the long listing of the **/usr** directory on the terminal and also appends it to the end of the file **clutter.**

TIME—will time a command. (297)
    time commandname
    Example:
        time cc woo.c runs the command **cc woo.c** and prints execution time when finished.

Adjusting Your Environment

You can customize your UNIX environment by changing your .profile (be careful) and by creating executable shell scripts.

Graphics

GRAPH will draw a graph. (376)
 graph filename | **plot**
 See Chapter 12 or the on-line manual for more details.

GRAPHICS—A Sophisticated Package of Graphics Commands.
  graphics [options]
 See the special Graphics Manual for details.

Mitchell Waite
Donald Martin
Stephen Prata

UNIX*
SYSTEM V
PRIMER

Reference Card

Owned or Sponsored by:

How To Remove and Fold Card

UNIX title underneath

book

A   B   C

* UNIX is a trademark of AT & T Bell Laboratories

ex Reference Card

The ex Line Editor—a Quick Summary

The command for editing the file "filename" is **ex** filename

If no such file exists yet, it will be created when this command is given.

Modes

Command Mode:
To Enter: Lets you use any commands described below. You are placed in the Command Mode when you invoke **ex**. To enter the Command Mode from the Text Mode, begin a new line with a period (.) and hit the <return> key.

Command mode prompt is a colon(:).

Text Mode:
To Enter: Lets you use the keyboard to enter text. Use an **a**, **i**, or **c** command.

Open/Visual Mode:
To Enter: type **o** or **vi**

to get back to **ex**, type **Q**.

Commands

In general, commands consist of an address and an instruction. The address identifies the lines to be affected.

Addresses

In the following, "n" and "k" are integers.

n   The nth line.
n,k   Lines n through k.
.   The current line.
$ The last (i.e., final) line.
+n   n lines after the current line.
-n   n lines before the current line.
$-n,$ The last n + $ lines.
/pat   search forward for pat.

Instructions

For clarity we will include simple forms of addresses with the instructions. Instructions shown with an address range will also accept a single address. Instructions operate on the current line if no other address is given.

n,kp   Print lines n through k.
na   Append (text is added after line n).
ni   Insert (text is inserted before line n).
n,kd   Delete lines n through k.
n,kc   Change lines n through k to new text.
n,kmj   Move lines n through k to after line j.
n,kcoj   Place a copy of lines n-k after line j.
s/pat1/pat2/   Replaces the first occurence of "pat2" with
                with "pat1" on the current line.
nr filename   Read and insert filename at line n.

Searches

/pattern   Causes **ex** to search for the next line containing a pattern.

A search pattern can be used in place of an address in a command. For example:
/slop/d   Delete the next line that contains "slop."
/dog/s/dog/hog/ Find the next line containing "dog" and replace the first
                occurrence of "dog" on that line with "hog."
/dog/s//hog/   Short form of the preceding command.

The Global Parameter g

The **g** parameter, when following an **s** command, makes the substitution affect all occurrences of "pat1" in a line. When preceding an **s** command, it makes the command affect all lines. Both uses can be made in the same command:

g/house/s//home/g   Substitutes "home" for "house" everywhere in the file.

The Undo Command u

A friendly command that lets you undo the last change made to the buffer.

Saving Text and Quitting the Editor

Editing work is done in a temporary buffer and must be "written" into a file to save it.

w   Writes the current text into a permanent file.
q   Quits the editor, if no changes since previous **w**.
wq   Write and quit.
q!   Emphatic form of quit. No changes recorded.
n,kw file2 Writes lines n through k into another file.
n,kw file3 Appends lines n through k to file 3.

vi Reference Card

The vi Screen Editor—A Quick Summary

The command for editing the file "filename" is **vi** filename.

If no such file exists yet, it will be created when this command is given.

Modes

Command Mode:	Lets you use the commands described below. You are placed in a Command Mode when you invoke **vi**.
To Enter:	To enter the Command Mode from the Text Mode, hit the <esc> key.
Text Mode:	Lets you use the keyboard to enter text.
To Enter:	Any of the following commands will put you in the Text Mode: **a, i, o, O, R,** and **c**.

Using ex Commands

While in the Command Mode, type a colon and follow it with the desired **ex** command;

for example:

:g/dog/s//mango/g

or

:14,42w newfile

You are returned to the regular Command Mode after the **ex** command is executed.

Cursor Movement Commands

vi commands take place at the cursor location. These commands help you to place the cursor where you want it to be in the text. The cursor will not move beyond the bounds of the existing text.

j	Moves the cursor down one line.
k	Moves the cursor up one line.
h	Moves the cursor left one space.
l	Moves the cursor right one space.
<control-d>	Moves the screen down a half page.
<control-u>	Moves the screen up a half page.
<control-b>	Moves the screen back a full page.
<control-f>	Moves the screen forward a full page.
nG	Moves the cursor to the nth line of file.

Text Entering Commands

a	Appends text after cursor position.
i	Inserts text before cursor position.
o	Opens a new line below cursor position.
O	Opens a new line above cursor position.

Text Deletion Commands

x	Deletes character under cursor.
dw	Deletes from cursor to beginning of next word.
dd	Deletes line containing cursor.
d)	Deletes rest of sentence.
d}	Deletes rest of paragraph.

These commands can be preceded by an integer to indicate the number of characters, words, etc., to be affected.

Text Alteration Commands

The **R,cw,c)** commands need to be terminated with an <esc>.

r	Replace character under cursor with next character typed.
R	Write over old text, beginning at cursor position.
cw	Change word (beginning at cursor) to new text.
c)	Change sentence (starting at cursor) to new text.
J	Join next line down to line with cursor.
u	Undo last command.
U	Undo all changes to line with cursor.

Search Commands

/pattern	Search for next occurrence of "pattern."
?pattern	Search for preceding occurrence of "pattern."
n	Repeat the last search command given.

Text Moving Commands (also see Text Deletion Commands)

yy	Yank a copy of a line, place it in a buffer.
P	Put after the cursor the last item yanked or deleted.
P	Put before the cursor the last item yanked or deleted.
"cY	Yank a copy of a line, place it in buffer c, where c is any letter from a to z.
"cP	Put after the cursor the contents of buffer c.

Saving Text and Quitting the Editor

Editing work takes place in a temporary work area and must be saved by "writing" it into a permanent file.

<esc>:w	Write the current text into the permanent file.
<esc>:q	Quit if no changes since last **w**.
<esc>:q!	Emphatic form of quit, no changes written.
<esc>:wq	Write and quit.
<esc>ZZ	Write and quit.
<esc>:n,kw file 2	Write lines n-k into another file.
<esc>:n,kw >> file 2	Append lines n-k to another file.

Screen Enhancement Options

<esc>:set wm = k	Provides wrap margin at **k** characters from right.
<esc>:set redraw	Keeps screen display current.

More Excellent Books in the Sams/Waite Primer Series

BASIC PROGRAMMING PRIMER (2nd Edition)
Gives you fundamental BASIC keywords, statements, and functions usable with the IBM* PC, Apple* II, or any other computer running a variation of Microsoft BASIC. Also covers advanced BASIC, new game program listings, more.
Waite and Pardee
No. 22014 . . . . $17.95

C ™ PRIMER PLUS
A clear, complete introduction to the C language that guides you in the fundamentals, covers use of Microcomputer C with assembly language, and contains many sample programs usable with any standard C compiler.
Waite, Prata, and Martin
No. 22090 . . . . $19.95

COMPUTER GRAPHICS PRIMER
A classic Sams best seller that helps you learn all types of graphics programming, including animation. Many program examples written in Applesoft.
Mitchell Waite
No. 21650 . . . . $15.95

CP/M BIBLE: THE AUTHORITATIVE REFERENCE GUIDE TO CP/M
Gives you instant, one-stop access to all CP/M keywords, commands, utilities, conventions, and more. A must for any computerist using any version of CP/M.
Waite and Angermeyer
No. 22015 . . . . $19.95

CP/M PRIMER (2nd Edition)
Completely updated to give you the know-how to begin working with new or old CP/M versions immediately. Includes CP/M terminology, operation, capabilities, internal structure, and more.
Waite and Murtha
No. 22170 . . . . $16.95

MICROCOMPUTER PRIMER (2nd Edition)
Shows you basic computer concepts, the electronics behind the logic, what happens inside the computer as a program runs, and a little about languages and operating systems.
Waite and Pardee
No. 21653 . . . . $14.50

SOUL OF CP/M* : HOW TO USE THE HIDDEN POWER OF YOUR CP/M SYSTEM
Teaches you how to use and modify CP/M's internal features, use CP/M system calls, and more. You'll need to read *CP/M PRIMER*, or be otherwise familiar with CP/M's outer-layer utilities.
Waite and Lafore
No. 22030 . . . . $19.95

SUPERCALC PRIMER
Makes it much easier for you to find your way out of a sticky calculation, hit the right keys to get a given answer, or otherwise get the most out of your SuperCalc spreadsheet program. Fully illustrated.
Waite, Burns, and Venit
No. 22087 . . . . $16.95

PASCAL PRIMER
Guides you swiftly through Pascal program structure, procedures, variables, decision making statements, and numeric functions. Contains many useful examples and eight appendices.
Waite and Fox
No. 21793 . . . . $17.95

TIMEX SINCLAIR BASIC PRIMER, WITH GRAPHICS
Easiest, most effective introduction ever to computers and programming. Graphics let you "see" your commands work as your own programs gradually develop into realities.
Waite and Chapnick
No. 22077 . . . . $9.95

UNIX ™ PRIMER PLUS
Presents the elements of UNIX clearly, simply, and accurately, for ready understanding by anyone in any field who needs to learn, use, or work with UNIX in some way. Fully illustrated.
Waite, Martin, and Prata
No. 22028 . . . . $19.95

YOUR OWN COMPUTER (2nd Edition)
Shows how to choose a computer for your own uses and explores applications, buzzwords, programs, hardware, and peripherals for 30 different models.
Waite and Pardee
No. 21860 . . . . $8.95

UNIX and C are trademarks of Bell Laboratories • CP/M is a registered trademark of Digital Research, Inc. • IBM is a registered trademark of International Business Machines Corporation • UCSD Pascal is a trademark of the Regents of the University of California, San Diego Campus • Apple is a registered trademark of Apple Computer, Inc. • SuperCalc is a registered trademark of Sorcim Corporation

---

SAMS BOOK & SOFTWARE ORDER CARD

Catalog No.	Qty.	Price	Total	Catalog No.	Qty.	Price	Total

☐ Check ☐ Money Order
☐ MasterCard ☐ Visa

Subtotal	
AR,CA,FL,IN,NC, NY,OH,TN,WV residents add local sales tax	
Add Handling charge	2.00
Total Amount Enclosed	

Account Number _____ Expires _____

Name (print) _____

Signature _____

Address _____

City _____ State _____ Zip _____

Offer good in USA only. Prices subject to change without notice. Full payment must accompany your order. | WC002

To locate the Sams retailer or distributor nearest you, call 1-800-428-SAMS (residents in IN, AK, HI call 317-298-5566).

If your retailer or distributor doesn't stock the Sams publication you need, you can order directly from SAMS. Orders placed directly with SAMS are subject to a $2.00 additional handling charge per order.

PHONE ORDERS

You may order by phone by calling either number listed above to charge your order to your VISA or MASTERCARD.

MAIL ORDERS

Use the order form below or send your order on a plain piece of paper. Be sure to:

(1) Include your name, address, city, state, and zip.

(2) The titles of the books you need, the product numbers (see other side of this card) and the quanity of each one you'd like.

(3) Add the total cost for the books, add local sales tax. Add $2.00 for handling.

(4) Include your check or money order for the full amount due, or

(5) Charge your VISA or MASTERCARD. Charge orders must include the account number, card expiration date and your signature. Shipping charges will be added to credit card orders.

(6) Mail your order to:
Howard W. Sams & Co., Inc.
Dept DM
P.O. Box 7092
Indianapolis, Indiana 46206

In Canada, contact Lenbrook Electronics, Markham, Ontario L3E 1H2

All books available from Sams Distributors, Bookstores, and Computer Stores. Offer good in U.S. only. Note Distributor Computer Store and Dealer inquiries are welcome.

See other side for list of Sams/Waite Primers and their prices.

Place Stamp Here

HOWARD W. SAMS & CO., INC.

P.O. BOX 7092
INDIANAPOLIS, INDIANA 46206